D0891906

INVESTMENT AND PROPERTY RIGHTS IN YUGOSLAVIA

Soviet and East European Studies: 86

Editorial Board

Soviet and East European Studies, under the auspices of Cambridge University Press and the British Association for Soviet, Slavonic and East European Studies (BASSEES), promotes the publication of works presenting substantial and original research on the economics, politics, sociology and modern history of the Soviet Union and Eastern Europe.

For decades Yugoslavia has been trying to develop its own model of socialism based on workers' self-management and increasing use of the market mechanism. As a result, many scholars have seen the Yugoslav economy as very different from other socialist systems. In this book, Dr Milica Uvalić shows, on the contrary, how some of the fundamental features of the Yugoslav economy have remained similar to those characterizing other socialist economies.

Dr Uvalić focuses on theoretical and empirical issues related to investment in Yugoslavia since 1965. She examines investment policies, sources of finance, macroeconomic performance, enterprise incentives and current property reforms in relation to Western theory on investment behaviour in the labour-managed firm and to Kornai's theory of socialist economies. In line with Kornai, the author reveals that, in spite of substantial institutional change, the investment process has continued to be characterized by an over-investment drive, severe capital market distortions and capital allocation according to non-market criteria, frequent state intervention in daily enterprise policies and limited enterprise autonomy, lack of financial discipline and the socialization of losses. The author argues that investment reforms have not led to substantially changed enterprise behaviour, which illustrates the limited results to be expected from partial reforms in a socialist economy. The fundamental causes of investment problems in Yugoslavia are thus typical of 'traditional' socialist economic systems, rather than the specific characteristic of self-management.

Investment and property rights in Yugoslavia is a most topical work. It presents a great deal of new material and addresses issues that have previously been dealt with in isolation. It will be widely read by students and specialists of Eastern Europe, comparative economic systems and finance.

Soviet and East European Studies

Series list continues after index

INVESTMENT AND PROPERTY RIGHTS IN YUGOSLAVIA

The long transition to a market economy

MILICA UVALIĆ

European University Institute, Florence

CAMBRIDGE
UNIVERSITY PRESS

2450/727✓

Published by the Press Syndicate of the University of Cambridge
The Pitt Building, Trumpington Street, Cambridge CB2 1RP
40 West 20th Street, New York, NY 10011–4211, USA
10 Stamford Road, Oakleigh, Victoria 3166, Australia

First published 1992

Printed in Great Britain by Woolnough Bookbinding

A catalogue record for this book is available from the British Library

Library of Congress cataloguing in publication data
Uvalić, Milica.
Investment and property rights in Yugoslavia: the long transition
to a market economy / Milica Uvalić.
        p.   cm. – (Soviet and East European Studies: 86)
Revision of the author's thesis (Ph.D) – European University
Institute, Florence, 1988.
Includes bibliographical references and index.
ISBN 0 521 40147 X
1. Business enterprises – Yugoslavia – Finance. 2. Investments –
Yugoslavia. 3. Property – Yugoslavia. 4. Yugoslavia – Economic
policy – 1945– . I. Title. II. Series.
HG4234.6.U93 1992
332.6'09497–dc20   91–34135   CIP

ISBN 0 521 40147 X hardback

WD

To the memory of my father Radivoj,
from whom I learnt both to
love ideals and respect reality.

Contents

Figures

Tables

Preface and acknowledgements

My main motive for choosing the topic of this book has been the desire to contribute to a better understanding of the behaviour of the Yugoslav enterprise. When I first started working on the topic of investment in labour-managed firms, I was surprised to find that, according to the dominant theories developed in the West, the labour-managed firm would be likely to underinvest as compared to its capitalist counterpart. At first sight this prediction seemed to be in sharp conflict with empirical evidence from Yugoslavia – the only existing economy where labour-managed firms are prevalent – since until the early 1980s the Yugoslav economy had been characterized by high rates of investment growth. I was curious to look deeper into the principal reasons for such a divergence of empirical evidence from theoretical predictions.

There are many people to whom I am indebted for their help while writing this book, although the responsibility for its contents, and for any remaining errors, is entirely mine.

This book has its origins in my PhD thesis – 'Investment in labour-managed firms: theoretical problems and empirical evidence from Yugoslavia' – and I would first like to thank my PhD examiners – Professors Wlodzimierz Brus (Wolfson College, Oxford), Benedetto Gui (University of Trieste), Marie Lavigne (University of Paris I) and Aleš Vahčić (University of Ljubljana) – for useful suggestions and comments in revising an initial draft of the manuscript. My very special thanks go to my supervisor Mario Nuti for his patience, guidance, help and encouragement, useful critical comments and long discussions (including disagreements), all of which have been essential for the writing of this work.

I am also grateful to Stojan Babić, Will Bartlett, Josef van Brabant, Alberto Chilosi, Miša Crnobrnja, Renzo Daviddi, Dinko Dubravčić, Saul Estrin, Donald George, Norman Ireland, Derek Jones, Timothy King, Miroljub Labus, Maria Lacko, Paul Marer, Milić Milovanović,

Dušan Mramor, Louis Putterman, Stephen Smith, Djordje Šuvaković, Jan Svejnar and Cristine Wallich for helpful comments on earlier versions of parts of this study. Useful suggestions on the econometrics part were provided by Giancarlo Gandolfo, Massimo Gerli, Grayham Mizon, Harold Sonnberger, and anonymous referees. I would like to thank Gianluca Caporello for having done the graphics, and James Newell for editorial help.

Last but not least, I must thank all my other Yugoslav friends who have helped me throughout the research, either through fruitful discussions, or by providing important sources of data and information, including Mitja Gašpari, Planinko Kapetanović, Vladimir Kravčuk, Dragan Liješević, Branislav Lukić, Branko Milanović, Žarko Papić, Tea Petrin, Marko Simoneti, Zorica Stevčić, Radmila Stojanović, Ivan Teodorović, Dragomir Vojnić, Ivan Vujačić and Duško Vujović.

Parts of the study have also benefited from the comments of participants of various conferences, workshops and seminars, including the conferences of the International Association for the Economics of Self-Management (1985, 1988, 1991), the conferences of the Italian Association for Comparative Economic Systems – AISSEC (1986, 1987, 1988), the Workshop on Financial Reform in Socialist Economies organized by the World Bank and the European University in Florence (1987), seminars of the Working Group on Comparative Economic Systems at the European University Institute (1984–88), and the meetings of PHARE consultants for Eastern Europe to the Commission of the European Communities (1990–91).

Introduction

Over the past forty years Yugoslavia has been trying to develop its own model of socialism based on workers' self-management, decentralization, social ownership and increasing reliance on the market. These characteristics of the Yugoslav economic system have led many scholars to consider Yugoslavia to be very different from other socialist economies, frequently ascribing, in line with the theoretical literature on the labour-managed firm, economic inefficiency of the Yugoslav economy to the specific features of its economic system.

At the same time, however, until 1989 Yugoslavia remained a socialist economy characterized by many of the systemic features (and problems) of a traditional centrally planned economy. Although in Yugoslavia some of the typical priority objectives of centrally planned economies have been abandoned – such as full employment and price stability – along with many of the traditional centralized institutions, other fundamental socialist goals have been retained, including the commitment to non-private property, planning, egalitarianism, and solidarity.

The intention of this book is to evaluate the impact of such 'dualism' – self-management and increasing use of the market on the one hand, and socialist features on the other – on the nature of the Yugoslav system, by focusing on the specific field of investment. The period examined is primarily post-1966, since it is with the reforms of the 1960s that substantial institutional changes were introduced into the economy, in particular in the field of investment.

The book is divided into three main parts. After these introductory remarks, the first part describes the institutional setting and presents the theoretical framework necessary for understanding Yugoslav investment behaviour. In chapter 1, the evolution of the Yugoslav economic system is briefly described through a discussion of the main directions of past economic reforms, economic performance and

1

problems encountered, and the present economic crisis and the measures taken to overcome it. The three subsequent chapters discuss the theoretical framework: on the one hand, the likely impact of self-management on investment behaviour, as developed by Vanek, Furubotn, and Pejovich (chapter 2) and some extensions of the theory (chapter 3); and, on the other hand, the likely impact of systemic features of the socialist economy, following the theory of János Kornai (chapter 4).

The second part of the book provides empirical evidence on the nature of the Yugoslav system, with the aim of determining which of the two theories is more suitable to Yugoslavia. A general assessment is first given of Yugoslav investment and savings performance, both at the aggregate and enterprise level (chapter 5). The analysis proceeds with an evaluation of factors which, according to the theories discussed, are likely to have influenced investment in Yugoslavia, namely a number of market variables on the one hand, and socialist features of the Yugoslav economy on the other (chapter 6). Finally, the theories are also verified using econometric tests (chapter 7).

The last part of the book discusses pressure for more radical reforms in the field of investment incentives and property rights in Yugoslavia, both in the past and today. Chapter 8 analyses early theoretical proposals for such reforms developed by Edvard Kardelj and their practical implementation during the 1970s, pointing to the lack of change in the property regime as one of the main reasons for their failure. Chapter 9 focuses on current property reforms: it discusses proposals advanced during the property debate of the 1980s, which have paved the way for a radical change in official policies; concrete measures taken by the Yugoslav government from 1988 onwards and its privatization programme; regional problems linked to its implementation; and evidence on property restructuring in Yugoslavia. Since Yugoslavia is presently going through a process of transition from a socialist to a mixed market economy, similar to the process under way in other former socialist economies, chapter 10 discusses some specific features of the Yugoslav transition. In the concluding chapter 11, an overview of the principal conclusions is given.

Part I

The institutional and theoretical framework

1 The Yugoslav road towards market socialism

Despite retaining a communist one-party political regime until 1989, Yugoslavia was the first socialist country to attempt far-reaching economic reforms, and because of its early start and the frequency of systemic changes, it was for years considered the most reformed socialist economy. Along with significant institutional innovation, a policy emphasis on rapid growth led to continuous economic progress up until 1980, when a serious economic crisis began to develop. In order to give an overview of these developments, the evolution of the Yugoslav economic system will be presented through a short description of the main characteristics of past economic reforms, economic performance until 1980, and the present economic crisis.[1]

Past economic reforms

Each decade in post-war Yugoslavia has brought with it a new series of institutional changes, designed to gradually transform the economy from a traditional centrally-planned one into a more market-oriented system.

For a brief period after the Second World War, the Yugoslav economy was organized along similar lines to that of the Soviet Union. The model adopted was based on centralized planning, state ownership of enterprises brought about through nationalization (except for agriculture, the largest part of which remained in the hands of private farmers), state monopoly in the most important spheres (investment, banking, foreign trade), and administrative control of most prices. The system effectively implied full control of the federal state over the economy.

Following the Tito–Stalin conflict in 1948 and the expulsion of Yugoslavia from Cominform, in the early 1950s the Soviet-type economic model was abandoned. A law of 1950 introduced workers' self-management, initially in a limited number of enterprises and sectors, giving the workforce the right to directly elect workers' councils as the main decision-making organs of the enterprise which were to decide on production plans, inputs, hiring policies, and to a limited extent, prices and income distribution. Self-management was reinforced with the replacement of centralized planning by a more flexible system based on the planning of overall targets only ('global proportions'). A single price structure was also introduced, parallel to some relaxation in price controls.

In line with these changes, in 1953 state property was replaced by 'social property' intended as property of the whole of society. This gave enterprises in the social sector not property rights, but rather the right to use socially-owned assets and to appropriate their product (at first subject to a small capital charge, and since 1971 free of charge). Expansion of the private sector, consisting mainly of agriculture and certain crafts and services, was restricted by law: the 1953 land reform reduced the limit on the size of private holdings from 35 to 10 hectares per family, while in other sectors limits were placed on the number of workers that could be employed (usually five workers other than family members).

In the early 1950s, the state monopoly of foreign trade was replaced by a more decentralized system giving more freedom to enterprises in their foreign trade operations. The banking system was also somewhat decentralized, with the setting up of sectoral banks for agriculture, investment, and foreign trade. There was also some devolution of the federal powers to republican and local governments.[2] Competences in certain fields, such as light industry, were transferred from the federal to the republican level, while local political authorities were given certain independent rights to taxation.[3] The local commune became responsible for the implementation of the social plan, supervision of enterprises, and the provision of social and other services.

The institutional changes implemented during the 1963–7 period were much more far-reaching, and it is this economic reform that has usually been considered as marking the passage to 'market socialism' in Yugoslavia. The right to self-management was extended to all sectors and types of organization; planning was further relaxed by a switch to a system of indicative planning; and the market was to become the main mechanism of resource allocation. Price liberalization was carried further, through adjustments designed to remove distortions in relative prices, although certain prices continued to be fixed administratively and a system of controls was maintained. The competences and responsibilities of republics and local governments were increased further, and after 1968 the rights of the two autonomous provinces were also strengthened. There was major innovation in the foreign trade sector, in line with the policy of directing trade primarily towards Western markets: the system of multiple exchange rates was replaced by a uniform exchange rate, and the Dinar was devalued in 1965 in order to establish a more realistic rate; some import restrictions were reduced; and in 1967 joint ventures with foreign partners were permitted.

The economic reform of the 1960s included important changes in the field of banking, investment and finance. Central banking was separated from commercial banking, and a diversified structure of decentralized all-purpose banks was set up. The investment sphere was extensively decentralized, with the intention that banks and enterprises would become the principal agents of investment decisions. In 1963, central investment funds were abolished and their resources transferred to banks, which were to become the main financial intermediary; the only federal fund was to be the Fund for the Development of Less-Developed Republics and Regions. Fiscal burdens on firms were reduced – which left a larger share of generated income at their disposal – and wage controls were substantially relaxed, giving enterprises greater control over the distribution of their income. In principle firms were able to choose their own investment projects, as well as the proportion of profits to be allocated to investment.

The economic reform of the 1960s was followed by a number of economic, social and political problems,[4] resulting in a need for further major institutional change. A new economic reform was implemented in the 1971–6 period,[5] introducing a number of innovations. In the macroeconomic field, new mechanisms of policy coordination were invented, designed to reinforce the planning instrument, to be based on self-management principles permitting the active participation of economic agents in the overall planning process. 'Social compacts', or agreements concluded at different levels between representatives of the political authorities (or 'socio-political communities', in Yugoslav terminology),[6] trade unions, enterprises and other organizations, were to be concluded on policies to be pursued in a given field, such as prices, income distribution, employment, foreign trade, and so forth. In addition, 'self-management agreements' were to regulate relations between enterprises and other organizations in different areas of mutual interest, such as terms for the foundation of enterprises and banks, joint investment projects, transactions and deliveries, and so forth. These agreements are negotiated through a process of bargaining between the parties concerned, and once concluded, their implementation is, in principle, obligatory.

The economic reform of the 1970s brought about a further devolution of powers from the federation to the republics, and to the lower-level socio-political communities. In order to take account of the different economic interests of the single regional components of the Yugoslav federation, and to promote local interests and responsibilities, the reform strengthened the rights of the single republics in many important fields, including prices, income distribution, taxation, employment, social security and welfare, and foreign trade. Other fields, such as national defence and foreign policy, remained under federal control. Monetary and exchange rate policies, while also within the competence of the federal government, were to be based on agreement between the republican governments; since such agreements relied on the principle of consensus, a veto power was effectively given to each republic.

Substantial decentralization took place, in particular in the foreign trade sector, after 1977, when self-managed communities of interest for foreign economic relations were set up at republican levels. The new system had a number of deficiencies, as it implied the fixing of import and export quotas of each republic, the administrative allocation of foreign exchange both among and within republics, and preferential access to foreign currency for final exporters. Enterprises were also allowed to retain a substantial part of their foreign currency earnings in bank accounts, which were also permitted to be kept outside of Yugoslavia.

In the microeconomic sphere, in order to facilitate self-management within enterprises, during the early 1970s firms were split up into smaller units (so-called 'basic organizations of associated labour' – BOALs), each having its own self-management organs and statutory acts. Other new forms were also introduced: organizations of associated labour (OALs), regrouping several BOALs; complex organizations of associated labour, regrouping several OALs; and contractual organizations of associated labour, financed by a combination of private resources and socially-owned capital. In the field of social services, 'self-managed communities of interest' were introduced, intended to be organizations directly linking the interests of users and providers of such services on a self-management basis.

In order to reinforce further the position of enterprises *vis-à-vis* the banking sector, and prevent the concentration of financial resources within banks – something which, in the late 1960s, was regarded as being in conflict with self-management – banks were transformed into non-profit 'service' agencies of enterprises operating under their direct control. Substantial financial innovation was also brought about through the diversification of financial instruments, both standard (such as bonds, treasury bills and promissory notes) and those adapted to the Yugoslav self-management system (different forms of pooling of labour and resources which permit direct investment by one enterprise in another, or private investment by an individual into a socially-owned enterprise).

Economic reforms were reinforced by specific features of Yugoslavia's international economic relations. It did not join the Council for Mutual Economic Assistance (CMEA) in 1949 (although it participated, after 1964, in some of its standing committees), remained full member of the International Monetary Fund (IMF) and in the 1960s, became member of the General Agreement on Tariffs and Trade (GATT) and associate member of the Organization for Economic Cooperation and Development (OECD). Yugoslavia also had a privileged relationship with the European Community, from the early 1970s through trade agreements and benefiting from the Generalized System of Preferences (GSP), and since 1980 through a Cooperation Agreement, which besides trade regulates other important fields of cooperation (such as financial loans, energy, transport and technology).

Economic performance up to 1980

In spite of variations and some deterioration in economic performance during the post-1965 period, until the early 1980s the Yugoslav economy developed rapidly (see table 1.1). The annual rate of growth of gross material product (GMP) or 'social product' in Yugoslav terminology,[7] was over or close to 6 per cent throughout the 1953–80 period. A substantial proportion of GMP, around 30 per cent or more, was devoted to investment in fixed assets, frequently at the expense of consumption. Pursuing a strategy of rapid industrialization, the authorities gave priority to the development of industry over agriculture, and to the social sector over the private. Development-oriented policies made possible important changes in the structure of the economy, the growth of industrial employment with significant transfers of the labour force from agriculture, and a continuous increase in average living standards. The opening up of the economy to the West in 1965 led to concentration on Western markets, to a gradual integration of Yugoslavia into the world economy, and to substantial trade diversification.

Achievements in terms of economic development were also accompanied by a number of problems, in particular following the economic reform of the 1960s. Along with decentralization, liberalization and increasing reliance on the market mechanism – but without the parallel introduction of an efficient mechanism of macroeconomic regulation and control – the Yugoslav economy began to be characterized by deterioration in performance and increasing instability. After 1965, there was a notable slowdown in the growth of GMP, industrial output, employment and commodity exports, and the authorities had to cope with new problems such as inflation, unemployment, increasing disparities in regional development, and balance of payments difficulties.

Following the partial liberalization of prices in the mid-1960s, the average annual inflation rate (retail prices) increased to 10 per cent by the end of the decade, and to 20 per cent during the 1970s. Lower rates of output growth had aggravated the problem of unemployment, and the registered unemployment ratio of the total labour force rose to 6.9 per cent in 1976 and to 8.4 per cent in 1980 (OECD 1982, p. 14). In spite of the existence of a federal fund which ensured the transfer of substantial resources from the more to the less developed republics and regions, regional disparities in levels of development increased. Thus the difference in income per capita between the most developed republic, Slovenia, and the least developed region, Kosovo, increased from 5 to 1 in 1955, to 7.5 to 1 in 1988. At the same time, there was also substantial income disparity across sectors and across enterprises, even within the same sector.

Finally, the slowdown in the growth of commodity exports, together with a substantial increase in imports in the late 1960s, led to a widening trade deficit and to increasing balance of payments difficulties. While the deficit on the trade account was initially compensated for by workers' remittances from abroad and by tourism, during the 1970s the situation progressively deteriorated as invisible earnings became insufficient to balance the current account. The Yugoslav authorities did not react to the 1973–4 oil shock by lowering domestic spending, but rather, earlier growth rates of consumption were maintained or even increased; in particular, there was a rapid expansion of investment. This was made possible by more frequent recourse to borrowing on international markets, leading to a rapid increase in Yugoslavia's external debt (net of lending) – from less than $2 billion in 1970 to

Table 1.1. *Average growth rates of macroeconomic indicators in Yugoslavia, 1953–1989 (percentages)*

	1953–6	1957–60	1961–5	1966–70	1971–5	1976–80	1981–9
GMP	6.6	11.3	6.8	5.8	5.9	5.7	0.5*
GMP per capita	5.2	10.2	5.7	5.9	5.1	4.3	−0.2*
Industrial output	12.9	14.1	10.6	6.1	8.1	6.7	2.0
Social sector GMP	5.6	13.7	9.0	6.1	6.5	6.2	0.6
Private sector GMP	8.7	6.1	−0.1	4.6	3.0	2.3	−0.1
Employment	6.3	7.6	4.3	1.0	4.3	4.0	1.9
Real personal income per worker	1.1	9.1	5.4	7.3	1.5	0.9	−0.6
Retail prices	2.3	3.0	11.1	10.0	20.2	17.4	120.0
Commodity exports	9.4	14.6	9.7	5.8	4.9	1.5	2.4
Commodity imports	7.4	14.5	5.8	14.3	5.8	0.8	−1.0

*1988

Source: Savezni zavod za statistiku (SZS), *Statistički Godišnjak Jugoslavije 1990*, Tables 102–9 and 102–10.

$14 billion in 1979 and, following the second oil shock, to $18 billion in 1980. At the same time, due to shortcomings in the system of resource allocation, certain structural imbalances began to emerge. Insufficient investment in crucial sectors, such as energy and raw materials, led to a rising dependence of the Yugoslav economy on imported inputs, whereas there was excess capacity in other sectors and the duplication of plants of suboptimal size across regions. These negative trends culminated in 1979 after the second oil shock, which brought about a record deficit on both the foreign trade and the current accounts ($7.2 billion and $3.7 billion respectively).

The present economic crisis

The balance of payments constraint led the Yugoslav government to implement policies aimed at raising gross savings and suppressing domestic demand. Since 1981 these policies have been supported by IMF stand-by loans and credits from western governments and foreign commercial financial institutions. The initial austerity package, introduced in 1981, consisted of severe cuts in all components of domestic demand (especially imports and investment), price liberalization, restrictive monetary policies, and a more realistic exchange rate brought about through several devaluations of the Dinar.

Table 1.2. *Main macroeconomic indicators in Yugoslavia, 1979–1989*

	1979	1980	1981	1982	1983	1984	1985	1986	1987	1988	1989
	(Annual percentage change)										
Demand and output											
GMP	7.0	2.2	1.5	0.5	-1.0	2.0	0.5	3.6	-1.1	-1.7	0.8
Private consumption	5.2	0.7	-1.0	-0.1	-1.7	-1.0	0.0	4.5	0.3	-1.3	1.0
Public consumption	7.9	2.7	-4.8	-0.7	-4.0	-0.2	1.9	4.6	-1.5	0.1	-1.0
Fixed investment	6.4	-1.7	-9.8	-5.5	-9.7	-9.6	-4.0	3.5	-5.1	-5.8	0.5
Stocks	4.3	1.4	5.5	-0.7	2.8	4.7	3.2	0.0	0.9	0.7	-1.9
Exports	3.3	8.9	-0.4	-11.2	1.4	10.1	8.2	2.0	-0.6	5.7	7.2
Imports	9.6	-9.9	-12.3	-13.5	-5.5	-0.4	2.3	8.8	-5.8	1.1	12.7
Cost of living (a)	20.4	30.3	40.7	31.7	41.0	53.0	74.0	89.0	120	195	1252
(b)	23.0	38.1	36.2	33.0	60.0	46.1	85.2	91.0	171	241	2714
Real wages (social sector)	0.0	-7.5	-5.0	-4.0	-11.0	-6.0	2.0	9.3	4.1	-5.3	-0.4
Domestic employment	1.7	1.0	0.7	0.7	0.8	1.1	1.5	1.8	2.1	-1.2	-0.3
Balance of payments and debt ($ millions)											
Trade balance	-7.2	-6.1	-4.8	-3.1	-2.2	-1.7	-1.6	-2.0	-1.2	-0.6	-1.4
Current account	-3.7	-2.3	-0.7	-0.5	0.3	0.5	0.8	-1.7	1.2	2.5	2.4
External debt (net of lending)	14.0	17.3	19.5	18.6	18.7	18.3	18.0	18.6	19.5	16.8	15.2

(a) Annual percentage change with respect to previous year.
(b) Percentage change in December of current year with respect to December of previous year.
Source: Official Yugoslav statistics, as reported in OECD, *Economic Surveys – Yugoslavia*, various issues, except for data on external debt, which are from NBY *Bilten Narodne Banke Jugoslavije*, various issues.

In subsequent stabilization programmes, these measures were supplemented by a more active monetary policy (from 1982 onwards), continuous adjustments of the exchange rate pegged to a basket of foreign currencies, and major prices and incomes controls, with occasional freezes on both.

By 1983, some of the principal objectives of the austerity package had been achieved: there had been a notable improvement in the current account – which had moved into surplus – and the rapid rise in foreign indebtedness had been halted. However, the price paid for balancing foreign trade was a serious deterioration in domestic economic performance. A severe economic crisis began to develop, a crisis which progressively led the economy into a profound and long-lasting recession. From 1980 onwards, most of the macroeconomic indicators rapidly deteriorated (see table 1.2).

Since 1980, the Yugoslav economy has been characterized by stagnating or declining GMP, negative rates of investment growth (except in 1986 and 1989), modest rates of employment growth, and rising unemployment (1,240 million by the end of 1989, or 11.2 per cent of the domestic labour force).[8] Given that the initial improvement on the current account was achieved primarily through several import restrictions, rather than improvements in export performance, restrictive policies had a negative effect on many of the industrial sectors that were highly dependent on imported inputs. Moreover, throughout the 1980s, inflation progressively increased. The annual rate of increase of consumer prices (the cost of living) by 1984 was 53 per cent, increasing further to 89 per cent in 1986 and to 195 per cent in 1988, and giving way to hyperinflation in 1989. The year-on-year rate of increase of consumer prices in 1989 reached 1,252 per cent; the increase from December 1988 to December 1989 was as high as 2,714 per cent.

Rapid inflation in combination with restrictive incomes policies led to declining living standards, and between 1980 and 1984 alone there was a 34 per cent drop in real personal incomes. At the same time, substantial increases in nominal interest rates, credit and other restrictions (such as price freezes) led to serious liquidity problems for a growing number of enterprises. In the foreign trade sector, although the rapid rise in foreign indebtedness had been stopped, problems of servicing external debt required debt rescheduling from 1983 onwards, conditional on the implementation of policy packages coordinated with the IMF.

The results achieved by means of the various stabilization programmes implemented in the 1981–9 period proved highly disappointing, owing to both inappropriate institutional arrangements and inconsistencies in government policies. In spite of the new direction taken in economic policies from 1981 onwards, the stop–go character of certain measures – monetary restrictions, prices and incomes controls, interest rate policies – had a number of counterproductive effects, especially on prices.[9] In the face of mounting social tensions, from mid-1988 the government had relaxed incomes controls and in 1989 wages were freely determined, adding further to inflation. These negative trends culminated in 1989 when the Yugoslav economy was confronted with hyperinflation.

The new stabilization programme implemented in 1990 consisted of a 'shock therapy' based on the pegging of the exchange rate to the German Mark and the introduction of resident convertibility for current transactions; freezing of money wages, after some adjustments had been made, at their December 1989 level; stricter monetary control; liberalization of most prices (except for public utilities, some metals and pharmaceuticals affecting about 20–25 per cent of all prices); and further liberalization of imports (95 per cent of total imports by the end of the year). In the first half of the year, the programme succeeded in bringing down monthly inflation from 59 per cent in December 1989 to zero by April 1990, and resident convertibility was sustained, facilitated by substantial foreign exchange reserves (around $9 billion).

However, in the second half of 1990, the stabilization programme was undermined by a series of negative developments. Under pressure from the republican governments, each of which felt adversely affected by continuation of the programme,[10] the Yugoslav prime minister Ante Marković accepted certain compromises. Thus in mid-1990, there was a deviation from the originally stipulated policies, which involved both monetary policy and the exchange rate.[11]

The relaxation of monetary restrictions from mid-1990 onwards led to new inflationary pressures; hence despite the positive results achieved during the first half of the year, the annual average rate of retail price inflation in 1990 was 588 per cent.[12] Inflationary pressures were also created by the Gulf crisis which, because of foreign trade links with Iraq and Kuwait, reduced the balance of payments surplus by some $3 billion. In addition, contrary to federal regulations, most republican governments officially permitted wage increases, and failed to respect their obligations concerning the financing of the federal budget, and the monetary regulations of the National Bank of Yugoslavia.

The fixed exchange rate could not be sustained, due to rising inflation and declining foreign exchange reserves, caused primarily by the loss of confidence of the population in announced policies. The growing awareness that there would be a devaluation led to increasing withdrawals of foreign currencies from banks, and by autumn 1990 there was a general shortage of foreign exchange, the black market had re-emerged (the black market premium was about 30 per cent), foreign exchange reserves had fallen to around $7 billion by December 1990, and resident convertibility was effectively suspended (though formally only in December 1990). There was also a threefold increase of the foreign trade deficit relative to 1989.[13] A change in the exchange rate was inevitable: in January 1991 the Dinar was devalued against the German Mark by 22 per cent, and in April by a further 30 per cent.

Alongside short-term stabilization policies, in 1982 a new economic reform was announced, a reform which like those in the past aimed at a 'greater reliance on market forces'.[14] However, implementation of the new economic reform has been extremely slow and fragmentary. The elaboration of new legislation has been lengthy due to long discussions and disagreements over concrete reform measures, and hampered by the complex decision-making process involving a large number of participating institutions. In spite of some legislative changes in the mid-1980s, it was only in 1988 that a long list of important laws was finally adopted.

Apart from the economic crisis, Yugoslavia has also been facing growing social and political unrest. In particular, during the second half of the 1980s, widespread economic and political grievances resulted in frequent strikes and demonstrations throughout the country which – in the absence of alternative methods – were used to put pressure on local politicians to increase wages, or to resign from office. Growing social discontent eventually led to the emergence of alternative political parties which, until they were legalized in 1989, appeared under the form of 'associations'. In addition, the unresolved problem of the autonomous region of Kosovo,[15] which since 1981 has demanded the right to become an independent republic, has led to increasing nationalist conflicts, ethnic persecution and discrimination, several military interventions, and the official reinforcement of Serbian rights over Kosovo through amendments to the Serbian Constitution adopted in March 1989.

In the mean time, a serious political crisis within the Yugoslav federation has also developed, this due to continuous conflicts between the governments of the more developed republics in the north and the less developed republics in the south, over both economic and political issues. Within the party, such conflicts led to the dissolution, in 1989, of the Central Committee of the League of Communists of Yugoslavia. Following political developments in other East European countries, Yugoslavia also opted for a democratic multi-party regime, and by the end of 1990 free elections had taken place throughout the country.

Nevertheless, political democracy has also further aggravated the national problem. In several republics parties representing strong nationalist sentiment have come to power, pursuing the objective of increasing republican independence through the abuse of fiscal obligations towards the federation, the illegal strengthening of local police forces and army units, adoption of laws not in conformity with federal legislation, and moves towards the establishment of independent states. The crisis resulted in the outbreak of civil war after the declaration of Slovenian and Croatian independence in June 1991. The situation is presently blocked by a lack of consensus on the future of the Yugoslav republics.

The latent nationalist problem, successfully handled under Tito's rule, has again come to the fore, this time in an extreme form. The economic crisis has been transformed into a more general crisis of a political, social, and moral character, a crisis for which no simple solution can be found.

How does one assess the Yugoslav model and explain the collapse of the Yugoslav 'miracle' (see Sapir 1980)? Are the principal causes of the present economic crisis in Yugoslavia to be sought primarily in the distinct characteristic of the Yugoslav economy, i.e. self-management, or are they rooted in the systemic features of socialist economies, inherited from the old system? By concentrating on the specific field of investment, the rest of this book tries to provide an answer to this question by examining theoretical predictions and empirical evidence from Yugoslavia concerning the twin characteristics of the Yugoslav economy – self-management and socialism.

2 The investment theory of the labour-managed firm

The economic theory of the labour-managed firm (LMF) has been developed by Benjamin Ward (1958), Jaroslav Vanek (1970), James Meade (1972) and a number of other scholars.[1] Although Ward's model was originally inspired by the Yugoslav ('Illyrian') system of self-management, the concept of the LMF has in the mean time been extended to include producer cooperatives in Western economies. Thus today, in the growing theoretical literature, the LMF refers to both the self-managed socialist firm in Yugoslavia and the workers' cooperative in Western countries; both types of firm are considered to have the following principal features in common (Nuti 1988b): (1) self-management, i.e. participation of all workers in decision-making on all major policy issues, usually on the basis of the principle of one person one vote, directly or through representative organs; (2) an egalitarian system of profit distribution; and (3) collective ownership of capital – which implies certain restrictions on the appropriability of net assets.

Given these specific features, the LMF has been distinguished for its objective function (Ward 1958, Vanek 1970). In contrast with the capitalist firm, which maximizes total profits, the LMF is assumed to maximize income per worker.[2] Such enterprise behaviour is capable of supporting the same kind of long-term equilibrium achievable by an economy with traditional capitalist firms (see Vanek 1970); in the short run, however, the difference in maximands is expected to lead to a number of inefficiencies of the LMF with respect to the capitalist firm (see Nuti 1988b).

The alleged drawbacks of the LMF include restrictive employment policies in competitive conditions on the part of any LMF paying out incomes per member higher than the supply price of labour outside the firm; more restrictive monopolistic behaviour than in the case of capitalist firms, due to maximization of monopoly profit per man instead of total profit; and the unsuitability of the LMF outside labour-intensive sectors and for risky ventures. Moreover, there will be inefficient allocation of labour, due to the 'perverse' or at any rate rigid response of the LMF to changes in product price, technology, and capital rental: for an LMF in equilibrium, total revenue minus fixed charges over membership (i.e. average earnings) must be equal to the marginal revenue product of labour. Thus a product price rise or a decrease in capital rental raise average net income per worker relative to its marginal product, and this provides an incentive to raise further average earnings per member through a reduction of membership size, instead of encouraging greater employment and output in the short run (the opposite happens for product price falls and capital rental rise). Either way, short-term adjustment leads to Pareto inefficiency. The LMF will also be characterized by inefficient use of capital, due to distortions in project selection: investment projects having a positive present value may be rejected if they reduce average earnings, while negative present value projects may be accepted if they raise average earnings. But even in the absence of such distortions in project selection, a bias against the reinvestment of net income can be expected, since LMF members are entitled to the current benefits of a project only for the duration of their membership, as they do not participate in subsequent benefits or in the residual capital value of the investment at the time of departure.[3]

We will primarily discuss the last set of drawbacks – the tendency of the LMF to underinvest, compared to a capitalist firm, and distortions in project selection – as developed in the theories of Vanek (1970, 1971) and Furubotn and Pejovich (1969–80). Both theories assert that the LMF will be less willing to invest in capital assets from retained earnings than its capitalist counterpart, for reasons connected with collective ownership of capital and limited property rights.

Vanek (1971) examines an LMF maximizing income per worker, a function of the capital–labour (K/L) ratio. All members have the same time preference R, while the title of an investment remains in the hands of the collective. It is assumed that assets are of infinite durability, and thus depreciation considerations are excluded.

If the firm self-finances its investment and constant returns to scale (CRS) are assumed, four dynamic forces operate on the equilibrium of an LMF. The first self-extinction force is the desire of the LMF to reduce membership in order to increase income per worker, until the point where the firm is reduced to one member; although the community will try to prevent this happening by prohibiting the expelling of members, departure of workers will in the long run nevertheless occur through natural wastage. The second self-extinction force is the desire to consume capital, which sets in after the first force has brought about a disequilibrium in the K/L ratio. The third underinvestment force arises because the collective nature of investment impels workers to recover the principal of an investment in the course of their expected employment, which would not be the case if they invested in savings accounts. Finally, the fourth is the never-employ force, because an increase in labour reduces the K/L ratio and therefore income per worker.

Let us consider a stationary-membership LMF. Faced with the possibility of reinvesting one money unit of enterprise revenue within the enterprise, obtaining an infinite stream of yearly net revenue A, a worker will consider investing only if the present value V of the net revenue over his time horizon T is at least as great as the cost of investment, i.e. if:

$$V = A \sum_{i=1}^{T} (1+R)^{-i} \geq 1$$

However, the worker also has the option of supporting instead the distribution of enterprise net revenue to members, in which case he can obtain not only an annual yield for t years, but also recover the principal at time T. Hence for the worker to approve the reinvestment of LMF net revenue, the stricter condition must be satisfied:

$$V = A \sum_{i=1}^{T} (1+R)^{-i} + (1+R)^{-T} \geq 1$$

For an LMF worker to be indifferent between self-financed investment and net revenue distribution, it is necessary for the internal rate of return on the investment to exceed R by a margin, say D. Otherwise, as long as his time horizon T is shorter than the productive life of the investment, there will be underinvestment in self-financed projects.

In the case of increasing and then decreasing returns to scale (IDRS), a self-financed LMF will operate in the increasing returns to scale zone which implies inefficiency (the analogue of the first two self-extinction forces), the only difference being that the firm will never reduce membership to one worker because of the non-realization of economies of scale. The under-investment force remains unchanged.

In contrast, if investment can be externally financed at a cost equal to the time preference R, all four forces disappear: in the CRS case, an equilibrium will be reached at a point where the marginal product of capital equals the rate of time preference R; in the IDRS case, the LMF would always operate in the locus of maximum physical efficiency (CRS), where for a prescribed K/L ratio average and marginal products of labour are equalized, and along which the average product of labour is at its maximum.

The LMF will also be characterized by distortions in project selection (Vanek 1970). Since an LMF undertaking investment will consider, unlike the capitalist firm, the return per unit of employment, positive present value projects may be rejected if pre-investment income per member is greater than the supply price of labour, and the positive present value is obtained only for lower earning levels, although not lower than the supply price of labour; this happens when an employment-expanding project involves a membership increase proportionally greater than the associated increase in the present value of expected total earnings. Conversely a negative present value project will be attractive to an LMF if it involves a membership decrease proportionally greater than the decrease it causes in the present value of expected total earnings. Therefore, there will be a bias against the generation of new employment through investment in existing firms (Nuti 1988b). In order to ensure a higher income per worker, the LMF will tend to invest more in capital-intensive projects.

The above arguments are presented as being crucial in explaining why cooperatives have had only a qualified success in the capitalist environment, remaining confined to small-scale, lower than average risk and capital activities. By contrast to a self-financed cooperative, an externally-financed LMF would show a pattern of behaviour identical to an 'ideal' capitalist firm (Vanek 1971). The investment mechanism of the labour-managed economy may produce Pareto optimality, but on the condition that LMFs are externally financed. Otherwise, Pareto optimality can only be a long-run phenomenon, obtained through the entry and exit of firms instead of short-term changes in capacity utilization and investment in existing firms (Vanek 1970).

Furubotn and Pejovich's (1969–80) theory is similar, although it assumes a somewhat different maximand (usually income per worker from a dynamic viewpoint) and in most articles looks at an LMF under the Yugoslav institutional setting. When workers do not have full ownership rights over the firm's assets (hence the term 'non-owned assets'), they cannot recover the principal of their investment at the end of their time horizon, whereas investment in individual savings accounts (or 'owned assets') ensures the recovery of both the principal and interest. This will cause a bias in favour of 'owned' as against 'non-owned' assets. The problem is first presented in Pejovich (1969) and its implications discussed in a series of later articles (see table 2.1).

The following formula gives the condition for the two investment alternatives to be equally attractive, for a sum invested in T periods (Furubotn 1971, p. 190):

$$S(1+i)^T = S[(1+r)^T - 1] \text{ where}$$

S is the principal invested
i is the interest from investing in savings accounts
T is the time horizon
r is the return from investing in the firm's capital stock.

In the case of a one-year time horizon, an investment in 'owned assets' brings back $S+iS$, whereas an investment in 'non-owned assets' brings back only rS; hence r has to be large enough to compensate for the loss of the principal, S. With the prolonging of the time horizon, the difference between the required returns from 'owned' and 'non-owned' assets diminishes, but disappears only for an infinite time horizon.[4]

It is to be noted, however, that earlier articles by Furubotn and Pejovich leave more room for optimism: as opposed to wage maximization (the one-period case), which is inconsistent with positive investment in the firm, wealth maximization (dynamic case) can ensure positive investment in capital assets and wages below the maximum attainable level (see Furubotn and Pejovich 1970a and 1970b; Furubotn 1971). In all later articles, the authors' conclusions are more straightforward, suggesting self-financed investment in an LMF is highly unlikely, especially if external funds are provided. If bank credit is available, the disincentive to invest from retained earnings will be even greater: the LMF will rely exclusively on bank finance, the more so the shorter the time horizon, the higher the rate of interest on savings, the lower the cost of credit, and the lower the marginal productivity of capital. This will cause a general retardation of voluntary savings, followed by inflation and inefficiency (Furubotn and Pejovich 1973; Furubotn 1974; Furubotn 1976; Pejovich 1976; Furubotn 1980a; Furubotn 1980b).

Contrary to Vanek's proposal, rental contracts based on the leasing of capital do not banish the inefficiency problem of the LMF, because collective property rights, the main cause of the problem, distort incentives to invest. Workers will have little interest in protecting and preserving leased capital. In addition, there will be a bias in project selection: efforts will be made to shift the repayment burden to future

Table 2.1. *The evolution of the Furubotn–Pejovich hypothesis on the investment behaviour of the labour-managed firm*

Article	Field	Maximand	Other assumptions	Investment criteria	Conclusions
Pejovich (1969)	Decentralized socialist state	Wealth/worker	• Only the right to use assets (usufruct law) • CMR	Shortened T in case of I in n.o.a. because of non-private property. r must be larger than i to elicit investment.	Voluntary allocation of resources between present and future C in a centralized socialist state tends to favour current C relative to a decentralized socialist state, and in the latter tends to favour current C relative to a private-property society. I projects with long gestation periods disfavoured, will have to be financed by banks of the central treasury. Limited role of monetary and fiscal policies.
Furubotn and Pejovich (1970a)	Socialist firm	Two cases: (1) income/worker (one period) (2) director's U function and wealth/worker (dynamic case)	• Usufruct law • CMR • No external financing	(1) First maximand: I in n.o.a. = 0. (2) Second maximand: I in n.o.a. positive as long as r is greater than i. Indifferent if $r=i$.	While the wage max. hypothesis is inconsistent with positive I, wealth max. can lead to I in n.o.a. even without government pressure, as long as r is greater than the opportunity cost of K (i). If the director is the central figure, I in n.o.a. even more likely, and need not be in conflict with motives of the whole community.

	Firm	Relevant goal	Assumptions	Result	Discussion
Furubotn and Pejovich (1970b)	Yugoslav firm	Relevant goal: wealth/worker	• Usufruct law • CMR • An interest tax on the book value of capital • No external financing	I in n.o.a. displaces savings schedule upwards, because of the change into non-private property rights.	N.o.a. can bring effectively higher r than the official i and thus there is no desire to allocate all pf to wages. However, the greater the attenuation of private property rights, the lower is the level of voluntary savings. Economic theories should be developed around the concept of property rights.
Furubotn (1971)	Yugoslav firm	Wealth/worker or community's U index: $U = (C1 \ldots Ct)$ $C = pf - I$	• Usufruct law • CMR • Identical U • No external financing	Indifferent if $S(1+i)^t = [(1+r)-1]^t$ I in n.o.a. yields rS, while I in o.a. $s+iS$. If T is short, there will be a problem of incentives.	Narrow self-interest can dictate I in n.o.a. but no logical mechanism exists which requires such I; for it to be likely, initial K has to be small, elasticity with respect to K large, T long. Existing property rights favour C more and more as individual property rights are weakened. As time passes, cessation of self-finance occurs, because later I must promise very high r.
Furubotn and Pejovich (1973)	Yugoslav firm and the labour-managed economy	Utility (wealth)	• Usufruct law • CMR • (1) No external finance • (2) External sources available	(1) Indifferent if: $S =$ $\sum_{t=1}^{T} (rS)t/(1+i)^t$ I in n.o.a. only if r exceeds i. (2) No I in n.o.a.	I in n.o.a. possible, but unlikely. If credit is available, self-finance decreases, leading to a general retardation of voluntary savings in the economy, inflation, inefficiency, etc. The pure LM system is an essentially unstable construction. r will tend to i only for T tending to infinity.

Table 2.1 (cont.)

Article	Field	Maximand	Other assumptions	Investment criteria	Conclusions
Furubotn (1974)	LMF through a model of the Yugoslav firm	Multiperiod preferences: U as a function of C	• Usufruct law • Cannot select to disinvest • Long-term credit • r^*: critical yield on I in n.o.a. • r: productivity of I in o.a.	Indifference formula same as in Furubotn and Pejovich (1973). $r^* = s$, but typical case: r^* larger than r. When r smaller than r^*, I in n.o.a. = 0.	Bank credit enables the LMF to enjoy higher future C without sacrificing present income. 'Credit first' rule applied, self-finance avoided. I in n.o.a. possible, but improbable if workers have freedom of choice, LR low and T short. When LR lower than r^*, credit will substitute savings completely, causing a retardation of voluntary savings in the economy.
Furubotn (1976)	LMF	Utility of the original majority, a function of C and of the economic and social environment, itself a function of employment	• Usufruct law • No liquidation of capital stock • r^*: critical return on I in n.o.a. • r: reduced r^* that accounts for change into non-private property	Efficiency: if $r^* = i$, but in an LMF r^* must be greater than i for I in n.o.a. to be made.	Pareto efficiency will prevail only under very special conditions, but highly improbable. Efficiency requires that $r^* = i$, while LMF r^* is motivated only if $r = i$. This will result in divergence between the needs of society and those of the firm, implying that it is possible for socially desirable I to be neglected, even if r^* *is larger than* i. Leads to restricted I in n.o.a. The LMF is not an inherently efficient organization.

Pejovich (1976)	LMF and labour-managed economy	Wealth	• Usufruct law • CMR • Firm's demand for liquidity related to K stock. • (1) No credit available • (2) Bank credit available • r^*: critical r	(1) rS, if I in n.o.a. $s+iS$, if I in o.a. Only if r^* larger than i, is I in n.o.a. likely. (2) loans available, r falls and I in n.o.a. not likely. As long as LR below r^*, preference for debt finance.	Failing the special condition that r is larger than r^* and the possibility of credit, the LMF will choose C as alternative. Demand for long-term loans will be accompanied by rising demand for liquid assets, which in a socialist firm have to be held in non-interest bearing forms; cost of holding liquid assets higher than in capitalist firm. This will produce a liquidity crisis and inflation.
Furubotm (1978)	LMF and labour-managed economy	Benefits over T	• Yugoslav institutional structure • K leased	Since K leased, no interest to preserve equipment. Repayment burden shifted to future. Preference for quickest yielding projects.	Labour-managed system cannot achieve Pareto optimality. Incentives distorted by institutional arrangements. LM: an artificial construction. Rental contracts do not banish the inefficiency problem. Incentives for the creation of new firms lower than in a capitalist firm.

Table 2.1 (cont.)

Article	Field	Maximand	Other assumptions	Investment criteria	Conclusions
Furubotn (1980a)	Socialist LMF	The earning's residual (total K minus maintenance and loan repayment)	• Usufruct • CMR • Long-term credit available • r^*: minimum r for loan to be justified.	$r^* = S + i \, dS/di$ r^* larger than r LR as long as the loan period is finite. r^* must cover: K maintenance, repayment of loan, surplus for higher wages.	LMF will borrow and invest less than is justified from a social standpoint. The LM system cannot achieve Pareto optimality, for incentives are distorted by specific institutional arrangements. Collective welfare criteria will differ from social welfare criteria.
Furubotn (1980b)	LMF	Expected utility	• Yugoslav institutions • Bank credit available	Typical case: LR will almost certainly be less than r^*, unless T very long.	LMF will prefer bank credit and no savings. Incentives are such as to disuade workers from I in n.o.a. Alternatives promising higher rewards than i not available. More difficult to mobilize voluntary savings. The explanation is found in the property rights structure.

| Furubotn (1980c) | LMF in a capitalist setting | Present value of the worker's claims | • Possibility of trading job rights. Difficulties emerge in disposing of claims because: (1) democracy increases risk; (2) high cost of the search process. | Compare present value of I in conventional stock and in LMF. LMF claims undervalued in the absence of an organized market. | Allocative efficiency cannot be brought about by introducing tradable claims: I in n.o.a. remains retarded. Inefficient resource allocation since claims difficult to sell. LMF less attractive because purchaser of a claim must join the firm. Tradable claims not consistent with broader needs of LM, since they decrease democracy. Possibility of degenerating into a conventional firm. If solution exists, must rest on external sources of finance. |

Abbreviations:

I – investment
n.o.a. – non-owned assets
o.a. – owned assets
T – time horizon
S – principal invested

pf – profit
K – capital
L – labour
U – utility
f – function of

r – return on n.o.a.
i – return on o.a. (interest rate)
LR – bank lending rate

C – consumption
max – maximization
CMR – capital maintenance requirement
w – wages

generations, leading the LMF to choose projects which pay off relatively quickly (Furubotn 1978).

However, neither does a simple change in property rights ensure optimal investment behaviour of an LMF (Furubotn 1980c). If we assume an LMF in a capitalist environment with tradable claims held by individual workers, underinvestment will still prevail because difficulties will emerge in selling workers' claims. In addition, there will be a high probability that the LMF will degenerate into a conventional capitalist firm.

Therefore, an LMF undertaking investment is expected to face a specific problem: since workers do not have full ownership rights over the firm's assets, they will not be able to recover the principal of their investment at the end of their time horizon. Unlike the capitalist entrepreneur whose investment is 'perfectly' liquid, a worker in an LMF cannot sell his job and the future income streams associated with it in order to capitalize his part of the firm's current and future earnings, but can only benefit from an investment over the period of employment in the same firm. This will lead the LMF to adopt a truncated time horizon – a problem which at least in theory does not arise in the capitalist firm – which in turn will cause underinvestment of the LMF, compared to its capitalist counterpart operating under similar conditions.

3 Extensions of the LMF investment theory

The Vanek-Furubotn-Pejovich hypothesis has laid down the basis for analysis of LMF investment behaviour and even today, after twenty years, it represents the dominant theory. Nevertheless, the conclusion on underinvestment cannot be generalized, as critical assessments of the theory have proposed conditions under which an LMF may not underinvest. Four groups of considerations are of particular importance, related to restrictions on capital withdrawals, the planning horizon, methods of finance, and some other critical assumptions.

A differentiation of restrictions

The collective nature of investment in an LMF can have different implications, depending on the type of restrictions regarding capital withdrawals. It can imply the limited recovery of capital (LRC), which prohibits withdrawals of workers' shares in past investment and the capitalization of future earnings, in case a worker leaves the firm; and the capital maintenance requirement (CMR), which requires refinancing of past investment through appropriate depreciation in order to maintain the value of enterprise assets. While the CMR is usually taken to represent the Yugoslav LMF, the LRC is considered a general characteristic of the LMF with collective ownership. Since both sets of rules imply a limitation of traditionally conceived capitalist property rights, they have often been considered jointly in the literature under the generic term of 'limited recovery of capital'.[1]

It has been argued that the disincentive to invest can only be established unambiguously under the CMR, i.e. if the LMF is obliged to maintain its capital stock indefinitely (Zafiris 1982; Uvalić 1986). A strong CMR, defined by Bonin (1985) as the maintenance of the real value of assets over time, *does* generate a disincentive to invest: workers will not be able to recover the principal of an investment, even if they

29

remain with the same firm for the full duration of an asset, and hence even if they adopt fairly long time horizons, since the value of capital cannot be reduced. An LMF with a strong CMR will therefore exhibit the underinvestment effect, applying a higher rate of return from real assets than the capitalist firm, the rate being inversely related to workers' time horizons (Bonin 1985).[2] The only exception is if infinite time horizons are assumed, in which case the investment criterion of an LMF will not differ from that of a capitalist firm.

In the absence of the CMR, the investment decision of the LMF will depend crucially on the relationship between its time horizon and the repayment period of an investment. If the LMF's time horizon is shorter than the repayment period of an investment, the expected tenure of workers will represent an essential (specific) investment criterion: for an investment in real assets to be opted for, the investment would have to earn gross profits having the same total present value as investment in bank deposits – not over the lifetime of the plant, as in a capitalist firm, but over the expected tenure of workers. The difference in criteria will lead to a different ranking of projects, since projects with high returns over the LMF's time horizon may be accepted because of shorter payback periods, even though those with higher rates of return are rejected. Therefore, an LMF may place liquidity concerns above the productivity of capital, discriminating against projects stretching beyond the workers' horizon (Bonin 1985; Zafiris 1982). This distortion, however, is not equivalent to underinvestment, as it influences the *type* of projects chosen but might not necessarily decrease the overall *level* of investment; and it is also conditional on relatively short time horizons, which need not be the case.

If the time horizon of an LMF which is not obliged to respect the CMR is longer than the repayment period of an investment, the investment behaviour of an LMF may not differ substantially from that of a capitalist firm, since in this case the relevant criterion of the LMF will no longer be the time horizon, but the repayment period of an investment (Zafiris 1982; Ellerman 1986).

In spite of his assumption of the infinite durability of assets – which could implicitly imply the CMR[3] – Vanek did not refer to the CMR, but to the more general principle of LRC.[4] Indeed, Vanek's analysis assumes that capital *can* be consumed; otherwise, the second force of reducing capital could not take place. However, if the LMF can consume assets set up by an investment, the underinvestment force will not be present, since the selling of an asset and the distribution of its proceeds will permit the recovery of the principal. Therefore, Vanek's assumption on the infinite durability of assets is misleading, not only because it implies the exclusion of depreciation,[5] but because such an assumption by definition provokes the disincentive to invest: assuming infinite durability of assets and finite time horizons of workers obviously implies that the principal can never be recovered within the workers' time horizons.

As to Furubotn and Pejovich's theory, the authors usually assume a Yugoslav-type LMF obliged to respect the CMR – and on this basis propose general hypotheses for the LMF's behaviour.[6] In most articles the CMR is explicitly assumed but, with the exception of Furubotn (1980a), the authors fail to stress the importance of the CMR as a disincentive (Bonin 1985). However, investment behaviour under a CMR cannot be generalized.

The CMR does not usually apply to an LMF in a capitalist environment, but is a specific regulation present only in Yugoslavia (see appendix to this chapter). Although there are various restrictions in workers' cooperatives – limited interest on workers' shares and their redemption at nominal value, and more importantly, the constitution of obligatory collective funds which are not distributable to workers in case of closure – these restrictions are of a different nature than the CMR and are present only in some countries. They imply that a worker will not realize capital gains from investing personal wealth in the cooperative, or may not be able to capitalize his share of the firm's (collective) capital, either in the case of the cooperative being liquidated or in the case of leaving. However, as long as the cooperative continues operating and the worker remains employed for a sufficiently long time, he could benefit from undertaken investment through appropriate reward schemes; indeed, there is evidence that schemes rewarding investment are applied successfully in practice.[7] In Western cooperatives, there are no systemic constraints such as those that existed in Yugoslavia until 1989, that workers could not be owners of a part of their enterprise's capital.

In the case of Yugoslav LMFs, the underinvestment effect needs to be evaluated by taking into account other features peculiar to the Yugoslav context. The CMR could be partially ineffective in Yugoslavia because of inflation, when replacement costs exceed historical cost (Bonin 1985; Zafiris 1982), or due to regulations regarding loan finance which permit the repayment of a loan from depreciation allowances (Stephen 1978; Connock 1982). The effectiveness of the underinvestment bias might also have been reduced because of other systemic features of the Yugoslav economy, such as interest rate policies, imperfect capital markets, rules limiting enterprise autonomy in profit distribution, etc.

An analysis of depreciation rules in Yugoslavia reveals, in fact, that over the whole period since 1965, the CMR has been only partially effective (see appendix). Until 1975, firms were obliged to maintain only the book value of assets; since then, in spite of annual revaluation of assets and the intention to introduce a strict CMR, the system of depreciation and revaluation has lagged and hence has been unable to assure the maintenance of the real value of assets, thus effectively permitting its reduction. Because there has been a partial relief from the CMR, the underinvestment effect is likely not to have exhibited its full effect even in Yugoslavia. It was only in 1987 that stricter rules regarding revaluation were introduced.

Therefore, in spite of the generalized approach which dominates the LMF theory, there are important institutional differences between the Yugoslav firm and the Western cooperative. In addition to differences in restrictions on capital withdrawals discussed previously, in Yugoslavia all capital is in non-private property, whereas the Western cooperative is usually based on a mixture of private property (shares) of members and collective property (specific funds). In Yugoslavia, when an enterprise is closed no part of the capital can be appropriated by workers, since the enterprise is not the legal owner of its capital; whereas in workers' cooperatives, only a part of the capital (collective funds) cannot be distributed to workers (and this restriction exists only in some countries). The Yugoslav LMF is also part of a socialist system, whereas the Western cooperative operates in a capitalist economy and consequently may face different types of problems to those faced by the Yugoslav firm.

Time horizon

In a capitalist firm, the owner-entrepreneur can capitalize his part of the firm's earnings, current and future, by selling his claim on income flows, and hence his investment is to a greater or lesser extent perfectly liquid (depending on the organization of capital markets). This effectively means that he has a planning horizon which is long enough to enable him to benefit from all future revenues expected of an investment, i.e. his planning horizon is theoretically infinite. In an LMF, conversely, perfect liquidity of an investment is absent and workers have no claim over future income after termination of employment; hence the planning horizon of an LMF, as a rule, is not as long.

A truncated time horizon is a fundamental assumption of the under-investment hypothesis. Vanek argues that with time horizons longer than one year, the ranges for the returns on investment in capital assets A will be between twice and four times the time preference rate R, which, however, does not hold if a sufficiently long time horizon is considered.[8] Furubotn and Pejovich do adopt a dynamic analytical framework, yet the LMF's time horizon is regarded as being 'typically short' because of the negative implications of collective property rights.[9]

Nevertheless, a truncated time horizon need not be the general case. Ideally, the cause of the problem could be removed by distributing to workers free shares and/or bonds, corresponding to the increase in the capital value of enterprises and ensuring their tradability,[10] but this solution involves a number of problems (possible in theory, but not applied in practice, except sometimes, within a cooperative).[11] Remuneration schemes based on individually-specified rewards for capital invested in the firm are in line with Meade's (1986) proposal regarding a labour–capital discriminating partnership: workers and capital providers would, instead of income, be given two types of shares: capital shares freely tradable on the market, and labour shares (pro rata, so as to exhaust all of the enterprise's net value added) which would be tied to an individual worker and surrendered upon depar-ture. The investment bias would be avoided by issuing either debentures (Meade 1982, p. 218), or free capital shares corresponding to self-financed investment, pro rata to all labour and capital shareholders (Meade 1986; Nuti 1988b).[12] The major drawback of this solution is the inequitable principle of distribution: workers who join the LMF early will earn more than those who join later.[13] The underinvestment prob-lem is resolved, but at the cost of income inequality, although this may be justified on the basis that workers joining earlier should indeed be rewarded for the fact that they had to bear the initial risk. Moreover, all workers would get the same income for the part which is related to their work. The resulting inequality is of the same order as that resulting from the existence of private property and free enterprise.

Besides such remuneration schemes – which could, in principle, resolve the underinvestment problem – the planning horizon of an LMF may be as good as infinite, or at least long enough to eliminate the disincentive to invest, if additional factors, mainly neglected in the literature, are taken into consideration. Such factors include: (1) the level of workers' commitment; (2) the age structure of the work force; and (3) the effective investment criteria of an LMF.

1 Commitment of workers in an LMF may be higher than elsewhere. In a socialist LMF, workers may sufficiently regard themselves as 'guardians' of society's capital to adopt infinite horizons with respect to their investment (Zafiris 1982), in which case even in an LMF with a strong CMR the disincentive to invest would not apply.[14] Moral incentives may play an equally important role in participatory organizations in the West.

Commitment may also be higher, because of factors which reduce the mobility of labour. Schlicht and Von Weizsacker (1977) suggest that the way in which the commitment problem will be solved in the labour-managed market economy is by a sufficient *de facto* immobility of labour. Capitalism makes the commitment principle compatible with high labour mobility, while excluding workers from decision-making; a labour-managed economy makes the commitment principle compatible with labour management, by reducing mobility of workers.[15] Low mobility of labour might also be present in an LMF more than elsewhere, because past investment, due to the LRC, ties workers to their firm (Horvat 1982; Nutzinger 1975), or because of solidarity issues (reluctance to fire workers). In addition, a worker deciding to invest will probably be concerned more about how such a decision will affect the firm's growth and, therefore, his own future earnings, than with the possibility of changing jobs; transferred to the level of the whole collective, it is highly improbable that the *majority* of workers, at the moment of an investment decision, will think of seeking another employment in the short term. Whereas an immobile labour force will create other inefficiencies and problems, its presence implies that the penalty for poor investment choice will have to be borne by workers and that it will be in their interest to make the best possible investments, in order to increase incomes in the future (Milenkovich 1971).

2 The second issue of importance for the LMF's time horizon is the age structure of the work force, something which is usually assumed to be such as to determine short time horizons.[16] If we accept the usual assumption that in an LMF, the system of decision-making is such as to provide each worker with one vote, it is the median-aged worker who will cast the decisive vote on investment.[17] If the hiring policies of an LMF are such as to replace older members (at retirement) on a consistent basis with younger members, the median age of workers will remain approximately constant. If, as seems plausible for an LMF, there are no non-voluntary dismissals and the above mentioned hiring policy is applied, it is not unreasonable to suggest

that the time horizon of the median worker will be around twenty years – a time horizon which should be long enough, on average, to allow workers to benefit from undertaken investment.[18]

3 Finally, let us reconsider the investment criteria of the LMF. Although the time horizon, if exceeding the repayment period of an investment, loses much of its relevance as a specific investment criterion of the LMF, let us for a moment consider a short time horizon of five years. Such a horizon will allow sufficient time for workers to recover their shares of an investment (under appropriate reward schemes) only if the firm selects projects with a pay-off period not longer than five years.

Here it is useful to consider a capitalist firm operating under conditions of high uncertainty and risk, and rapidly developing technology. It has been observed that capitalist firms are increasingly using discounted cash flow techniques in conjunction with other methods, such as the pay-off period, since it provides a way of handling uncertainty and risk.[19] For a project to be undertaken, its pay-off period should not exceed the standard period which is customary in a given sector, ranging from under two, to five years (Nuti 1987a). This implies that a contemporary capitalist firm may not be in a position to maximize the present value of an investment project, but will be constrained to consider primarily the period over which the investment is repaid through gross profits as the decisive criterion for guiding investment.

In order to survive, an LMF operating under similar conditions of rapid technological progress will have to behave similarly to its capitalist counterpart, and therefore opt for the fastest-yielding investment projects. Yet the proposed pay-off period of no more than five years is highly unlikely to be longer than the time horizon of an average worker in an LMF. In this case, the ranking of projects by an LMF will not differ substantially from that of a capitalist firm, even when the LMF has a finite (and rather short) time horizon, in comparison with the capitalist firm having an infinite one.

It is also worth noting that a key problem for the capitalist firm is that it has to bargain frequently with labour unions. Since investment weakens the firm's bargaining position, a bias may be created towards more liquid forms of investment or towards easily saleable capital, or simply towards investment. This may be a bigger problem for the capitalist firm than the time horizon problem is for the LMF (see Ireland 1984).

Financing of investment

In Vanek's internally-financed solution, the opportunity cost of capital may in fact be equal to R (and not $R+D$), for reasons already discussed.[20] Similarly, external financing might not be provided at a cost reflecting the time preference R. Imperfections arising from transaction costs and different lending and borrowing rates could lead to situations where external financing will not be preferred. Such situations will arise where the weight of the repayment cannot be transferred to the future beyond the time horizon of the majority of the collective's members, or where the repayment periods are shorter than the life of the asset (see Gui 1984; Chilemi 1981). The existence of external finance does not remove the obligation of the LMF to pay back the principal eventually; the shorter the payback period of a loan, the more external financing approaches internal financing of investment.[21] In addition, the high dependence of LMFs on financial institutions can lead to banks' involvement in the internal policy of the firm – something which is against the principle of self-management – and hence to a conflict between the owner of capital and its user (Schlicht and Von Weizsacker 1977; Jensen and Meckling 1979; Dumas and Serra 1973; Horvat 1982; Ellerman 1986; Bonin 1985). There will also be a 'moral hazard' problem, arising from the risk associated with debt financing: an LMF may lack the incentive to operate successfully if in risky situations a substantial part of the losses can be avoided by bankruptcy; hence lending to a firm of yet unknown future profitability may involve a higher degree of risk (Schlicht and Von Weizsacker 1977; Gui 1985; Keren 1985). In addition, the main reason for underinvestment on the part of traditional cooperatives may not be the high implicit cost of capital from internal sources, but limited internal funds; for where the supply of funds is not infinitely elastic, reliance on internal funds clearly hampers the growth of the firm's capital stock (Stephen 1984).

Furubotn and Pejovich's claim that the availability of external sources of finance will drive self-financed investment to zero has also been widely criticized, for internal financing need not always be excluded by the LMF. The argument concerning exclusive reliance on bank loans is weakened by the likely existence of a margin between banks' borrowing and lending rates; such a margin will reduce the differential between the investment rate of return and the interest rate required for a worker to be indifferent between self-financed investment and distribution of net revenue to members. Indeed, if the margin is large enough, reinvestment of retained earnings will be actually encouraged. Whether bank finance will be the cheaper source will in addition depend on the payback period of a loan, on the time horizon of the LMF, and on whether or not a CMR is imposed on the LMF.

Stephen (1980, 1984) has argued convincingly that when the loan repayment period is shorter or equal to the workers' time horizon, any investment must be seen as a combination of credit and self-finance. When the bank lending rate exceeds the bank deposit rate, internal funds will have an opportunity cost lower than the cost of borrowing, and therefore the LMF may rely on internal finance. When borrowing and lending rates are the same, the required return for a project financed by a loan which is repaid within the planning horizon is the same as that for an internally financed project, and the availability of credit does not affect the level of investment (Stephen 1984).[22] On the other hand, perhaps enterprises can only borrow a maximum multiple of their internal finance, in which case they must reinvest net revenue to have access to external finance at all (as has been the case in Yugoslavia).

Bonin (1985) shows that in the absence of a CMR, under conditions of perfect financial intermediation (i.e. the bank lending rate being equal to the bank deposit rate), an efficient investment equilibrium will be possible in a labour-managed economy equivalent to the one in the capitalist economy. In an LMF with a CMR, only if the CMR is not obligatory for externally-financed investment will there be an absolute preference for bank loans,[23] and the argument on exclusive reliance on bank loans will be valid only if no payment of principal is ever made (Bonin 1985). Furubotn and Pejovich's implicit assumption that maturity dates for loans are matched not with tenure, but rather with the expected life of the assets, is a heroic assumption, since the CMR makes the life of an asset infinite, implying that the loan maturity date will also be infinite (Bonin 1985). For an LMF to rely only on external financing, either financial institutions will have to offer especially advantageous conditions (long maturity and low lending rates), or the representative worker's tenure will have to be quite short, or both.[24] An LMF with a CMR is therefore likely to rely on both internal and external sources of finance, but problems linked to capital misallocation are likely to remain, even in the presence of financial intermediation (Bonin 1985).

Aoki (1984) has suggested that the LMF's choice of the method of financing will depend essentially on whether an investment project is labour-saving or not. If an investment requires the employment of new workers and is financed internally, the entry of new workers is financed at the expense of existing members, whereas future yields of the investment will be shared equally by all workers (including newcomers). In this case external debt will be preferred, since future interest payments will be borne equally by new and existing members. If, however, an investment requires the introduction of labour-saving technology, there is less opportunity to mitigate the burdens of cost-bearing by putting off the actual payment of the capital cost. Since the number of new entrants will be smaller than the number of outgoing workers, workers who have prospects of longer tenure will be better off by sharing the current capital cost with the relatively larger number of existing workers, and hence will prefer to finance investment from retained earnings.

Other critical assumptions

Vanek's degeneration process essentially depends on certain critical assumptions. It is the choice of income per worker as maximand that leads to the disappearance of the firm under CRS, and to its small size under IDRS. This maximand is not consistent with Vanek's own assumption regarding membership reductions, which are likely to take place only through natural wastage. The assumed maximand can be accepted only if the adjustment of membership is viewed as a short-run phenomenon, whereas Vanek's view regarding the prohibition against expelling workers assumes just the contrary, i.e. that downward adjustments take place only in the long run.

If the LMF does have some preference for changes in membership, several models have shown that the objective of an LMF will not simply be the maximization of income per worker.[25] In addition, under the assumption of a reluctance to dismiss workers, degeneration will take a long time. In such a long-term framework the LMF is even less likely to maximize income per worker, since growth objectives requiring positive investment may be essential for higher incomes in the future.[26]

Furthermore, in the original model developed by Ward (1958), Vanek (1970) and Meade (1972), the choice of membership size is the outcome of two competing forces: one which seeks to reduce membership and hence increase revenue per worker, and the other which seeks to increase membership, thereby reducing non-labour costs per worker. Vanek (1971) explicitly assumes the absence of non-labour costs, because the community does not pay for the collectively-owned assets. Nevertheless, the LMF is bound to have certain non-labour costs, even if assets are not paid for (capital maintenance, rent, heating, insurance, and so forth). Minimizing such non-labour costs by spreading them over a larger number of workers would represent an incentive *against* membership reductions.

Another implicit assumption of Vanek's model is the perfect homogeneity of the labour force. Specialization would represent a further obstacle in membership reductions since certain types of worker, indispensable for production, would have to be replaced on retirement. Similarly, the assumed perfect responsiveness in adjustments of capital may not always be possible; a machine that cannot be replaced by one operating with fewer workers may block membership reductions.

Several inconsistencies relating specifically to the second self-extinction force have also been pointed out. The maximand of income per worker does not require the reduction of capital, at least not in the CRS case, given that income per worker is a function of the K/L ratio, while the second force involves a *reduction* in that ratio (Stephen 1984, p. 81). Here again the assumed maximand is placed in question: contrary to Vanek's analysis of the degeneration process, where the opportunity cost of capital is assumed to be equal to zero, a more realistic objective function would be one which maximizes income net of opportunity cost of capital per worker, or $Y=(pX-rK)/L$, since capital has an opportunity cost, even if no financial payment is made for its use: it is the return to be earned from liquidating the asset and investing its proceeds (Stephen 1984, pp. 80–4).

The degeneration process will not necessarily take place in the case of IDRS, since the outcome of the second self-extinction force need not benefit the collective, depending on the particular production function assumed: where the technology is not of a CRS type, the theory only provides an explanation of the small size of cooperatives, not of their short life-span; but small size does not necessarily imply a short life (Stephen 1984, pp. 78, 81). An LMF under IDRS may obtain a technically efficient level of production if capital has an opportunity cost equal to R (Stephen 1984, p. 84), or if we consider that the two conditions necessary for the maximization of income per worker, $F_L = X/L$ and $F_K = 0$, imply that CRS hold (Bartlett 1984a). Therefore, under IDRS, the process described by Vanek does not, and under CRS need not necessarily involve degeneration. And since CRS is a very special, rather than general case usually encountered in practice, the degeneration process itself can occur only under specific conditions.

Vanek's analysis provokes confusion since it assumes two different

Table 3.1. *The impact of appropriability restrictions on LMF investment behaviour*

Restrictions	Time horizon (T)	Investment criterion	Underinvestment
1 LRC and CMR			
1.1 Maintain real value of assets	Finite	Horizon	Fully present
1.2 Maintain book value of assets	Finite	Horizon	Present only partially
1.3 Maintain real or book value of assets	Infinite	Standard*	Not present
2 LRC without a CMR			
2.1 T relatively short, due to LRC	(a) T<Invest. pay-back period (PP)	Horizon	Distortion in ranking projects, which is not equivalent to under-investment and could be avoided by schemes designed to prolong T[27]
	(b) T<Loan maturity (LM)	Horizon	Not necessarily present, if lending rate is high enough
2.2. T relatively long, due to age structure, commitment, etc. or reward schemes designed to prolong T (e.g. shares)	(a) T>PP	Standard	Not necessarily present, if workers are adequately rewarded
	(b) T>LM	Standard	Not present if lending terms are sufficiently unfavourable
	(c) T>PP, but techno-logical properties of a project are considered:		
	If labour-intensive	Present
	If labour-saving	Indefinite

*Criteria usually used in capitalist firms based on discounted cash flow techniques (net present value, internal rate of return).

opportunity costs of capital, one prior to an investment equal to $R+D$, and another one for an asset already committed to the firm, equal to zero. Yet for CRS to hold, under the assumption of self-financing and the maximand of income per worker, the optimal capital stock requires that the marginal product of capital be equal to zero, and not to $R+D$, and hence it will be *larger*, not smaller than in the externally-financed case where the marginal product of capital equals R (Bartlett 1984a).

In conclusion, a summary of the different possibilities concerning an LMF's investment decision is presented in table 3.1. The table shows that the time horizon may, but need not always be the decisive criterion of the LMF's investment decision. Contrary to the surveyed theories which draw their conclusions by focusing exclusively on the workers' time horizon as the dominant criterion of an LMF's investment decision, two other horizons are equally important: namely, the payback period of an investment, in the case of self-financed investment, and the repayment period of a loan, in the case of external finance. However, even when the time horizon is the dominant criterion of an LMF undertaking investment, it need not, under certain conditions, lead to underinvestment. Therefore, the LMF's investment behaviour needs to be evaluated by taking into account the concrete institutional setting in which an LMF operates.

Appendix: restrictions on capital withdrawals in labour-managed firms

It is of interest to contrast the theoretical LMF with actual Western and Yugoslav LMFs, with particular reference to restrictions on capital withdrawals by workers, since the theoretical prediction on underinvestment essentially depends on the nature of these restrictions.

Yugoslav regulations

There is some confusion in the literature concerning the nature of the capital maintenance requirement (CMR). For some authors, the requirement is directly linked to Yugoslav practice, whereas others argue that collective ownership of assets implicitly contains such an obligation, so that the rule is more widely applicable. There has also been some doubt as to the real meaning of the CMR in Yugoslavia; it has been questioned whether it refers to the physical maintenance of existing equipment or the maintenance of the value of capital, to the book or the real value of assets, to gross or net assets, to capital provided by the state or also future increments of capital.

The CMR is a specific regulation present only in Yugoslavia. The 1974 Constitution (Article 15) and the 1976 Associated Labour Act (ALA) (Article 3) state that 'workers are obliged to . . . continuously renew, increase and improve social assets'. Details are given in chapter 6 of the ALA, which specifically refers to the management of social resources (Article 227 onwards). Further regulations concerning the CMR are contained in various laws on the depreciation and revaluation of assets, laws which have been changing continuously over the past 25 years. Since the law on depreciation was adopted at the end of 1966, there has been a special law on depreciation rates (1966), a further four laws on depreciation (1974, 1976, 1984, 1986), and almost twenty amendments to these various enactments. The first law on the revaluation of fixed assets was adopted in 1975, followed by a new law in 1984; the latter was replaced by new provisions on revalorization included in the 1986 law on income, which effectively introduced an obligation to revalue assets every three months, starting from the beginning of 1987.

In the post-1967 period, depreciation allowances were to remain in the enterprise for the purpose of maintaining the value of the firm's fixed assets (instead of being placed in special accounts, as was the case before 1967). Besides the prescribed minimum rates, enterprises could allocate additional amounts to depreciation. Until 1975, the basis for calculating depreciation was the book value of assets (although revaluations of all fixed capital were undertaken in 1953, 1957, 1962, 1966 and 1971). In 1972, new regulations were adopted which provided for a revaluation of fixed assets if their market price had exceeded their book value by over 5 per cent. However, it is only since 1975, when the first law on the revaluation of fixed assets was adopted ('Zakon o revalorizaciji društvenih sredstava i sredstava zajedničke potrošnje od strane korisnika društvenih sredstava', Službeni list SFRJ no. 32, 1975) that enterprises have been obliged to revalue fixed assets on a continuous basis, if a difference greater than 10 per cent emerges between the book and market values of assets. Capital is revalued at the end of each year, and as such serves as the basis for calculating the following year's depreciation. For assets acquired using foreign loans, the book value of net assets is adjusted to the corresponding change in the foreign exchange rate. In 1985 obligatory revaluation was extended to working capital (raw materials, work in progress, finished products), and in 1987 to depreciation allowances not yet used for replacement.

The 1966 laws on depreciation ('Zakon o amortizaciji osnovnih sredstava radnih organizacija', and 'Zakon o stopama amortizacije osnovnih sredstava radnih organizacija', Službeni list SFRJ, no. 29 and no. 52, 1966) effectively served as the basis of all subsequent laws. Initially, depreciation rules applied to fixed assets and resources for collective consumption in use. If assets were withdrawn from use before they had fully depreciated, either the undepreciated amount was compensated for from the business fund, to be refunded from income during the following six years, or such assets were offered for sale; if no buyer was found, assets could be written off without corresponding compensation from income. Depreciation was to be used primarily for the replacement of existing assets and the acquisition of new fixed assets, but it could also be used temporarily for other purposes (for example as working capital).

The 1976 depreciation law enlarged the list of resources to be depreciated (so as to include, for example, expenditure on innovation and founder-members' investment) and changed certain specific provisions (for example, those relating to the writing-off of assets). More importantly, enterprises were given more freedom in using depreciation allowances, since these could now be used for the repayment of, or as a down-payment for, investment credits, as well as in joint investment projects. With the amendments adopted at the end of 1982, preferential treatment was accorded to enterprises in the process of liquidation or financial restructuring (50 per cent of depreciation obligations could be postponed until the following year), and to enterprises not using fixed assets at full capacity (depreciation rates could be reduced by up to 50 per cent).

According to the 1986 law on depreciation ('Zakon o amortizaciji društvenih sredstava', Službeni list SFRJ no. 72, 1986), resources that must be depreciated include fixed assets (buildings, equipment, cattle), material rights which are part of capital assets (buildings or equipment), material rights to technology (patents, etc.), innovation resources, investment for enhancing agricultural production, founders' investments, forests, slow-growing plants and fast-growing trees. Exceptions are land, buildings and equipment that serve national defence and state security, cultural monuments, and certain categories of fast-growing trees and cattle. The depreciation rate is set on the basis of the purchase price, or the revalued value of such resources. An enterprise can lease assets not being used to other enterprises or to individuals wanting to set up private businesses; or, as was provided for by previous laws, it can offer such assets for sale. Depreciation allowances can be used for a variety of different purposes, including the repayment of investment credits and as working capital. Some restrictions have also been introduced: depreciation obligations can no longer be postponed or calculated at a lower rate when assets are not being used at full capacity (Article 14); the only exception to this concerns resources damaged due to *force majeure*, and assets in their first year of use (Article 11). Voluntary depreciation no longer forms a part of income, but of material costs of an enterprise. Enterprises which are in the process of financial restructuring or liquidation, which were not privileged by the 1984 depreciation law, are now again exempt from depreciation obligations. Finally, stricter regulations have been set for assets not being used: if the price obtained by selling an asset is lower than the non-written-off value of that asset, the difference must be compensated for.

Uniform depreciation rates have been laid down for the whole country; the only exceptions are depreciation rates for apartments, buildings, forests, and roads, which are determined by republican laws. Depreciation rates are differentiated by type of assets, which are classified into more than 100 different groups. The depreciation rates have remained almost unchanged in the 1971–85 period. The average rate of depreciation has been around 5 per cent in most years since 1971 (Žarković and Vujičić 1987, p. 144), although the rates for different groups of assets range from a minimum of 1 per cent to a maximum of 50 per cent. The 1985 regulations, for example, applied a 1 per cent rate to earth sluices for water supply and canalization, to branch lines for railway tracks, and to sports facilities made of concrete (diving boards, skating tracks); a 50 per cent rate was applied to certain types of cattle, and to packaging for the transport of radio and television equipment. In 1986, these rates were increased for most groups of assets, in some cases by more than 100 per cent.

Several weaknesses of the system of depreciation and revaluation of fixed assets in Yugoslavia have been emphasized. Revaluation has not adequately reflected inflation, since until 1975 it was undertaken only occasionally, while thereafter, it was lagged and therefore insufficient: fixed assets were revalued annually for inflation during the previous year; and the capital so revalued served as a basis for depreciation only in the following year. Moreover, until the beginning of 1987, revaluation was not applied to unused depreciation allowances; according to some calculations, this has decreased the real value of depreciation funds annually by more than one half (Žarković and Vujičić 1987, p. 29).

Such a system of revaluation has therefore meant that depreciation was insufficient to maintain the real value of assets. Whereas in the 1971–80 period the nominal value of fixed assets increased 14.1 times, depreciation increased by only 10.7 times, and the average depreciation rate actually declined from 6.5 per cent in 1970, to 4.2 per cent in 1980. Although since 1981 depreciation rates have been increased, the average rate has remained low and has thus resulted in a rather low average depreciation period of fixed assets: 23.6 years in 1980, and 21.7 years in 1981 (Drakul 1984). The more favourable conditions granted to some categories of enterprises – such as the possibility of postponing depreciation obligations – have meant that an enterprise could effectively calculate depreciation at a much lower rate.

The existing systems of depreciation and revaluation have also been criticized as being active generators of inflation, because of deficiencies in accounting. Since in the balance sheets of enterprises depreciation appears as a material cost, its calculation lower than that necessary for maintaining the real value of assets has meant an understatement of costs, while income could for the same amount be artificially over-stated, enabling the payment of higher personal incomes (see Žarković and Vujičić 1987). In other words, when net assets are revalued, the counterpart on the liabilities side is entered by increasing the value of the business fund (i.e. the enterprise's own resources); but in contrast, depreciation of an asset enters costs in a given year in its non-revalued amount (see Bajt 1985; Ranković 1985; Rankov 1986). Thus the system has encouraged the outflow of a substantial part of income from fixed assets into consumption. The existing accounting system has also discouraged voluntary depreciation above the legally prescribed rates, until 1986, since this part of depreciation was not included in costs, but in taxed income.

Existing depreciation regulations have also encouraged a high degree of reliance by Yugoslav enterprises on bank loans. An enterprise could effectively use depreciation allowances for different purposes, and compensate for the amount so used by means of new bank credits (thus saving on interest). Existing legislation is also very complicated; in order to facilitate the implementation of existing laws, several handbooks on their application have recently been made available (for example, Milošević and Živković 1984; Pančić 1985; Žarković and Vujičić 1987). It is also worth noting that Yugoslav depreciation laws, and problems encountered in implementing them, are very similar to those in other socialist countries (on the problems encountered in, for example, the Soviet Union, see Lavigne 1962, 1968, 1978).

Regulations in Western cooperatives

In Western Europe, restrictions on capital withdrawals from workers' cooperatives vary considerably, not only across countries, but also within countries, as specific rules are sometimes laid down only by enactments of individual cooperatives themselves (see table 3A.1). In practice, there are almost no cases of 100 per cent collective ownership of assets, in the sense of Vanek's theory; the more frequent form is a mixture of private and collective ownership. Members contribute a certain amount of capital when joining the cooperative, usually in the form of a share, which remains the worker's private property and in most cases is redeemable and sometimes indexed. Collective property of a cooperative is usually constituted by that part of capital which is allocated to various funds, and in cases of closure, in some countries, such funds cannot be distributed among workers.

The ratio of private capital to collective funds varies considerably across countries. In contrast with Spain (Mondragon) where 85 per cent of original capital is held on members' individual capital accounts and only 15 per cent goes into the compulsory reserve fund, in Danish trade-union cooperatives the entire capital is collectively owned, and in British ICOM ('Industrial Common Ownership Movement') cooperatives the percentage of collective funds is generally quite high because individual capital stakes are limited. Differences are found even within different sectors: for example, Estrin, Jones and Svejnar (1984) found that private property of workers in French cooperatives represented 30 per cent of capital in the building sector, but almost 60 per cent in the electric energy sector. Therefore, the collectively-owned capital to which Vanek's theory refers represents only a part of the total capital of a cooperative.

Concrete restrictions which may constitute a disincentive to the individual worker to invest in a cooperative can be classified into two groups. The first group consists of restrictions concerning members' shares (initial capital contributions). In most countries there are no limitations on the maximum amount that can be contributed, although there are exceptions; thus in British ICOM cooperatives the individual capital stakes were limited to one share of £1 per member. Limits are sometimes also set on the total capital that can be held by a single member: in Italy the maximum was L4 million, subsequently raised to L30 million; in Ireland it is IR£3,000; in British CPF cooperatives the legal maximum is £5,000. More importantly, interest on members' shares is usually limited (as this is one of the principles of the

International Cooperative Alliance), but there are exceptions to this (in Ireland, Germany, Belgium, and some cooperatives in the UK). Low interest rates are also applied, in some countries, on members' loans (Italy, Netherlands). If a worker decides to leave the cooperative, his shares and/or initial capital contributions are usually reimbursed, but not always (in Ireland), sometimes only at their nominal value (Belgium, France, Italy), or only partially (in Mondragon, 80 per cent if leaving before retirement). Finally, shares cannot be sold to outsiders, and are not tradable except sometimes among members.

The second group of restrictions regards profit distribution and the related issue of the distribution of residual assets if a cooperative is liquidated. With the exception of French, Italian, Mondragon, and British ICOM cooperatives, where precise rules exist on the percentage of profits to be contributed to certain collective funds, in other European countries these matters are not regulated by law. Nevertheless, the percentage of profits allocated to funds, even when obligatory, is not very high. Thus the allocation to the reserve fund (indivisible reserves) ranges from 15 per cent of profits in Mondragon and France, to 20 per cent in Italy; in France, however, it ceases to be obligatory once the value of the fund has reached that of the cooperative's initial capital. In Spain, an additional 10 per cent must go into the Social Fund. In France, 25 per cent of profits *must* be distributed to workers (or reinvested for them through the Workers' Participation Fund). In Italy, profits distributed to workers must not exceed by more than 20 per cent the average wage bill on the market, as otherwise the cooperative can no longer claim tax benefits. In these three countries, if a cooperative is liquidated, the residual remaining in collective funds cannot be distributed among workers, but must be transferred to other cooperatives or to charities. Whereas the strictest rules are to be found in Italy and France (the residual, once shares have been redeemed and debts paid, is used entirely for charitable purposes), the rules in Spain allow, in addition to full recovery of the capital held on individual members' accounts, the distribution of 50 per cent of the compulsory reserve fund and of 100 per cent of optional reserves; only what remains is used for charitable purposes. In all the other West European countries, if a cooperative is closed, residual assets can be distributed to workers, usually in proportion to shares held.

The above limitations imposed on cooperatives need to be weighed against the advantages they enjoy in terms of fiscal benefits and financial support. It is precisely cooperatives in those countries in which the strictest rules are applied (Italy, France, Spain) that also enjoy

Table 3A.1 Regulations in workers' cooperatives in western Europe

| | Limitations | | | Profit distribution | | Distribution of capital in case of liquidation | Advantages | |
| | Capital provided by members | | | | | | | |
	Worker's capital stake	Interest on shares	Recovery of shares on leaving	General rules	Reserves (RF) and other funds		Fiscal benefits	Financial support
Belgium	No legal minimum	Not limited	Nominal value	No rules except for legal reserves	Same as in other types of firms	No rules	If member of association: • reduced corporation tax • interest on workers' invest. non-taxable • first BF1,500 interest on capital invested exempt from income tax	*Sociatra*, a special fund for coops
Denmark	Rules as in other firms[a]	Usually limited to 2 per cent above the DNB rate	n.a.	As in other firms		No rules	No special benefits respect to other types of firms	Workers' National Bank: loans at 1 per cent lower interest rates

France	One share or more per memb. One member cannot hold more than ¼ of total share capital	Limited to 2 points above the NBF rate	Nominal value but only if this doesn't decrease capital to less than ¼	RF: 15 per cent until it has reached the level of capital. At least 25 per cent: workers' bonuses (or put in Partici-pation Fund). Dividend on capital: not to exceed 25 per cent, and must be lower than amount for bonuses		Surplus in RF after shares and debts are paid goes to charity	• No business licence fee • Workers payments deductible from taxed profit • Partic. fund, if blocked for five years, not taxed • Investment RF (can be set up if Partic. Fund exists) is tax-free	Guarantee Fund which provides coops with revolving loans. Coops favoured in public contracts. SCOP: state support.
Germany	At least one share per member. Level set in internal rules	Interest on shares not limited; but on workers' investment paid only if profits allow	Original shares paid plus part of reserve fund	Free to decide	Level of RF specified in internal rules	Once all obligations are met, assets can be distributed to members	Same fiscal treatment, but for few exceptions (construction coops exempt from tax)	No special provisions

Table 3A.1 (cont.)

| | Limitations | | | | | Advantages | | |
| | Capital provided by members | | | Profit distribution | | | | |
	Worker's capital stake	Interest on shares	Recovery of shares on leaving	General rules	Reserves (RF) and other funds	Distribution of capital in case of liquidation	Fiscal benefits	Financial support
Italy	One share or more per member. Min. and max. stake set: L5,000 and L30 million	Interest limited on shares and loans. Until 1983 to 5 per cent, after 1983 to 2.5 per cent above interest on postal bonds (presently 12 per cent)	Nominal value		RF: at least 20 per cent. Profits distributed to workers must not exceed by more than 20 per cent the average market wage; otherwise the coop is no longer legitimate for tax exempt.	Surplus, after shares and debt are repaid goes to charity or to other cooperatives.	Interest on members loans privileged (taxed at 12.5 per cent). If adhering to cooperative principles benefits from total/partial tax relief (corporate tax, local revenue tax, tax on distributed profits).	State fund for the promotion of coops, through a special department of the *Banca Nazionale del Lavoro*
Ireland	Maximum per worker set to IR£3,000	Not limited (set by coop)	Not refunded	No rules	RF: usually a part of profits	No difference respect to other firms (in proportion to shares)	Tax on dividends not paid Dividends and premia tax-deductible	Grants under a scheme for promoting small industry

Netherlands	No legal provision	Sometimes workers have no shares; if they do, modest i	n.a.	No rules	Must be set in internal rules	Profits distributed to workers exempt from tax (taxed only as income). Members' loans not taxed if interest not received	A recently created Fund for promotion of ABC coops
Spain (Mondragon)	15 per cent of initial capital goes to RF; rest to workers' personal accounts	Limited to i of the Bank of Spain or the max. of 11 per cent	Revalued members' capital is redeemed on retiring; if leaves earlier receives 80 per cent	Compuls. RF: min. 20 per cent. Compuls. Social fund: 10 per cent. Optional RF may be set up. Remaining profit: indiv. accounts, according to pay and i' due on shares (this part is usually reinvested)	Optional RF and 50 per cent of compuls. RF can be distr. to workers. Shares repaid. Rest: for charity	Corporate tax is 18 per cent (not 33 per cent). Social fund is tax-deductible. Exempt from tax: transactions among coops and profits distributed to workers. A rebate of 95 per cent on the taxation licence	*Caja Laboral Popular:* provides investment capital and various services
UK ICOM	One £1 share per member			Members may share in profits, but a certain percentage must go into RF (left to the coop to decide)	Residual must go to charity purposes		Indus. Common Owner. Finance (govern. funds): loans at lower interest rate

Table 3A.1 (cont.)

| | Limitations | | | | | Advantages | | |
| | Capital provided by members | | | Profit distribution | | | | |
	Worker's capital stake	Interest on shares	Recovery of shares on leaving	General rules	Reserves (RF) and other funds	Distribution of capital in case of liquidation	Fiscal benefits	Financial support
CPF/ Coop. Union	No limits other than legal max. (£5,000 in 1981)	Not limited	Usually reimbursed (nominal value)	Apart from legal requirement for individual holdings assets held in collective form. Can issue bonus shares to workers.		Can be distr. to workers in proportion to shares	Workers' bonuses deducted from corporation tax (taxed as personal income); interest on investment in coop tax-free	Sometimes get a £1,000 start-up grant. Coop Bank: sometimes finances up to 50 per cent of investment.

[a] In Denmark, however, in the largest part of workers' cooperatives, ownership and control rests entirely with trade unions, and hence they are not really comparable with cooperatives in other countries.

Source: Compiled on the basis of information provided in Commission of the European Communities (1984), European Communities (1986), Bartlett and Uvalić(1986).

major fiscal benefits, that have experienced the most rapid growth in the past twenty years, and that today account for the largest share of workers' cooperatives in Western Europe (see Estrin 1985).

As to empirical data, early evidence on British footwear cooperatives provided by Jones and Backus (1977) seemed to offer support to Vanek's underinvestment theory (although these results have not been universally accepted as a confirmation of the theory; see Stephen 1984, p. 147). Indeed, a major problem of the cooperative sector, both historically and today, has been the problem of finance: because of the lack of capital, cooperatives have become widespread almost exclusively in labour-intensive sectors, such as trade, construction, transport, light manufacturing, and services (see Nuti 1988b). However, more recent evidence suggests that, for example, the system in Mondragon has secured a high level of internally-financed investment (see Commission of the European Communities 1984, vol. II, p. S16; Thomas and Logan 1982). Similarly, the latest evidence from France suggests that the basic determinants of investment in workers' cooperatives are similar to those in conventional firms, and that in general, no tendency to underinvest is apparent (Estrin and Jones 1987).

Therefore, restrictions on capital withdrawals applied by workers' cooperatives in different countries are not always, and not in all countries, as restrictive as is usually assumed. Even in countries where the strictest rules are applied, these restrictions essentially concern (1) the original capital of members (limited interest, redemption of shares at nominal value); and (2) subsequent increments of capital (obligatory collective funds, and the prohibition on distribution of the residual in cases of closure). Such restrictions are only likely to affect the worker if he leaves, or if the cooperative is liquidated. These restrictions are also different to those imposed on Yugoslav firms through the CMR. Although French cooperatives are required to maintain the value of assets at the level of 25 per cent of the highest value they have reached (see Estrin and Jones 1987), this minimum requirement regarding capital values is not equivalent to the CMR; and, although Mondragon cooperatives effectively revalue all their capital assets, in case of closure they are allowed to distribute a large part of the capital among members, and hence are not obliged to maintain indefinitely the value of capital.

4 The investment behaviour of the socialist firm

The theoretical framework, within which the likely impact of self-management on enterprise investment was analysed in the preceding two chapters, will now be supplemented by an analysis of the effects of socialist features of the Yugoslav economy on enterprise behaviour. For this purpose, we will rely mainly on Kornai's (1980) theory, but without giving a comprehensive survey of his work. Since not all of Kornai's hypotheses are fully applicable to Yugoslavia,[1] we will focus only on those parts of the theory which are directly relevant to Yugoslavia. In particular, Kornai points to certain general features of the traditional centrally planned economy, suggesting that these are likely to persist even after economic reforms aimed at decentralization and a higher reliance on the market have been implemented. Although Kornai initially (1980) developed his theory primarily for Hungary and other members of the CMEA, he later (1986) extended it to other socialist economies, suggesting that the theory is also applicable to Yugoslavia.

Kornai's theory of the socialist system

According to Kornai (1980), social relations and institutional conditions generate definite forms of behaviour, economic regularities and norms. The behaviour of the enterprise in a socialist economy is determined by the nature of the socialist system. One of the most fundamental features of the socialist system is the 'paternalistic' relationship between the state and the firm. Both before and after economic reforms aimed at greater reliance on market forces, the firm has been constantly protected and supported, to various degrees, by the state. While paternalistic tendencies appear from 'above' (state organs), this is complemented with the demand for paternalism from 'below' (enterprises). Social ownership of the means of production is concomitant with the active role of the state in the economy.

State 'paternalism'[2] provides an immediate explanation for the persistence of what Kornai calls the 'soft' budget constraint typical of the traditional socialist economy. Partial decentralization, like the 1968 Hungarian reform, has somewhat altered the normal degree of 'hardness' of the firm's budget constraint, but only a little. Among the main conditions for a soft budget constraint are 'soft' terms set in the tax, credit, and financial system in general, or in other words, the toleration by political authorities of financial indiscipline on the part of enterprises, and their non-fulfilment of obligations. The main consequence of the soft budget constraint is that the firm does not bear risk alone, but shares it with the other agents, or sometimes even shifts it on to others altogether. The 'socialization' of losses, as an alternative to bankruptcy, is implemented through various forms of redistribution of profits from profitable to loss-making sectors and firms. Firms cannot be sure of keeping additional profits, whereas if they find themselves in unfavourable financial conditions, they will be able to shift the consequences on to someone else: the buyer (through higher prices), creditors (postponement of repayments), or the state (through tax subsidies). Survival and growth of the firm will therefore not depend solely on its market performance, profitability and internal savings, but also on power influences.

These general features of the socialist system have a direct impact on investment behaviour. Because of state paternalism and soft budget constraints, demand for investment is not limited by fear of loss or failure. Since the firm's interests are not primarily linked to profits, repayment of money received for investment purposes can never cause much worry; a possible financial loss is compensated for by a variety of means. Managers will fight continuously for new investment, and the budget constraint of expenditures earmarked for investment is soft.

'Expansion drive' is the joint effect of the motivations listed above. It is a form of behaviour preconditioned by social relations, which became rooted so deeply in the thinking and acting routine of participants in the socialist economy that it has become a 'natural instinct'. Consequently, no firm is to be found that does not want to invest, and investment hunger is permanent. Expansion drive is present at all levels: nobody renounces investment voluntarily, nor does anyone need to be encouraged to invest. There is permanent self-stimulation, since there is no internal economic force to hold back investment hunger. Those who ask for investment resources run no financial risk. Expansion drive and investment hunger are among the main explanations of fast growth in socialist economies. In a socialist economy, growth is rapid even at times when the production of a capitalist economy declines because of demand constraints.

The granting of investment credits and government subsidies is influenced by the investment targets of the plan. Whereas the soft budget constraint is a sufficient cause of investment tension, such tension will be increased if economic policy itself heads expansion efforts, if it forces the fastest possible rate of economic growth and if official expectations regarding investment are high.

There is a close relationship between the hardness of the budget constraint and the activity of money. In a socialist economy, money supply passively adjusts itself to money demand, since the system of short-term credits granted to firms is also 'soft'. Thus for the enterprise sector, the rate of interest on investment funds is not an effective regulator of total investment demand. The firm is almost totally irresponsive to interest rate levels: a change in price has no income effect on the demand for borrowed funds, since the additional cost can be compensated for by a price subsidy, tax allowances, or price increase. Non-market methods of allocation of investment resources and capital rationing will therefore prevail. For the household sector, on the contrary, money is active, since the budget constraint of the household is hard.

A further indirect symptom of the softness of the system of financing of the socialist firm is the proliferation of interfirm credits. If an enterprise gets into financial difficulties, it will put off payments to other firms. Thus in conditions of restrictive monetary policies, firms will help each other through the mutual toleration of indebtedness, which will lead to an expansion of interfirm credits.

Another characteristic of the investment process in a socialist economy is the frequent and substantial overrun of both costs and time in completing investment projects. Claimants will underestimate expected costs, since the chances of acceptance when applying for funds will be greater if costs appear relatively small. Approval must be obtained to start an investment project; once started, it will also end in some way and at some time.

The tendencies described above will produce investment cycles in socialist economies. The upward swing of investment growth will last as long as the process does not hit one of the tolerance limits. Three kinds of tolerance limit are of particular importance: the balance of payments situation, the consumption level of the population, and resource constraints and bottlenecks. It is enough that the economy reaches only one of the above-mentioned tolerance limits for the brake to be suddenly applied. If drastic intervention is necessary, the most obvious field will be investment.

Following economic reforms aimed at introducing a more market-oriented system, expansion drive and investment hunger have persisted, since the budget constraint has remained soft. Investment is still not held back by fear of financial failure or by perceived risks, and no internal economic compulsion puts a voluntary constraint on investment hunger. The budget constraint has not hardened enough to render the interest rate on investment funds an effective regulator of total investment demand. The effect of the profitability criterion on investment decisions has somewhat strengthened, since investment is now financed partly from the firm's own resources. However, the effect is still much weaker than that of non-price selection criteria independent of profitability, since firms will continue to rely on state funds, and the share of profits redistributed by various means is still high. The role of the political authorities therefore remains extremely important; with economic reforms, plan bargaining has simply been replaced by redistribution bargaining.

Systemic features of socialist economies have been illustrated by reference to Kornai's work, but the problems he discusses have also been emphasized by other scholars. Nuti, for example, discusses the reasons for the accumulation bias of the Soviet-type economy: 'Both at the macro and the micro level the same urge to accumulate typical of the capitalist system is present, but without the checks and constraints of the capitalist system (such as stock market valuation, takeover bids, bankruptcy discipline, and so on)' (in Nuti 1985, p. 115). Other problems emphasized by Kornai – soft budget constraints, redistribution of profits, rationing of investment resources, underestimation of the investment costs, and other capital market imperfections – have also been discussed by a number of authors with particular reference to Yugoslavia.[3]

Application of Kornai's theory to Yugoslavia

The hypothesis advanced is that in spite of substantial institutional change in Yugoslavia, the essence of the investment process has remained very similar to that suggested by Kornai for other socialist countries. This is because until 1989, Yugoslavia remained a socialist economy, characterized by many systemic features (and problems) of the traditional centrally planned economy. With the implementation of economic reforms in Yugoslavia, some priority objectives of centrally planned economies were abandoned (primarily, full employment and price stability), along with many of the traditional institutions (centralized planning, state monopoly in some of the most important sectors, state ownership of enterprise assets). Nevertheless, other fundamental socialist goals were retained, including the commitment to planning, egalitarianism, solidarity, and non-private property.

Socialist goals in Yugoslavia, as in other East European countries, have been pursued through the traditional instrument of the Soviet-type model of persistent state intervention in the microeconomic sphere. What has changed with economic reforms in Yugoslavia is the level, institutions, and channels of state influence; but the nature of the enterprise–state relationship has essentially remained the same, characterized by state paternalism similar to that lamented by Kornai for the more conventional Hungarian economy.

Such state paternalism does not necessarily involve vertical relationships of formal supervision or direct subordination of enterprises to the central political authorities (see Hare 1990). In the Yugoslav case, state paternalism has continued to operate through various mechanisms of economic regulation, including a number of indirect and informal channels of political interference, no longer at the level of federal ministries, but more frequently at the level of local communes.

In Yugoslavia there are various mechanisms of economic regulation (not to use the word planning, as planning in the traditional sense has lost much of its meaning). Some of the existing mechanisms, such as certain economic policies of the federal government, resemble the state intervention practices of capitalist countries. Others are similar to planning instruments in socialist countries, such as medium-term (five year) plans which define the main objectives and priority sectors for the period concerned, and until 1989, annual economic resolutions which set the annual targets.[4] Still others are specific to self-management, such as social compacts and self-management agreements, reached through a bargaining process during which policies of the different agents are coordinated. But in addition to these regular macroeconomic instruments, which in one form or another are present in most economies, the Yugoslav government, like those in other socialist countries, has retained the right to intervene by means of *ad hoc* administrative measures, often on a selective basis favouring some sectors at the expense of others. Since such measures are hard to anticipate, they produce a high level of uncertainty, and at the same time frequently leave little room for autonomous decision-making on the part of the individual firm.[5]

In Yugoslavia, these mechanisms of economic regulation ensure the transmission of social objectives and interests to the individual enterprise, which is usually done through the local commune. Although officially the local socio-political community enters the enterprise decision-making process only when a consensus cannot be reached between the working collective, the management, and the socio-political organizations, it is directly involved in enterprise decisions through the planning mechanism (see Prašnikar and Svejnar 1988). Since an enterprise's medium-term plan is also part of the medium-term plan of the community, the two units are legally obliged to collaborate in the preparation of their plans and to harmonize them, which eventually leads to the conclusion of social compacts on the plan's implementation. The local community ensures control over the fulfilment of the enterprise plan in various ways. First, through the manager, as the community delegates two members of the commission responsible for the election of the general manager. Second, each enterprise must periodically furnish the community with its balance sheet and income statements. Third, the community ensures that social plans have a higher priority than enterprise plans; when the two diverge, the community can impose the specified social objectives on an enterprise. Moreover, the local political community is also involved in enterprise policies because of its own direct interests. Since employment and tax generation are the principal goals of the local community, the achievement of such goals depends directly on the economic performance of firms, which makes the harmonization of all the activities of the community highly desirable (Prašnikar and Svejnar 1988, p. 245).

Besides the above direct channels of state regulation, political structures exercise their influence over enterprise policies in Yugoslavia through a number of indirect channels. Broader social interests in Yugoslavia make themselves felt on enterprises not only through the local commune, but through two other institutions: the trade unions and the League of Communists of Yugoslavia (LCY). The trade unions are directly involved in enterprise decisions on a variety of issues, such as the electoral process, the distribution of income, and other fields regulated by social compacts. The LCY does not have any direct influence over enterprise decisions, but its direct influence is substantial, since top managers, trade union representatives and self-management officials are usually active members of the Party. The LCY therefore plays a crucial role, ensuring that party members in the firm pursue the established social goals; should there be a deviation from these goals in a particular firm, the LCY ensures that its members strive to bring the firm's policy back into line (Prašnikar and Svejnar 1988, p. 244).

Therefore, state interference in the microeconomic sphere in Yugoslavia no longer takes place through the stipulation of precise and detailed plan targets and norms to be fulfilled, but rather, through policy guidelines (established by social compacts) which must be respected. Moreover, state interference is no longer necessarily direct, but very frequently indirect, in the form of recommendations, or informal persuasion and simple 'advice' on the part of local political officials.

Among the most important reasons for the persistence of state paternalism in Yugoslavia is that the property regime has remained essentially unchanged. After the official abolition of state property in the early 1950s, all capital assets became 'social' property, granting enterprises only the right to use socially-owned resources, and not property rights. Under the system of social property, capital is owned by the 'whole society', but no one is officially the holder of property rights. In the 1974 Constitution, it is explicitly stated that 'no one has property rights over social means of production – neither socio-political communities, nor organizations of associated labour, nor groups of citizens, nor individuals'.[6]

While this main principle remained intact during subsequent decades, the implications of the system of social property for the individual enterprise were somewhat different. In the 1965–71 period, enterprises were subject to a tax for the use of social capital. However, the conclusion reached in the early 1970s was that a tax on social capital was not entirely in conformity with self-management. In order to further increase the autonomy of enterprises in investment decision-making, in 1971 the tax on social capital was abolished. The individual enterprise was thus expected to operate as an autonomous collective entrepreneur, using its investment resources freely according to tendencies prevailing in the market.

After the elimination of the charge for social capital, enterprises acquired full rights (at least in theory) to the income stream generated by social capital. This has been interpreted by many scholars as the introduction of 'group' property, the effective redistribution of property rights in favour of enterprises vis-à-vis the state.[7] Bajt (1968) has insisted on the distinction between economic and legal property, arguing that economic ownership, reflected in the system of distribution, such as the right to entrepreneurial income in the Yugoslav case, need not necessarily correspond to the legal title of property, and consequently that Yugoslav enterprises behave as if they were the effective owners of capital.[8]

However, by acquiring rights to the income stream generated by socially-owned capital, enterprises have not been assigned other functions that ownership usually includes, namely exposure to rewards and penalties according to market performance, which is the essence of entrepreneurship. This is the fundamental difference between the right to use and the right to own: along with positive rewards for entrepreneurship, negative rewards (penalties) for poor decisions are also necessary. In fact, what was never introduced in Yugoslavia was an appropriate incentives system of both profits and losses.

Under the existing system of social property, capital is officially owned by 'the whole society', but the real owner of capital is the state. Although the Yugoslav enterprise may be the effective owner of a smaller or larger part of income generated by socially-owned capital, the state (society) has remained in charge of 'the rules of the game'. Indeed, the political authorities have remained responsible for a number of fundamental issues: the coverage of losses through income redistribution from profitable to loss-making firms; the use of enterprise income through regulations limiting enterprise autonomy (such as a minimum rate of savings, limits on increases of personal incomes, the obligation to maintain the value of social capital, obligatory investment in less developed regions); and the entry and exit of enterprises, where the policies pursued have contributed to industrial concentration, monopolistic practices and a capacity structure inappropriate to domestic and world demand. The industrial structure in Yugoslavia is almost as distorted as in other ex-socialist countries, and characterized by an almost complete absence of small enterprises (see Vahčić and Petrin 1989).[9] The dominance of large enterprises by itself is thus evidence against LMF theoretical predictions (see chapter 2).

One of the major consequences of state paternalism, also present in Yugoslavia, is the persistence of the soft budget constraint, i.e. financial indiscipline on the part of economic agents, and the socialization of losses as an alternative to bankruptcy. Although deficits in Yugoslavia are no longer covered directly by the federal budget, but indirectly – through the banking mechanism (loans at favourable terms, rescheduling or writing-off of debt), by reserve funds of other enterprises or reserves of the commune, and by a lowering or abolition of fiscal burdens – they are more frequently covered by (or shared with) other agents, than borne by the individual firm. The socialization of losses has had the same investment encouragement effect in Yugoslavia that access to bank credit is expected to have in the traditional LMF theory, or indeed more so – encouraging overinvestment – due to the reduction or outright elimination of downward risk (i.e. the risk of returns being inadequate to cover interest, or even losses).

This is closely related to an additional element generating soft budget constraints, one which is specific to Yugoslavia, namely the existing banking system. Banks in Yugoslavia are non-profit 'service' agencies of enterprises, founded and controlled by member enterprises, including loss-making firms. Banks' funds are provided by the founding enterprises, and bank profits are distributed among member enterprises irrespective of individual capital shares. In conditions of monetary restrictions, loss-making firms are therefore in a position to put pressure on banks for additional resources.[10]

Moreover, whereas banks in Yugoslavia are controlled by member enterprises, they have at the same time never really been freed from the influence of political structures. Although some of the measures under-taken in the past – such as the exclusion of socio-political communities, from 1977 onwards, from organizations permitted to invest directly in banks – seemed to support the aim of reducing the role of the political authorities, they have continued to decide on a number of other important issues concerning banks' functioning. Thus the republican political organs are responsible for issuing certificates testifying that the necessary conditions for the establishment of a bank have been fulfilled; communal representatives participate actively in social compacts that determine the role of banks in the financing of priority sectors; and political structures are also initiators of interbank social compacts (for example, on interest rate policy) (Mramor 1984). Since the Yugoslav bank has limited capital of its own and cannot freely decide on the use of its funds – for it is subject to pressure from both enterprises and political structures – the consequence of such limited autonomy is that it is not exposed to risk and is not fully responsible for decisions taken. Indeed, the same type of socialization of losses present in enterprises is also present in banks.

These problems have become even more evident in the past decade. During the 1980s, under the pressure of the severe economic crisis, state intervention in day-to-day enterprise policies became even more frequent, persistent and unpredictable than in previous periods, while with the liquidity crisis of an increasing number of enterprises and banks, the budget constraint became even softer. In recent years, government intervention in enterprise policies has consisted of a number of administrative measures considered necessary as part of stabilization policies, such as frequent price freezes or direct limits on personal incomes, as well as various indirect measures, for example ceilings on bank investment credits. It is primarily this type of administrative *ad hoc* state intervention in an enterprise's policies that the current reform aims to eliminate.

Recent Yugoslav experience therefore confirms that the real owner of capital in Yugoslavia is the state, for the Yugoslav enterprise has lost practically all control over its income, including entrepreneurial income. As stressed by Bajt, 'the Yugoslav self-managed enterprise is no more than a form of workers' participation in state management of the economy' (1988a, p. 35).

Socialist features of the Yugoslav economy inherited from the traditional Soviet-type economy have had a direct impact on investment behaviour. The essence of the investment process has remained much the same, characterized by expansion drive and a 'natural instinct' to invest. Yugoslavs have for generations been educated in the spirit of the sacredness of growth objectives. Such an attitude, while initially imposed on firms through precise targets to be fulfilled, has with time become part of the socialist morale and has continued to be transmitted to firms, although often in an informal and indirect way.

Ostojić (1984) describes the mechanisms of political pressure on enterprises to save and invest. One of the main instruments for implementing the objectives of high growth and investment rates is employment policy. Managers and directors are frequently nominated directly by political authorities in a non-self-management way, with the task of convincing (democratically or otherwise) the working collective to invest as much as possible. In this way it is effectively the state that assumes the role of the social entrepreneur: it invests, bears the risk and covers the losses. As stressed by Ostojić, 'The mechanism is well known: the president of the commune or the secretary of the LCY committee are usually the persons who back up all more important investment projects in their territory. Directors of enterprises which invest insufficiently will not retain their positions for long. This explains why there is continuous and systematic interference by the state in economic life, in a more or less open and direct way' (1984, p. 101).

What has enabled such an overinvestment drive in Yugoslavia, as in other socialist countries, is the absence of a hard budget constraint. While all the conditions necessary for the soft budget constraint listed by Kornai are more or less present in the Yugoslav firm, what is of major importance are the *consequences* of such a soft budget constraint, that are fully present in Yugoslavia: no risk-bearing by the individual firm, its protection from bankruptcy, and hence – due to the absence of financial failure – no voluntary constraint on investment hunger. The losses incurred through inefficient investment have continued to be covered in a variety of ways, and not primarily by the individual firm. The Yugoslav enterprise is subject to risk, but more frequently due to investment of other enterprises than its own. Although the 'allocator' of resources in Yugoslavia (to use Kornai's expression) is no longer the state, but banks, capital continues to be rationed, predominantly according to non-market criteria.

Until fairly recently, a Yugoslav enterprise had little to lose from an ambitious investment project, no matter how risky or unprofitable. On the contrary, it could expect substantial gains, not only of a material kind; for example, praise from local authorities if its projects led to increased employment opportunities or to a higher living standard of the local community. If initial investment credits were not sufficient to complete the project, additional resources were required; the larger the project the more important it may have seemed to bank officials, and the larger the firm the more likely it was to get additional finance (because of the influence of enterprises on banks). If the project turned out to be a failure, however, losses were to be socialized.

Therefore, in spite of the introduction of self-management and a higher reliance on market forces, the behaviour and motivation of Yugoslav firms regarding investment has not substantially changed. Yugoslav workers today are more interested in increasing profits, and are in principle free to determine their investment levels, since investment projects to be undertaken are usually discussed by all workers at the general assembly of the enterprise. However, this fact does not in itself determine enterprise behaviour. As put by Kornai, 'the main question . . . is not the actual form of incentive, but the rules for the survival and growth of the firm, and, linked to these phenomena, the relation between firm and state' (1980, p. 319). In fact, it is precisely the enterprise–state relationship that has remained almost intact in Yugoslavia. The investment process has remained soft, for extensive decentralization and self-management have not resulted in the transfer to the individual enterprise of responsibility for investment and of the risk associated with it. The enterprise continues, in most cases, to be protected from financial failure; the price paid for such protection is limited freedom and persistent government intervention.

Tyson's (1983) analysis has led to similar conclusions: although the economic reforms in Yugoslavia have constantly modified the decision-making authority of other agents, they have not affected the effective discretion of enterprises. Similarly, Burkitt (1983) found that every administrative instrument used in the period before 1965 in the field of investment policy, was also occasionally used in the post-reform period.

The socialist features of the Yugoslav economy inherited from the traditional centrally planned economy have seriously undermined the ultimate goal of all economic reforms in Yugoslavia of introducing a self-managed market economy, thus reproducing problems, typical of the socialist economy, of economic inefficiency, inadequate incentives and lack of entrepreneurship.

Part II

Empirical evidence on the nature of the Yugoslav system

5   Yugoslav investment and savings performance

The theoretical framework for understanding the investment behaviour of the Yugoslav firm discussed in part I will now be confronted with empirical evidence from Yugoslavia.[1] The period examined is primarily post-1965, for it is as a result of the reforms of the mid-1960s that the investment sphere was extensively decentralized, giving more autonomy to enterprises. (For the sake of comparison, however, the first half of the 1960s is also briefly considered.)

Investment and savings at the aggregate level

According to official Yugoslav statistics,[2] the Yugoslav economy achieved high investment and savings rates during most of the period under examination. In the years immediately following the 1965 reform, however, some moderation of these rates was registered. In comparison with the 1961–5 period, in 1966–70 the relative share of gross investment in GMP declined from 43 per cent to 38 per cent,[3] of which investment in fixed assets declined from 32.2 per cent to 30.6 per cent (see table 5A.1 in the appendix to this chapter). After this initial decline, during the 1970s investment shares in GMP showed a steadily increasing trend, rising to 40.6 per cent and then to 43.3 per cent of GMP in the two five-year periods of the 1970s, with investment in fixed assets accounting for 30 per cent and 37 per cent of GMP respectively.

The level of investment reached at the end of the 1970s was well above the domestic savings potential of the Yugoslav economy. The failure to control the overall investment effort, especially in the second half of the 1970s, had important implications for macroeconomic stability and balance of payments performance. Expansionary policies had been financed increasingly through foreign borrowing, leading to a rapid rise in external indebtedness ($17.3 billion by 1980) and to a record deficit, in 1979, on the foreign trade and current account.

Stabilization policies implemented since the early 1980s have brought about an improvement in the foreign balance,[4] but at the cost of a deep recession. Restrictive measures applied since 1980 cut domestic demand drastically, in particular investment in fixed assets, which registered negative growth rates throughout the 1980s except in 1986 and 1989 (as reported earlier; see table 1.2). Moreover, although the gross investment/GMP ratio remained around or above 40 per cent, the share of investment in fixed assets declined continuously and by 1988 had fallen to an unprecedented low level of only 18 per cent of GMP, with a corresponding increase in stocks (see figure 5.1).

However, the above gross investment rates, based on official Yugoslav statistics, represent overestimates for two main reasons. The first is that in Yugoslav statistics stocks are calculated according to end-of-year prices, which inflates their value, and for GMP biases invest-ment and savings rates upwards. Inflation brings about an increase in the value of stocks expressed in current prices, even if their physical volume has remained unchanged or has even decreased, and such a method of automatic revaluation of stocks leads to significant over-estimates of GMP, gross investment and savings in Yugoslav statistics (see Madžar 1985, 1986; Lydall 1989; Schrenk et al. 1979). The second problem is that the Yugoslav concept of GMP is narrower than the Western concepts of GDP or GNP, for it excludes value added in 'non-productive' activities (such as education, health, banking, adminis-tration, defence and other services), and consequently, the Yugoslav investment rate in relation to GDP or GNP is lower.

When adjustments of Yugoslav statistics are made in order to take these problems into account, the gross investment ratio is indeed lower (see table 5A.2 in the appendix).[5] According to World Bank estimates of Yugoslav GNP, which include an adjustment for stock overvaluation, the gross investment/GNP ratio declined from 33.7 per cent in 1961–5 to 29.7 per cent in 1966–70, and further to 28.4 per cent in 1971–5, but it rose to 35.6 per cent in 1973–80 and further to 37 per cent in 1980–7.[6] The gross national savings/GNP ratio showed a similar decline – from 32.6 per cent in 1961–5 to 28.7 per cent in 1966–70, and further to 27.1 per cent in 1971–5 – whereas over the 1973–80 period it rose to 32.9 per cent, and in 1980–8 further to 38 per cent.[7] Thus in comparison with the investment/GMP rate as reported in Yugoslav statistics, the investment/GNP rate was systematically lower by some 10 per cent or more (see table 5.1).

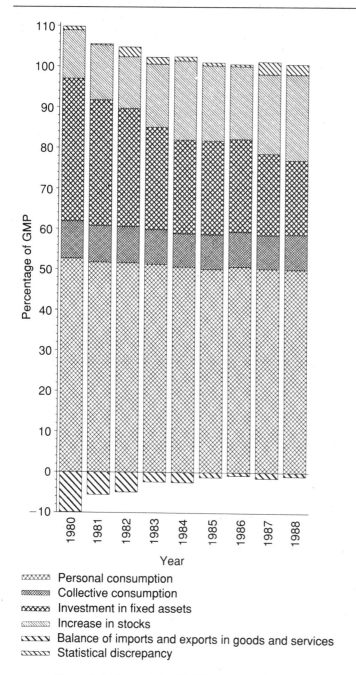

Figure 5.1 Yugoslavia: GMP by use, 1980–1988

Nevertheless, the adjusted investment ratios of the Yugoslav economy can still be considered high by international standards. When compared with countries at a similar level of development, such as Greece, Portugal, Spain, and Turkey, Yugoslavia has performed well in terms of several indicators measuring investment and savings effort (see table 5A.3 in the appendix). Throughout the period from 1965 to 1987, Yugoslavia had a higher investment/GDP ratio than all four countries; even during the 1980s, Yugoslavia's growth rate of domestic investment was less negative than those of Greece and Portugal. Bajt (1988a) has compared the investment rate in Yugoslavia and the above four countries for the 1960–80 period, both in relation to the Yugoslav concept of GMP (by deducting, for the four countries, the non-productive part of GDP) and to the Western concept of GDP (by adding, in the case of Yugoslavia, value added of non-productive sectors): in both cases Yugoslavia had the highest investment ratio. Vacić (1989) has made similar comparisons based on UN data for the 1971–87 period, reaching identical conclusions.

The crucial problem in the investment sphere in Yugoslavia has not been one of maintaining high levels of investment, but rather of mobilizing and allocating capital efficiently. Empirical evidence on capital allocation efficiency in Yugoslavia suggests that after 1965 the capital allocation process continued to produce a distribution of capital among regions, sectors and enterprises that was suboptimal from several points of view.[8] As can be seen from table 5A.3 in the appendix, investment efficiency in Yugoslavia, measured using a variety of methods, was lower than in Greece, Portugal, Spain and Turkey throughout the period under examination. Bajt (1988a) has compared the efficiency of investment in Yugoslavia and these four countries for the 1960–80 period, again taking into account the differences in the concepts of GMP and GDP, showing that investment efficiency, measured as the ratio between GDP or GMP growth and the gross investment/ GMP or GDP rate, has indeed been lowest in Yugoslavia, at around 70–75 per cent of the average for the other four countries.

In addition to economy-wide inefficiencies, Yugoslavia has also suffered from sectoral and regional capital misallocation, for significant differences in profit rates continued to prevail across sectors and regions. This has been influenced by severe capital market imperfections – inadequate interest rate policies, non-price credit rationing rules, excessive demand for credit – which have created barriers to capital mobility and have led to the persistence of 'political factories' and the duplication of facilities among republics, excess capacity in

Table 5.1. *Gross investment ratios in Yugoslavia according to Yugoslav and standardized concepts, 1961–1988*

	1961–5	1966–70	1971–5	1976–80	1980–8
Gross investment/GMP ratio	43.2	38.1	40.6	43.3	42.0
Gross investment/GNP ratio	33.7	29.7	28.4	35.6[a]	37.0[b]

[a] 1973–80
[b] 1980–7
Sources: Tables 5A.1 and 5A.2 (in the appendix to this chapter), based on official Yugoslav statistics of the SZS, and World Bank data (Schrenk *et al.* 1979 and World Bank 1990).

some sectors and bottlenecks in others, and a number of misconceived investment projects.[9]

The analysis leads to the conclusion that until the early 1980s the Yugoslav economy suffered not from underinvestment (predicted by Furubotn and Pejovich's theory), but from overinvestment (Kornai's 'expansion drive') and a series of other problems typical of socialist economies (capital market imperfections, inefficient use of capital, excess demand for credit). Although the decline in the investment and savings rates after 1965 might be thought of as constituting evidence in support of the underinvestment hypothesis, one of the main objectives of the 1966–70 Social Plan was to give priority to consumption and to redistribute national output in favour of personal incomes.[10] This decline in savings and investment was, therefore, at least partially intentional; rather than supporting Furubotn and Pejovich's predictions, it can be considered a sign of the achievement of planned objectives, thus confirming Kornai's contention regarding the importance of planning in a socialist economy. Moreover, the short-term moderation in these rates immediately after 1965 did not significantly influence the long-term trend (until 1980) of relatively high investment rates.

The drastic reduction in investment spending from the early 1980s only supports Kornai's hypothesis that the upward swing of investment growth will last until the system reaches one of the 'tolerance limits'. In Yugoslavia, such a limit was, in fact, reached in 1980 when there was a serious deterioration in the trade and current account deficit, requiring a reduction in all forms of consumption, and primarily severe cuts in investment spending.

Enterprise savings

The savings performance of Yugoslav enterprises can be analysed by examining four different savings ratios:[11]

1 **Gross savings/GMP ratio:** depreciation plus allocation to enterprise funds (business fund, reserve fund, collective consumption fund) in relation to GMP produced (the sum of depreciation, personal incomes, enterprise funds, and taxes and contributions).

2 **Net savings/GMP ratio:** allocation to enterprise funds in relation to GMP produced.

3 **Gross savings/net enterprise income ratio:** depreciation plus allocation to enterprise funds in relation to enterprise net income (the sum of depreciation, net personal incomes, and allocation to funds).

4 **Net savings/net enterprise income ratio:** allocation to enterprise funds in relation to enterprise net income.

The gross savings/GMP ratio of Yugoslav enterprises registered a substantial decline in the years following the reform (from 28.5 per cent in 1966 to 20.5 per cent in 1969), but this tendency was reversed in the 1970s and the average ratio for the decade was around 24 per cent. During 1981–5, enterprise gross savings reached a high average level of 28.1 per cent of GMP, but thereafter a notable fall was registered, and by 1988 the ratio of gross savings in enterprise GMP had declined to only 14.7 per cent (see table 5A.4 in the appendix).

It is also of interest to look at enterprise savings net of depreciation, since in Yugoslavia depreciation is not a voluntary component of savings. Similar to the trend in the gross savings/GMP ratio, the net savings/enterprise GMP ratio also declined in the late 1960s, from 19.7 per cent in 1966 to 9.7 per cent in 1969; thereafter it rose, oscillating around 13–15 per cent during the 1970s. In the first half of the 1980s, the ratio registered a substantial increase (exceeding 18 per cent in 1980–1), followed by a remarkable drop thereafter: by 1988 it had fallen to only 3.6 per cent.

Of major interest, however, is the distribution of net enterprise income after taxes and contributions are deducted from enterprise GMP. Similar to the trends observed in the other two ratios, the gross savings/net enterprise income ratio also declined initially (from 45.1 per cent in 1966 to 36.0 per cent in 1969). However, this ratio subsequently showed a tendency towards constant increase, rising from an average of 40.6 per cent in 1966–70 to 42.6 per cent in 1971–5, to 44.3 per cent in 1976–80, and further to 47.8 per cent in 1981–5. This long-term trend has largely been due to increasing shares of allocation to funds, as depreciation shares tended to be relatively constant.[12] However, after 1985 this savings ratio also fell, by 1988 to a low 34.4 per cent.

Finally, the net savings/net enterprise income ratio, once again of major interest because of exclusion of both taxes and depreciation, has been oscillating in a similar way; the five-year average rose moderately but continuously until the mid-1980s, from 23.7 per cent to 24.3 per cent, and further to 26 per cent in the three five-year periods following the 1965 reform, reaching a high 28.3 per cent in 1981–5; it then declined drastically, falling to 8.4 per cent by 1988.

In spite of the variations observed, all four savings ratios of Yugoslav enterprises have exhibited a similar tendency over time: a fall in the 1966–9 period, constancy or a modest increase in 1969–74, a decline in 1974–6, a general increase in the 1976–84 period, and a very notable fall from 1985 onwards (see figure 5.2).

Since the above ratios are based on official Yugoslav statistics, they represent a certain overestimation, because of the above-mentioned problem of stock appreciation. According to calculations by Schrenk *et al.* (1979) in which adjustments are made for stock overvaluation, in the 1966–75 period the gross savings/GMP ratio of Yugoslav enterprises was lower (especially in 1969–75), usually not exceeding 20 per cent.

Tyson's (1977a) econometric test of the savings performance of sixteen industrial sectors in Yugoslavia for the period 1965–74 shows that the long-run gross savings rates (the sum of depreciation and allocation to enterprise funds) out of enterprises' net income (the sum of savings and net personal incomes) were approximately 25 per cent or more in all but two of the eleven sectors that yielded statistically significant results. The hypothesis that the long-run savings rate was zero could be rejected in all but three sectors. This led Tyson to conclude that 'savings rates in many Yugoslav firms are positive and substantial rather than zero as predicted by theory' (1977a, p. 407).

However, unambiguous refutation of the underinvestment theory requires that *voluntary* savings of forms are positive. Even if we consider the narrow definition of savings, i.e. net savings, or 'accumulation' in Yugoslav terminology, this part of savings has not been entirely voluntary in Yugoslavia. Although for a short period (1966–71) enterprises were in principle 'free' to allocate their net income between accumulation and gross personal incomes, a substantial proportion of accumulation was nevertheless predetermined in advance for specific purposes (taxes and contributions paid from net income, interest payments and other contractual obligations). In addition, since 1971 accumulation has been legally subject to a minimum requirement depending on realized net income, in line with the terms set in republican social compacts on income which determine either the maximum permissible percentage of personal income payments, or a minimum savings rate.[13]

It is virtually impossible to identify the exact proportion of voluntary enterprise savings in Yugoslavia, but a better insight can be obtained by looking at the structure of accumulation (see table 5.2). Accumulation can be divided into four distinct categories: (1) various taxes and contributions paid out of enterprise net savings; (2) depreciation above the legal minimum (voluntary depreciation); (3) allocation to enterprise funds (business fund, reserve fund and other funds); and (4) contractual obligations (interest payments on bank loans and insurance premiums).

The first accumulation category – taxes and contributions – is clearly a non-voluntary component of enterprise net savings; until 1977, such taxes represented 10–19 per cent of accumulation, but have since progressively been reduced, and by 1986 had declined to only 0.3 per cent of enterprise net savings. Among the other categories, only the second – depreciation above the legal rates – is an entirely and unambiguously voluntary component of savings. During the 1967–86 period, depreciation above the legal minimum varied from 1 per cent to 14 per cent of total accumulation of Yugoslav enterprises, being close to or over 10 per cent until 1975, thereafter declining and usually not exceeding 5 per cent of accumulation. Fiscal disincentives contributed to such trends, since until 1986 voluntary depreciation did not form part of costs, but rather of taxed income. Among a sample of 147 Yugoslav firms, Prašnikar (1983) found that depreciation above the legally prescribed rates accounted for 2 per cent to 21 per cent of accumulation during the years 1975–9 (see table 5A.5 in the appendix).[14] Similar evidence is provided by Miović, who reports that Slovenian firms in the industrial sector on average depreciate at more than twice the minimum rate of depreciation (1975, in Tyson 1977a, p. 402).

For the other components of accumulation it is difficult to determine whether they can be considered 'voluntary'. A substantial part of accumulation has been dedicated to interest payments, which progressively increased from 16 per cent in 1966 to 66 per cent in 1986. Other categories, such as enterprise funds, have represented around 30–60 per cent of accumulation; although the minimum to be allocated to enterprise funds is imposed on firms, enterprises are free to allocate

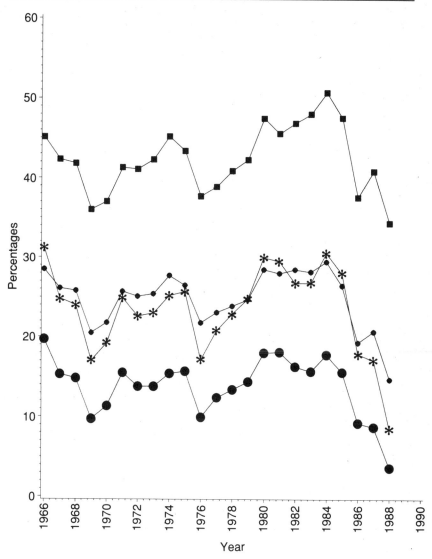

Figure 5.2 Savings ratios of Yugoslav enterprises, 1966–1988

Table 5.2. *Structure of accumulation of productive enterprises in Yugoslavia, 1966–1986 (ratios in per cent)*

	1966	1967	1968	1969	1970	1971	1972	1973	1974	1975	1976	1977	1978	1979	1980	1981	1982	1983	1984	1985	1986
Depreciation above legal minimum	—	4.6	8.5	9.7	12.7	14.3	13.0	12.1	10.5	10.7	6.1	1.8	4.3	3.6	4.9	4.7	2.7	2.8	3.3	1.3	1.4
Enterprise funds																					
Business fund	48.3	36.9	28.4	31.3	37.7	40.1	34.6	30.9	38.1	31.2	25.7	35.5	33.9	41.9	48.2	49.1	45.0	37.5	35.2	27.5	19.8
Reserve fund	11.9	11.7	12.5	10.5	6.4	6.2	5.6	8.8	6.0	6.0	6.2	9.1	10.8	10.3	9.1	9.7	9.4	10.7	9.9	7.2	7.5
Other funds	0.7	0.6	0.4	0.8	0.6	0.6	0.7	0.7	0.8	1.2	1.1	0.7	0.6	0.5	0.3	0.7	0.8	0.7	0.8	0.8	0.9
Contractual obligations																					
Interest on bank credit	16.5	20.4	23.3	23.2	22.9	21.3	25.1	24.8	23.0	27.9	36.5	35.6	36.8	35.1	30.6	29.6	35.4	42.5	46.3	59.3	66.0
Insurance premia	5.9	7.2	7.4	6.7	6.9	7.0	8.3	7.7	6.9	8.3	10.4	9.9	9.2	8.2	6.6	6.0	6.5	5.6	4.3	3.7	4.1
Taxes/contributions																					
Business fund	10.2	13.0	12.9	11.4	8.9	0.9	—	—	—	—	—	—	—	—	—	—	—	—	—	—	—
Commune	0.6	0.8	0.9	0.9	1.0	0.9	2.6	3.6	3.4	1.0	1.1	0.6	0.6	0.4	0.3	0.2	0.2	0.2	0.2	0.2	0.3
Land	1.3	0.9	2.3	2.1	2.1	1.3	—	—	—	1.4	0.2	—	—	—	—	—	—	—	—	—	—
Skoplje earthquake	—	—	—	—	—	—	—	—	—	—	—	—	—	—	—	—	—	—	—	—	—
Water utilities	0.9	1.1	0.9	0.9	0.7	0.6	—	—	—	—	—	—	—	—	—	—	—	—	—	—	—
Less developed regions	—	—	—	—	—	6.5	7.2	8.3	7.9	9.3	10.0	6.8	3.8	—	—	—	—	—	—	—	—
Contractors	—	—	0.1	0.1	0.1	0.2	0.2	0.4	0.7	0.5	0.5	—	—	—	—	—	—	—	—	—	—
Common reserves	3.7	2.8	2.2	2.4	0.0	0.1	2.7	2.7	2.8	2.8	2.2	—	—	—	—	—	—	—	—	—	—

Accumulation = 100

Source: Compiled from SDK balance sheet data of productive enterprises, reported in: Ekonomski Institut Zagreb (1981) and (1986).

more to these funds than is legally required. However, since the business fund often serves for loan repayment, it has been suggested that such savings (and interest payments in general) are not voluntary at the time they take place, for they are obligations carried over from a previous period (Stephen 1984, p. 124).

Data on credit repayments suggest that in order to be able to repay bank loans, firms must allocate a sufficient amount to the business fund: in fourteen out of the nineteen years following 1965, all resources allocated to the business fund seem to have been used for repaying investment credits, and in most years were not even sufficient, so that a part of depreciation had to be used (see table 5A.6 in the appendix). However, the decision to take a loan could also be considered as anticipated savings, as an intertemporal shift of voluntary savings from the present to the future, in which case loan repayments could be considered a voluntary component of savings. Resources allocated to the business fund are also a reflection of the obligation of Yugoslav firms to contribute a certain percentage of their own savings in order to obtain bank credit. Indeed, in Prašnikar's (1983) questionnaire to Yugoslav workers, 57 per cent declared that own sources for financing investment were just sufficient to cover the share needed for obtaining bank credits (see table 5.3).

Prašnikar's questionnaire offers additional evidence of interest (see table 5.3). Although 50 per cent of workers thought personal incomes had priority over accumulation in income distribution, 37 per cent considered the two categories equally important, whereas 7 per cent viewed accumulation as primary. A large majority (over 70 per cent) considered the level of accumulation to be too low. Over 62 per cent of workers thought there was a need for investment (medium to quite high), and moreover, 47 per cent were actually ready to renounce personal income in favour of investment, partly or completely. The survey therefore suggests no tendency to underinvest in Yugoslavia.

Yugoslav policy-makers have constantly criticized productive enterprises for low savings rates, as only about half of gross national savings is generated by productive enterprises belonging to the social sector. Nevertheless, the share of productive enterprises in both gross domestic savings and in social sector savings registered a continuous increase in the 1966–80 period, and has declined only in recent years.[15] As to the share of social sector productive enterprises in gross investment, it has remained fairly constant at around 70 per cent.

Using disaggregated data, Estrin (1983) found that Yugoslav firms tended to invest relatively more after 1965, when there was an acceleration in the rate of growth of capital stock. He observed similar changes in the pattern of growth of each of the nineteen individual industrial sectors. After 1965, capital accumulation actually accelerated in absolute terms in eleven of these sectors, while the rate of growth of the capital stock accelerated relative to output in every sector and absolutely in a few (Estrin 1983, pp. 154–8).

The analysis therefore confirms that Yugoslav enterprises' savings have been positive in the whole period under examination, and until 1985, not exceptionally low. However, this does not yet mean that Furubotn and Pejovich's theory can be refuted, since the conditions under which Yugoslav enterprises have been operating do not correspond to those assumed by the theory. Throughout the whole post-1966 period, Yugoslav enterprises have *not* been free to decide on the use of a large part of their income, as a number of requirements concerning even the formation and distribution of net income have been imposed on firms by external regulations. Enterprises have been obliged to save because of legal depreciation, taxes and contributions, the minimum savings requirement explicitly or implicitly laid down in social compacts, contractual obligations, and the rule linking approval of bank loans to availability of internal funds. In most cases, therefore, resources for undertaking investment represent only a residual of net income, after the various obligations are met. During the 1980s, external influence on enterprise savings policies in addition included direct administrative measures (such as personal incomes controls and freezes).

In Yugoslavia, as in other socialist countries, the priority given to high growth has been realized through a forced savings mechanism, imposed through a variety of regulations limiting enterprise autonomy. The observed oscillations in enterprise savings have been directly influenced by social objectives, priorities, and economic policies pursued in a given period, transmitted to enterprises through continuous and frequent changes in rules on income distribution, depreciation, taxes, and other regulations.[16] In line with Kornai's hypothesis, the state has continued to have considerable influence over enterprise decision-making in Yugoslavia. But although a large part of enterprise savings is not entirely voluntary in Yugoslavia, evidence on positive depreciation above the legal minimum confirms that Yugoslav firms do save a part of their income voluntarily. External pressure from local political authorities is likely to have favoured such (and other) savings.

The very notable fall in enterprise savings registered from 1985 onwards might be taken as evidence to support the underinvestment

Table 5.3. *Yugoslav workers' perceptions of accumulation and investment*

Questionnaire data (percentage of workers' answers)

1 Accumulation principle

Accumulation is a residual, after personal incomes are paid	49.6
Both planned personal incomes and planned accumulation realized	37.0
Planned accumulation is realized even at the expense of personal incomes	6.7
No accumulation	5.9
Other	0.8

2 Accumulation level

Too low, after personal incomes and obligations are met	71.5
Corresponds to needs	18.5
Too high as compared to investment plans	2.3
Too high as compared to income	1.5
Other	6.2

3 Need for investment

Small	27.6
Medium	22.2
High	21.5
Quite high	18.8
No need	9.9

4 Renouncing personal incomes in favour of investment

No	23.7
Little	29.7
Partly	25.3
Quite	11.8
Much	9.5

5 Proportion between down payments for credits and accumulation

Generally equal	53.0
Rarely equal	28.5
Occasionally equal	18.5

6 Preference for

Own sources	35
Borrowed sources	65

7 Own sources of investment finance

Higher than share needed for obtaining credits	42.5
Just sufficient to cover the share needed for bank credits	57.5

Results obtained from a questionnaire administered to workers in a 1979 sample of 147 Yugoslav enterprises, except for questions 6 and 7 which refer to the initial sample of 40 enterprises.

Sources: Questions 1–5: Prašnikar (1983), pp. 52–3, 68–9; Questions 6–7: Prašnikar (1980), p. 20.

hypothesis; indeed, Pejovich asserts that 'the property rights analysis has correctly anticipated economic problems in Yugoslavia' (1987, p. 248). But the reasons are more complex than those suggested by Furubotn and Pejovich; property rights have been limited in Yugoslavia throughout the period, yet only in recent years have enterprise savings been drastically reduced. The explanation for the reduced willingness to save can be found in the negative effects of a series of factors in combination: deficiencies in accounting, the worsening of the economic crisis, and economic policies applied in recent years.

Until 1987, the system of accounting was not adapted to inflationary conditions, permitting inadequate provision for depreciation, the understatement of costs and a corresponding overstatement of enterprise income, and hence the shifting of resources from capital to income. These accounting deficiencies have also stimulated inflationary pressures and led to increasing reliance on bank credits.[17] It was only in 1987 that the accounting system was changed, introducing a more appropriate revaluation of assets and the obligation to revalue a number of other items (costs, stocks, interest on dinar credits, and the exchange rate). However, in the absence of parallel changes in interest rate policies, bank credits continued to be provided on soft terms and hence the new accounting system had a number of counterproductive effects: for example, it destimulated savings by enabling enterprises to realize inflation gains through increasing reliance on external funds (see Mates 1987). In the high inflationary environment (with inflation exceeding 100 per cent in 1987) even short delays in paying back credits could bring about substantial gains.

At the same time, the worsening of the economic crisis (rapid inflation, falling output and productivity, declining real personal incomes, serious liquidity problems of enterprises), in combination with certain government policies, has also destimulated enterprise savings. The stop-go character of economic policies – price and personal income controls and freezes – has created a highly uncertain climate in which enterprises have been inclined to raise personal incomes as much as possible while they can, anticipating the imposition of new freezes. Although moral suasion has continued to be applied to influence firms to increase capital accumulation and decrease personal incomes, since 1985 many firms have tended to flout solidarity principles and pay higher personal incomes at the expense of savings (Prašnikar and Svejnar 1988, p. 307). This is understandable, considering that accelerating inflation has brought about a substantial and continuous drop in living standards.

Investment finance

One of the standard methods of calculating the self-financing ratio of Yugoslav firms is based on National Bank of Yugoslavia (NBY) data on productive enterprises' gross savings, financial savings, and gross investment, where their self-financing ratio is calculated as the ratio of gross savings to gross investment (see table 5A.7 in the appendix). The self-financing ratio of productive enterprises increased substantially in the decade following the mid-1960s reform, and it was on average 70 per cent or higher throughout the 1970s. During the 1980s, after an initial rise from 74 per cent in 1980 to a high of 86 per cent in 1982, a drastic reduction followed, and by 1986 the ratio had declined to the lowest level recorded, 57 per cent.[18]

The above ratios again represent overestimates, because of over-valuation of stocks in Yugoslav statistics. Schrenk *et al.* (1979, p. 153) report a lower enterprise self-financing rate, calculated on the basis of adjusted gross savings and adjusted gross investment, of 66.8 per cent in 1966–70 and 63.8 per cent in 1971–5. Moreover, these self-financing ratios are based on data on the formation of gross savings, not all of which are effectively used for investment purposes.[19] In order to get a better insight into the amount of investment financed by enterprise sources, it is more appropriate to analyse data on investment in fixed assets by source of finance, as provided by the Federal Institute of Statistics (SZS) (see table 5A.8 in the appendix, and figure 5.3).

The share of enterprises in total sources of fixed investment finance increased substantially immediately after 1965 – from only 28 per cent in 1965 to over 50 per cent in 1966. Such an outcome was precisely one of the intentions of the reform, and was in part the direct consequence of the reduction in the fiscal burden on firms.[20] The enterprise share remained relatively constant until the 1980s, at a level of around 50 per cent. Restrictive policies implemented from 1980 onwards, including limits on investment credits and greater emphasis on enterprise self-financing, increased the enterprise share in investment finance to 66 per cent by 1985 and further to 76 per cent by 1988. Given that during the 1980s investment activity was practically halted (investment growth rates were negative in most years), this is not inconsistent with the remarkable drop in enterprise savings observed earlier.

Available enterprise data (Prašnikar 1983) on the proportion of self-financed investment in Yugoslavia reveal that in the 1975–9 period, enterprises' own sources of investment finance oscillated from a minimum of 31.18 per cent in 1977 to a maximum of 42.7 per cent in

1979 (see table 5A.9 in the appendix).[21] Prašnikar's questionnaire offers additional evidence: more than half of workers interviewed expressed the view that enterprise savings for financing investment were about equal to down payments for loans. Although 65 per cent of workers did express a preference for borrowed funds, 35 per cent actually preferred own sources for financing investment (see table 5.3 above).

The positive level of self-financed investment noted above may not be accepted as a refutation of the Furubotn and Pejovich theory, since no distinction has been made between self-financed net and self-financed gross investment. Stephen (1984) suggests that self-financed investment in Yugoslav firms has been roughly equal to their depreciation allowances, and that self-financed net investment (the part self-financed by enterprises on a voluntary basis) has been close to zero. He tests the hypothesis empirically by using sectoral data from the nineteen industries in the Yugoslav mining and manufacturing sector in the years 1969, 1970, and 1971, and concludes that the hypothesis cannot reasonably be rejected (Stephen 1984, pp. 125–6).

Evidence on the use of gross savings in Yugoslav enterprises indirectly supports Stephen's hypothesis. Around 33 per cent to 59 per cent of resources allocated to the business fund and depreciation, which are the principal internal sources of enterprises for financing gross investment, have actually been used for repaying investment credits in the post-1965 period (see table 5A.6 in the appendix). In fourteen out of nineteen years following the reform, resources allocated to the business fund were not sufficient for repaying loans, but a part of resources allocated to depreciation had to be used. Therefore, enterprises' own resources remaining after loans had been repaid and obligatory depreciation covered, may not have been very high. In other words, in most years *net* investment, i.e. investment other than replacement of worn-out capacity, probably had to be financed externally.

Nevertheless, a different picture emerges if we contrast productive enterprises' depreciation allowances with investment in fixed assets financed by enterprises. The difference should represent the part of investment which is self-financed by Yugoslav firms, yet is not directly imposed on firms as in the case of legal depreciation.[22] This part of self-financed investment exceeding depreciation was 26.9 per cent, 31.6 per cent, and 32 per cent of gross investment of productive enterprises in the three years considered, suggesting that enterprises' own sources for financing investment, other than the ones used for legal depreciation, have been well above zero. In addition, investment in new capacity and enlargement, as opposed to capital maintenance (see table 5A.10 in the

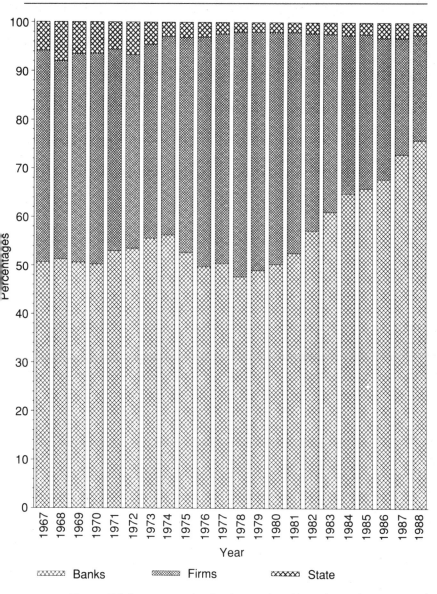

Figure 5.3 Investment in fixed assets in Yugoslavia, by source of finance, 1967–1988

appendix),[23] accounted, in the three years considered by Stephen, for over 80 per cent of total investment in fixed assets. Recalling that in 1969–71, around 51 per cent of fixed investment was financed by enterprises, it would seem that at least a part of these resources provided by enterprises had to be used for investment in new capacity and enlargement, and not exclusively for capital maintenance.[24]

In conclusion, Furubotn and Pejovich's hypothesis regarding the exclusive reliance on external funds cannot really be verified, since it is not possible to determine which part of investment is actually self-financed on a fully voluntary basis in Yugoslavia. Moreover, Furubotn and Pejovich's hypothesis applies to an extreme hypothetical case: that bank credit will exclusively be used if available. In practice, Yugoslav firms have relied on both own and external sources of finance, among other things because of the above-mentioned obligation to participate with their own sources when applying for bank credit, and because external funds have not been available in unlimited quantities. In addition, considering the specific features of the Yugoslav banking system (banks as non-profit 'service' agencies of enterprises, operating under their direct control), it is difficult to make a distinction in Yugoslavia between 'internal' and 'external' sources of finance. Finally, the proportion of self-finance in different capitalist economies varies considerably between countries,[25] and hence there are no universally acceptable prescriptions on the 'ideal' debt–equity ratio.

Apart from these problems, which render it difficult to refute the Furubotn and Pejovich theory, it is very likely that Yugoslav firms have relied on external sources of finance not primarily because of the structure of property rights, but because of other factors, such as very low interest rates on loans, and other capital market imperfections, which have significantly stimulated bank financing of investment (and investment itself). These issues are analysed further in the next chapter.

Appendix

Table 5A.1. *Yugoslav gross material product by use, 1961–1988 (ratios, in per cent of GMP in current prices)*

	1961–5	1966–70	1971–5	1976–80	1980	1981	1982	1983	1984	1985	1986	1987	1988
GMP = 100[a]													
Personal consumption	50.2	54.2	54.7	53.6	52.7	51.8	51.7	51.4	50.7	50.2	50.8	50.3	50.2
Collective consumption[b]	9.0	9.6	9.1	9.6	9.2	9.0	8.9	8.5	8.3	8.6	8.7	8.4	8.7
Gross investment[c]	43.2	38.1	40.6	43.3	47.0	44.5	41.9	40.8	42.6	41.6	40.8	39.7	39.5
of which:													
Fixed assets	(32.2)	(30.6)	(30.3)	(36.9)	(35.1)	(31.0)	(29.2)	(25.3)	(23.1)	(23.1)	(22.9)	(20.1)	(18.3)
Increase in stocks	(11.0)	(7.5)	(10.3)	(6.4)	(11.9)	(13.5)	(12.7)	(15.5)	(19.5)	(18.5)	(17.9)	(19.6)	(21.2)
Foreign balance[d]	-1.5	-3.2	-7.5	-7.1	-9.9	-5.6	-4.9	-2.4	-2.5	-1.2	-0.8	-1.4	-0.9
Other[e]	-0.9	1.3	3.1	0.6	0.9	0.3	2.4	1.7	1.0	0.8	0.5	3.0	2.5

[a]Gross material product, or 'social product' in Yugoslav terminology, is the value added in market prices of productive sectors, in both the social and the private sector; it does not include non-productive sectors, such as housing, health, education, administration, banking, defence.
[b]Collective consumption includes 'general consumption' and 'collective consumption' of non-productive sectors of the economy.
[c]Gross investment refers to investment by the private and social sector in productive and non-productive sectors of the economy.
[d]Balance of imports and exports in goods and services.
[e]Statistical discrepancy.

Sources: 1961–80: Savezni zavod za statistiku (SZS) i Savezni zavod za društveno planiranje (1982), p. 88.
1980–8: Calculated from *Statistički godišnjak Jugoslavije* 1985 and 1990, Table 106-1.

Table 5A.2. *Yugoslav standardized and adjusted aggregate savings and investment rates, 1961–1988 (ratios, in per cent)*

	1961–5	1966–70	1971–5	1973–80	1980–8
Gross national savings/GNP	32.6	28.7	27.1	32.9	38.0
Foreign financing/GNP	1.1	1.0	1.3	2.7	–1.0
Gross domestic investment/GNP	33.7	29.7	28.4	35.6	37.0*

*1980–7.

Sources: 1961–75: Schrenk *et al.* (1979), p. 137.
1973–88: World Bank (1990), p. 167.

Table 5A.3. *Savings and investment performance of Yugoslavia and selected countries, 1960–1988 (in per cent)*

	Gross national savings/ GNP ratio	Gross investment/ GDP ratio		Growth rates of investment		Indicators of investment efficiency[b]		
	(1) 1965–73	(2) 1965–73	(3) 1971–87	(4) 1965–80	(5) 1980–8	(6) 1968–73	(7) 1971–87	(8) 1960–80
Greece	18.8	28.3	19.4	5.3	−3.9	3.3	6.5	0.270
Portugal	—	26.6[a]	25.7	4.6	−1.3	2.8	6.9	0.298
Spain	21.4	23.3	22.9	—	—	3.4	7.4	0.258
Turkey	19.3	20.1	21.4	8.8	4.4	2.9	3.9	0.305
Yugoslavia	28.4	29.5	27.8	6.5	−0.4	4.2	9.0	0.198

[a] In relation to GNP.
[b] The figures are not comparable over time, as they are based on different indicators.

Sources:

(1) and (2): Schrenk *et al.* (1979), p. 112, except for Portugal, which is from World Bank (1990), p. 167.
(3): Vacić (1989), p. 89.
(4) and (5): World Bank (1990), pp. 192–3.
(6): Schrenk *et al.* (1979), p. 169; incremental capital-output ratio (i.e. ratio of gross investment to GDP increase).
(7): Vacić (1989), p. 89; ratio of the investment/GDP rate to GDP growth.
(8): Bajt (1988a), p. 19; ratio of GDP growth to the investment/GDP rate.

Table 5A.4. Distribution of GMP of productive enterprises in Yugoslavia (social sector), 1966–1988 (ratios, in per cent)

	1966	1967	1968	1969	1970	1971	1972	1973	1974	1975	1976	1977	1978	1979	1980	1981	1982	1983	1984	1985	1986	1987	1988
Enterprise GMP=100																							
1. Depreciation	8.8	10.8	11.0	10.8	10.5	10.2	11.3	11.6	12.3	10.8	11.9	10.7	10.5	10.3	10.5	9.9	12.2	12.5	11.7	10.9	10.1	12.0	11.1
2. Net personal incomes	34.7	35.6	35.8	36.5	37.1	36.5	36.0	34.6	33.6	34.5	36.1	36.2	34.6	33.6	31.6	33.3	32.4	30.4	28.6	29.4	32.1	30.4	28.4
3. Funds (net savings)	19.7	15.3	14.8	9.7	11.3	15.5	13.8	13.8	15.4	15.7	9.9	12.4	13.4	14.4	18.0	18.1	16.3	15.7	17.8	15.6	9.2	8.7	3.6
4. Taxes and contributions	36.8	38.3	38.4	43.0	41.1	37.8	38.9	40.0	38.7	39.0	42.1	40.7	41.5	41.7	39.9	38.7	39.1	41.4	41.9	44.1	48.6	48.9	57.2
Gross savings (1+3)	28.5	26.1	25.8	20.5	21.8	25.7	25.1	25.4	27.7	26.5	21.8	23.1	23.9	24.7	28.5	28.0	28.5	28.2	29.5	26.5	19.3	20.7	14.7
Net enterprise income=100																							
1. Depreciation	13.9	17.5	17.8	19.0	17.8	16.4	18.5	19.3	20.0	17.7	20.6	18.1	18.0	17.5	17.5	16.1	20.1	21.3	20.2	19.6	19.7	23.5	26.0
2. Net personal incomes	54.9	57.7	58.2	64.0	63.0	58.7	58.9	57.7	54.8	56.6	62.3	61.1	59.1	57.7	52.5	54.4	53.1	51.9	49.2	52.4	62.4	59.4	65.6
3. Funds (net savings)	31.2	24.8	24.0	17.0	19.2	24.9	22.6	23.0	25.2	25.7	17.1	20.8	22.9	24.8	30.0	29.5	26.8	26.8	30.6	28.0	17.9	17.1	8.4
Gross savings (1+3)	45.1	42.3	41.8	36.0	37.0	41.3	41.1	42.3	45.2	43.4	37.7	38.9	40.9	42.3	47.5	45.6	46.9	48.1	50.8	47.6	37.6	40.6	34.4

Source: Calculated from SZS, SGJ, various years, Table 'Osnovni podaci o organizacijama udruženog rada društvenog sektora'; the numbering of the table has changed over time (in SGJ 1990 it was Table 113-1).

Table 5A.5. Distribution of GMP in a sample of 147 Yugoslav firms, 1975–1979 (ratios, in per cent)

	1975	1976	1977	1978	1979
Gross value added (GMP)=100					
Taxes and contributions	9.97	9.56	10.36	10.11	10.55
Accumulation and depreciation	33.08	30.74	29.10	31.00	31.02
Gross personal incomes and collective consumption	56.94	59.50	60.52	58.88	58.52
Statistical discrepancy	0.01	0.20	0.02	0.01	−0.09
Gross value added after tax=100					
Accumulation and depreciation	36.7	34.1	32.5	34.5	34.8
Gross personal incomes and collective consumption	63.3	65.9	67.5	65.5	65.2
Net value added after tax=100					
Accumulation	32.0	25.1	26.0	28.4	28.2
Gross personal incomes	68.0	74.9	74.0	71.6	71.8
Accumulation=100					
Interest payments	27.2	51.3	45.1	48.0	46.5
Depreciation above legal minimum	21.5	5.4	2.6	3.0	2.7
Founders' income	0.2	0.9	2.4	0.9	0.8
Contributions	0.8	2.3	5.3	7.9	3.6
Business fund	39.5	29.9	32.8	29.9	34.9
Reserve fund	6.2	6.0	9.2	9.5	10.1
Other funds	4.6	4.2	2.6	0.8	1.4

Source: Compiled from Prašnikar (1983), pp. 124–5.

Table 5A.6. *Productive enterprises' repayment of investment credits in Yugoslavia, 1966–1984*

	1966	1967	1968	1969	1970	1971	1972	1973	1974	1975	1976	1977	1978	1979	1980	1981	1982	1983	1984
Billions of dinars																			
Business fund	7.7	5.8	5.9	8.2	10.9	15.7	15.3	17.5	29.1	25.3	21.4	33.5	43.6	74.9	138.8	212.4	255.9	342.3	609.5
Depreciation[a]	6.3	8.2	9.1	11.9	13.8	19.9	13.4	29.2	41.9	46.1	59.9	67.0	84.4	104.8	143.1	187.4	303.6	430.1	636.3
Available for debt repayment	14.0	14.0	15.0	20.1	24.7	35.6	28.7	46.7	71.0	71.4	81.3	100.5	128.0	179.7	281.9	399.8	559.5	772.4	1245.8
Debt repayment[b]	4.6	6.2	7.5	9.4	12.2	16.6	19.4	21.2	25.3	30.3	39.7	58.9	86.1	106.7	145.5	171.4	236.2	349.5	464.4
Ratios, in per cent																			
Repayment/ business fund	60	107	129	115	112	106	127	121	87	120	185	176	198	142	105	81	92	102	76
Repayment/ available funds	33	44	50	47	49	47	50	45	36	42	49	59	67	59	52	43	42	45	37

[a]Includes both the legally prescribed minimum and voluntary depreciation.
[b]Payments remaining from previous year and payments due in current year.
Source: Balance sheet data of productive enterprises provided by the Federal Accounting Office (Savezno Društveno Knjigovodstvo-SDK), in Vojnić (1986), p. 463.

Table 5A.7. *Self-financing ratio of Yugoslav productive enterprises (social sector), 1961–1986*

	1961–5	1966–70	1971–5	1976–80	1979	1980	1981	1982	1983	1984	1985	1986
Billions of dinars												
Gross savings	52.0	110.6	334.8	1125.3	259.7	401.0	559.0	754.1	1035.2	1643.9	2666.7	4397.0
Financial savings	−31.5	−51.2	−117.5	−464.0	−125.4	−138.6	−149.0	−120.1	−301.9	−600.6	−1505.3	−3335.6
Gross investment	83.5	161.8	452.3	1589.3	385.1	539.6	708.0	874.2	1337.1	2244.5	4172.0	7732.6
Ratios, in per cent												
Self-financing ratio (GS/GI)	62.3	68.4	74.0	70.8	67.4	74.3	78.9	86.3	77.4	73.2	63.9	56.9

Social sector productive enterprises (OALs – organizations of associated labour) include OALs of the productive sector, internal banks, work communities of banks and of other financial organizations and self-managed communities of interest for material production, housing and communal development. OALs' *gross savings* represent the difference between proceeds from sales of goods and services and expenditures, such as operating costs (excluding depreciation), contributions, taxes, personal incomes. OALs' *financial savings* represent the difference between their savings and investment. OALs' *gross investment* is the sum of their gross savings and financial savings.

Source: NBJ, *Bilten Narodne Banke Jugoslavije*, various issues, Table 'Novčana amumulacija i finansijska štednja'. 1986 was the last year for which this table was compiled by the statistical office of the NBJ.

Table 5A.8 Payments for investment in fixed assets in Yugoslavia, by source of finance (social sector), 1967–1988

	1967	1968	1969	1970	1971	1972	1973	1974	1975	1976	1977	1978	1979	1980	1981	1982	1983	1984	1985	1986	1987	1988
Billions of dinars																						
Total	21.3	26.2	30.9	39.0	47.7	56.3	63.0	85.8	130.0	167.4	220.7	303.8	377.9	454.6	552.9	673.5	818.4	1211.6	2254.4	4271	7393	2117
Firms	10.8	13.4	15.6	19.6	25.3	30.2	35.0	48.3	68.5	83.2	111.5	145.0	185.2	228.6	290.8	385.5	500.3	786.7	1487.1	2900	5398	1608
Credits	9.3	10.7	13.3	16.9	19.8	22.4	25.2	35.0	57.5	79.1	103.9	152.7	185.1	216.9	250.9	273.2	298.8	393.7	713.7	1241	1764	457
Grants	1.2	2.1	2.0	2.5	2.6	3.7	2.8	2.5	4.0	5.1	5.3	6.1	7.6	9.1	11.2	14.8	19.3	31.2	53.6	130	231	52
Ratios in per cent[a]																						
Firms	50.7	51.3	50.6	50.2	53.0	53.5	55.6	56.3	52.7	49.7	50.5	47.7	49.0	50.3	52.6	57.2	61.1	64.9	66.0	67.9	73.0	75.9
Credits	43.5	40.7	42.9	43.4	41.4	39.8	39.9	40.8	44.2	47.3	47.1	50.3	49.0	47.7	45.4	40.6	36.5	32.5	31.6	29.0	23.9	21.6
Grants	5.8	8.0	6.5	6.4	5.6	6.7	4.5	2.9	3.1	3.0	2.4	2.0	2.0	2.0	2.0	2.2	2.4	2.6	2.4	3.1	3.1	2.5

[a]Total = 100. Firms refer to OALs in both productive and non-productive sectors, including self-managed communities of interest. Credits are loans from banks, from other enterprises, and from socio-political communities. Grants are non-reimbursable funds of socio-political communities. All figures refer to payments for investment in fixed assets, excluding investment in collective consumption objects.
Source: SZS, SGJ, various years, Table 'Izvršene isplate za investicije po osnovnim oblicima finansiranja'; the numbering of the table has changed over time.

Table 5A.9. *Investment in a sample of 147 Yugoslav enterprises, by source of finance, 1975–1979 (ratios, in per cent)*

	1975	1976	1977	1978	1979
Enterprises' own sources	41.03	36.09	31.18	32.81	42.70
Of which: investment in other enterprises[a]	(1.25)	(0.88)	(0.73)	(0.87)	(7.82)
Credits from suppliers (domestic and foreign)	23.45	18.00	25.90	20.10	18.65
Bank credits (short and long-term)	35.37	43.74	41.31	45.85	38.50
Other	0.15	2.17	1.61	1.24	0.25
Total sources of finance	100.0	100.0	100.0	100.0	100.0

[a]The so-called 'pooling of labour and resources'.
Source: Prašnikar (1983), p. 122.

Table 5A.10. *Realized investment in fixed assets in Yugoslavia (social sector), by type of investment, 1967–1989 (ratios, in per cent)*

	1967	1968	1969	1970	1971	1972	1973	1974	1975	1976	1977	1978	1979	1980	1981	1982	1983	1984	1985	1986	1987	1988	1989
New capacity	37.3	34.1	33.4	35.2	32.1	34.2	45.0	45.9	51.1	57.5	56.9	59.3	60.0	61.3	62.2	61.2	60.4	54.1	47.7	45.2	44.0	42.5	45.4
Enlargement	44.5	49.1	47.9	46.8	50.4	47.4	37.0	36.0	33.2	27.8	28.0	26.3	25.3	24.0	22.9	23.5	22.9	26.9	31.2	32.7	35.8	30.2	31.6
Maintenance	18.2	16.8	18.7	18.2	17.3	18.4	18.0	18.1	15.7	14.7	15.1	14.4	14.7	14.7	14.9	15.3	16.7	19.0	21.1	22.1	20.2	27.3	23.0

Investment in fixed assets = 100.

New capacity refers to both investment on a new location (creation of new enterprises) and on an old location (new units in existing enterprises). *Enlargement* refers to enlargement, reconstruction and modernization through changes in the composition, technology, and techniques of production, rearrangement of equipment and purchase of new fixed assets within existing working units. *Maintenance* refers to the replacement of capital. *Realized investment* in a given year refers to the period when assets were constructed or purchased, regardless of the dates of payment.
Source: SZS, SGJ, various years, Table 'Ostvarene investicije po karakteru izgradnje, tehničkoj strukturi i nameni'; the numbering of the table has changed over time.

6 The determinants of investment in Yugoslavia

Empirical verification of the investment theories will now proceed with a more detailed analysis of the role of certain market variables which are regarded as crucial by Furubotn and Pejovich, and of socialist features of the economy emphasized by Kornai, in determining investment in Yugoslavia.

The role of market variables

Furubotn and Pejovich's theory analyses an LMF under the Yugoslav institutional setting (social property, the capital maintenance requirement), while at the same time implicitly assuming that Yugoslavia is a market economy. Under such an assumption, investment in savings deposits and in firms' capital stock is expected to depend primarily on the interest rate, the lending rate, the marginal productivity of capital, and the time horizon of the representative worker (Furubotn and Pejovich 1973, p. 281).

In order to determine the role of these variables in Yugoslavia, they are presented (or approximated) for the 1966–85 period in table 6A.1 in the appendix to this chapter. Since interest rates applied by banks have varied from a lower to an upper bound,[1] the maximum nominal interest rates in a given year are reported.[2] Because of rising inflation, interest rates have been deflated so as to obtain returns on savings deposits and the cost of borrowed funds in real terms.[3] Capital returns are presented through three sets of figures: (1) the pre-tax profit rate, as a rough approximation of the marginal productivity of capital;[4] (2) the post-tax profit rate, which has the advantage of excluding taxes, contributions, and other obligations (such as interest payments);[5] and (3) realized returns on 100 dinars of utilized assets, as the official indicator of the Federal Accounting Office (SDK). The proxy used for the time horizon is labour turnover, i.e. the average monthly fluctuation of workers in Yugoslavia, on the assumption that the time horizon is inversely related to such fluctuations.[6]

The reported data reveal that until 1982, interest rate policies in Yugoslavia were highly passive; rates were fixed for many years, and there was practically no adjustment for inflation. The presence of high and rising inflation meant that, with the exception of 1967, 1968 and 1984, the maximum returns from investment in savings deposits were negative in real terms. In addition, inflation significantly reduced the maximum real cost of borrowed funds, which was also more often negative than positive (except in 1967–9, 1972, 1976–8, and 1983–4), implying that enterprises were often paying a negative price for borrowed capital (see figure 6.1).

Such an interest rate policy was therefore a cause of significant redistribution from households (as net lenders) to enterprises (as net borrowers). Whereas negative interest rates on savings deposits represent a loss for households, negative interest rates on loans by contrast represent a gain for enterprises. To capture the distributional effects of interest rates on the two sectors, in figure 6.2 the two real interest rates are presented in terms of gains/losses of the two sectors, revealing that in most of the years following 1965, enterprises were subsidized, through the banking mechanism, by household savings. However, the graph underestimates the extent of such redistribution, since it is based on the maximum interest rate in a given year (and not on the average, which was lower, especially in recent years; see below).

The rigid system of fixed interest rates was abandoned only in 1982, as part of the policy orientation contained in the Long-Term Stabiliz-ation Programme to move towards positive real interest rates. Since July 1982, an active interest rate policy has been applied through con-tinuous adjustments of nominal rates to rising inflation. Although this has occasionally resulted, for short periods, in positive real interest rates, the adjustments have been insufficient to ensure a permanent change in policies. Since banks in Yugoslavia are managed by firms, which are the main borrowers, they have tended to keep rates as low as possible. In addition, low interest rates have also been occasionally supported by the federal government, as in 1985 when positive real interest rates were suppressed because they were considered to be among the main causes of high inflation.[7]

OECD calculations of real average monthly interest rates in Yugoslavia from 1980 onwards do indeed show that all interest rates remained highly negative in real terms throughout the 1980–4 period (see OECD 1984, p. 23). Although in the first quarter of 1985 a positive

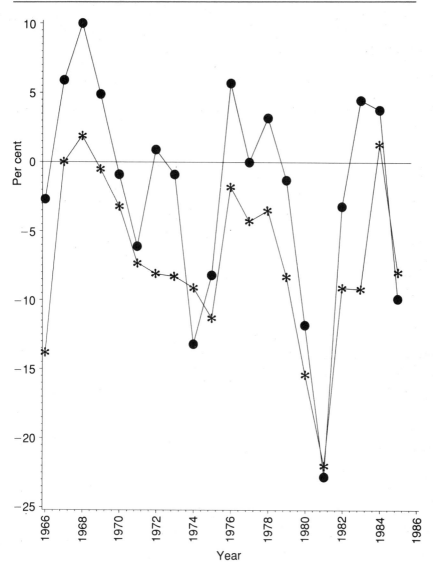

* Real rate of interest on time deposits of households
● Real rate of interest on short-term bank loans to enterprises

Figure 6.1 Real interest rates in Yugoslavia, 1966–1985

(a)

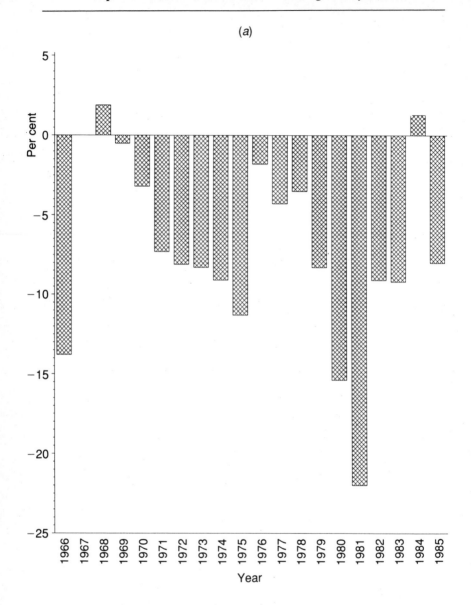

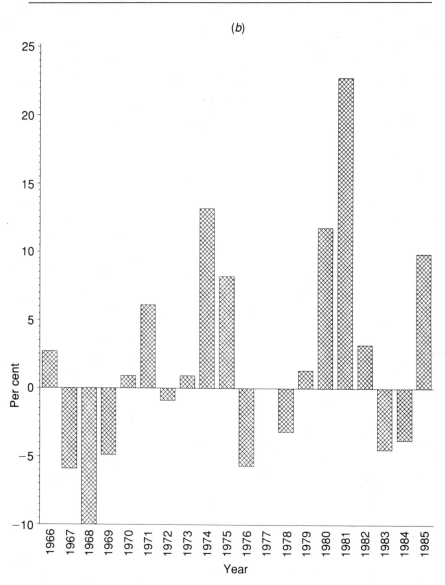

Figure 6.2 Distributional effects of interest rate policies in Yugoslavia, 1966–1985, (a) household losses, (b) enterprise gains

real interest rate on both household deposits and bank credit was applied, it again became negative in the second quarter of the year and stayed negative until the beginning of 1988 (see OECD 1988, p. 17). Moreover, there was no radical change in policies favouring the enterprise sector; thus in 1986, the household real deposit rate was substantially lower than banks' real short-term credit rate paid by enterprises.[8] With the rapid acceleration of inflation from 1988 onwards, policies were variable and discontinuous. Whereas the real interest rate on household sight deposits remained highly negative throughout the 1988–90 period, on household time deposits and on enterprise bank loans, it was occasionally positive (see OECD 1990, p. 28).

The privileged position of the productive sector *vis-à-vis* households, which lasted at least until fairly recently, is one of the main factors that have favoured investment in 'non-owned' assets as compared to investment in 'owned' assets in Yugoslavia. Interest rates on household savings have been kept low partly for ideological reasons: rental income was regarded as 'exploitation', i.e. appropriation unrelated to work done. What the above data show, in fact, is that it was the enterprise sector that was 'exploiting' the household sector, and not *vice versa*.

Nevertheless, for the investment decision the essential consideration is the gap between the borrowing rate and the rate of return, whether in monetary or real terms. If we consider the pre-tax profit rate, or average returns on capital, until 1982 these were higher than the nominal interest rate on bank loans. It is only in recent years, due to the substantial increase in nominal interest rates, that the relationship has been reversed. Even if the lowest among the profit rates is considered – the after-tax profit rate – it was higher than the nominal interest rate on loans in most of the period under examination (except in 1976, 1978–9, and 1982–5). Moreover, according to prevailing estimates, the real rate of return on enterprise investment in Yugoslavia was somewhere between 9 per cent and 12 per cent during the ten-year period following the 1965 reform (see Miović 1975; Vanek and Jovičić 1975; as reported in Tyson 1977a). When compared with the real interest rate on bank loans for the same period – which was usually negative – it is likely that the gap between the borrowing rate and the rate of return in real terms often favoured investment in 'non-owned' assets, thus weakening or falsifying the underinvestment argument based on the LMF investment theory (see chapters 2 and 3 above).

Another feature of interest rate policies in Yugoslavia is that rates on household deposits have been practically identical across banks, whereas those on bank loans to enterprises have varied considerably, resulting in very different terms of access to finance. In particular, the system of selective credits for financing priority sectors of the economy, credits which are rediscounted by the NBY, has granted those sectors particularly favourable credit conditions. Nominal interest rates on selective credits were until recently set at a very low level (even at 0 per cent), usually below the official discount rate, and commercial banks were until 1987 obliged to apply these low rates, irrespective of the cost of such credits (Mates 1987). Although during the 1980s selective credits were abolished for all sectors except agriculture and exports, the magnitude of these credits remained substantial. Between 1981 and 1985, selective credits for agriculture and exports accounted respectively for about one-third and one-quarter of the increase in total dinar credits to enterprises, and selective credits in 1985 represented 45.8 per cent of all NBY credits to banks (OECD 1987a, pp. 44, 49). The OECD calculated the implicit subsidies which result from such mechanisms,[9] showing that between 1980 and 1988, bank subsidies to enterprises increased from 5.8 per cent to 16.1 per cent of total bank assets respectively (OECD 1990, p. 40).

The serious underpricing of capital in Yugoslavia was a result not only of concessionary forms of external finance, but also of internal funding. The tax on the business fund, or interest paid on social capital 'inherited' from the state, was progressively reduced after the 1965 reform, and in 1971 completely abolished. Since no charge was set for the use of social capital, this effectively implied rental income for enterprises depending on their capital endowments, something which is likely to have stimulated investment, in particular in capital-intensive projects.[10] Personal incomes, by contrast, are taxed on a progressive basis (although rates are fairly low). Such fiscal policies are another element that has stimulated investment in 'non-owned' as compared to 'owned' assets in Yugoslavia.

The last variable – labour turnover – approximately inversely related to workers' time horizons, has been fairly low in Yugoslavia. After an initial increase due to the opening of Yugoslavia's borders and the outflow of workers to Western Europe in the late 1960s, the monthly fluctuation of workers after 1973 stabilized at a level of a bit over 1 per cent (see table 6A.1).

Low mobility of labour in Yugoslavia derives not only from specific historical, cultural and national factors that have set up regional barriers to labour mobility, but also from policy measures which have led to serious labour market imperfections. Labour relations legislation ensures a high level of job security. The disciplinary measures envisaged for not respecting work obligations include a public warning, cash fine (set in relation to a low maximum percentage of the worker's monthly personal income),[11] and dismissal. The most frequently applied measure until very recently was the public warning, while dismissal as the ultimate sanction was applied rarely (and then only in cases of very severe violations). Enterprises were required by law to attempt to redeploy or retrain a worker within the enterprise before dismissing him. In addition, there was a low rate of voluntary labour turnover, due to the enterprise-specific nature of some social benefits (such as funding for housing provided from the enterprise's collective consumption fund). Employment security has also been ensured by policies of supporting loss-making firms, thus preventing redundancies which would otherwise have occurred owing to bankruptcy.

The existence of a low level of labour mobility in Yugoslavia is confirmed by Prašnikar's (1983) questionnaire to Yugoslav managers and workers (see table 6.1). In 96 per cent of cases, managers did not consider firing workers in the event of bad business results, and 58 per cent of managers thought that worker fluctuation occurred rarely. Around 65 per cent of workers hadn't considered searching for employment in another firm; 40 per cent of workers had been employed in the same firm for six to fifteen years, and another 29 per cent for over fifteen years; moreover, the level of worker commitment seemed quite high, since 80 per cent considered their enterprise to be a relatively good firm (Prašnikar 1983).

Since low labour mobility implies an extension of time horizons, it is very probable that the average Yugoslav worker in fact has a fairly long time horizon. With the prolonging of the time horizon, the difference between investment in 'owned' and 'non-owned' assets diminishes substantially: thus for a twenty-year time horizon, an 8 per cent return from 'non-owned' assets is required to make the worker as well off as he would be with a 5 per cent return from 'owned' assets. Since the Yugoslav worker in most years would have received a negative real interest rate on savings deposits, and investment opportunities yielding above 8 per cent in real terms, as reported earlier, do seem to have existed, investment in 'non-owned' assets would have been not only acceptable, but also a more profitable alternative to investment in 'owned' assets (especially given that, until very recently, there were limited opportunities for private investment and hence no alternative

Table 6.1. *Factors influencing time horizons of Yugoslav workers*

Questionnaire data (percentage of total answers)

Firing workers because of bad business results[a]	
No	96.4
Little	2.9
Much	0.7
Employment fluctuation[a]	
Rarely	58.2
Sometimes	34.3
Usually	7.5
Employment in another firm	
Don't think of it	39.2
Don't yet think of it	25.8
Cannot decide	8.0
Have not yet decided	13.8
No such intention	13.2
Years employed in the same firm	
Less than 1	4.6
1–5 years	26.0
6–15 years	40.3
More than 15	29.1
Level of workers' commitment	
Not a good firm	20.6
A good firm	37.8
Quite a good firm	27.5
Very good firm	14.2

[a]Questions posed to managers.
Source: Prašnikar (1983), pp. 49, 51, 71, 72, 74, questionnaire data from a sample of 147 Yugoslav enterprises.

outlets for individual savings, other than bank accounts yielding negative real returns).

Some observers are surprised by the fact that empirical evidence from Yugoslavia does not support the Furubotn–Pejovich underinvestment hypothesis (Tyson 1977a).[12] This is not surprising, since the theory assumes the normal functioning of capital and labour markets – neither of which in Yugoslavia have been fully introduced. Hence it was to be expected that the variables considered crucial by Furubotn and Pejovich have had a limited role in determining investment in Yugoslavia. Furubotn and Pejovich place exclusive emphasis on two institutional features of the Yugoslav system – limited property rights and self-management – while disregarding all other factors which have favoured investment in capital stock in Yugoslavia.

Interest rate policies in Yugoslavia confirm that, at least until 1982, if not longer, the Yugoslav economy remained typically socialist. In line with Kornai's theory, concessionary forms of enterprise finance and mechanisms enabling the redistribution of income in their favour continued to be prevalent, and the interest rate played a limited role in regulating investment demand.

The role of socialist features of the economy

Further evidence on the socialist nature of the Yugoslav system will now be presented, supporting some of Kornai's other hypotheses on the investment behaviour of the socialist enterprise. The evidence includes various symptoms of soft budget constraints, such as a limited number of bankruptcies, the socialization of losses, uncontrolled proliferation of interfirm credits, time and cost overruns of investment projects, and non-market allocation of investment resources.

Bankruptcies. Prior to 1986, official statistics for Yugoslavia included bankruptcies within the broader category of 'liquidated' firms. In the 1976–84 period, a total of 1,332 firms were liquidated, a figure which represented a low percentage of both organizational changes and of the number of enterprises that had ceased to exist; a more frequent way of closing down an enterprise was to merge or affiliate it with another firm (50 to 60 per cent of cases; see table 6A.2 in the appendix to this chapter). Moreover, although 'liquidation' also included bankruptcies, only a small percentage of liquidated firms are closed due to bankruptcy: out of 283 liquidated enterprises in 1983–4, OECD sources suggest that only around thirty firms actually went bankrupt in the same years (OECD 1987a, p. 37). The OECD reported a total of fifty bankruptcies in Yugoslavia over the 1983–5 period, which took place after new legislation in 1983 imposed more stringent conditions on firms operating at a loss.[13] The reported number of bankruptcies in Yugoslavia may seem considerable in comparison with the situation in other socialist countries, but it is still low with respect to the number of loss-making enterprises, the majority of which, until very recently, were bailed out (see below).

With the new law on rehabilitation and liquidation adopted in December 1986 – which applies stricter criteria for defining losses, introduces major controls, and substantially shortens the period of

Table 6.2. *Bankruptcies and other forms of firm exit in Yugoslavia, 1986–1989*

	1986		1987		1988		1989	
	Number	Per-centage	Number	Per-centage	Number	Per-centage	Number	Per-centage
Exit, total	1,655	100	1,988	100	2,210	100	4,809	100
Bankruptcy	28	1.7	20	1.0	52	2.3	41	0.85
Liquidation	34	2.1	23	1.2	60	2.7	41	0.85
Closure	48	2.9	42	2.1	48	2.2	276	5.7
Reorganization	1,545	93.3	1,903	95.7	2,050	92.8	4,451	92.6
Initiation of bankruptcy procedures	35		59		100		43	

Source: Table 6A.2, appendix to this chapter.

rehabilitation of loss-making enterprises – the budget constraint of Yugoslav firms has been somewhat 'hardened'. Compared to previous years, when bankruptcies affected only a small number of workers (2,000 on average, between 1982 and 1986), in 1987 some 16,000 workers were laid off (OECD 1987a, p. 38). Since 1986, in Yugoslav statistics (*SGJ*) bankruptcies have been reported as a separate item, revealing that over the 1986–9 period, 141 enterprises were closed due to bankruptcy. This figure, however, is extremely low compared to those for both organizational changes and total exit of firms, as the prevalent form of exit for firms until the end of 1989 was reorganization (over 90 per cent of the total) (see table 6.2).

Moreover, not all enterprises for which bankruptcy procedures are initiated – a total of 237 over the 1986–9 period – actually go bankrupt. The number of bankruptcies effected in a given year was systematically lower than that of bankruptcy proceedings initiated in the previous year; for example, out of 100 firms for which bankruptcy procedures were initiated in 1988, only forty-one actually went bankrupt in 1989 (see table 6.2). This suggests that a number of firms are bailed out even after the bankruptcy procedure has started.

Similarly, not even for those enterprises for which the initiation of bankruptcy procedures is specifically required (usually by the Federal Accounting Office (SDK)), are such procedures always implemented, since alternative, less painful solutions are first sought. By June 1990, requests for the initiation of bankruptcy procedures had been submitted for a total of 582 Yugoslav enterprises, but only in a few cases had they actually been initiated (see table 6.3). Preliminary evidence relating to Slovenian firms suggests that, for example, out of thirty-one requests, by the end of June bankruptcy procedures had been initiated for only one enterprise, and the situation seems to be similar in several other republics. While this may in part be due to delays in implementation, it is reported that in several cases alternative solutions of financial rehabilitation were indeed found (see *Ekonomska politika* 2,000, 30 July 1990, p. 22).

With a rapid increase in total losses of the economy, which at the end of 1990 amounted to around $7 billion (see *Ekonomska politika* 2,037, 15 April 1991, p. 26), in the second half of 1990 there was a threefold increase in the number of requests for the initiation of bankruptcy procedures, which by the end of 1990 involved a total of 1,659 firms employing some 750,000 workers. As a result, bankruptcies and massive lay-offs began to occur more frequently, particularly in Slovenia and Croatia; preliminary data suggest that in January–April 1991, 300 bankruptcies were registered in Croatia alone (*Ekonomska politika* 2,036, 8 April 1991).

Socialization of losses. The above policies of applying bankruptcy only as an ultimate measure conforms to the practice of 'socialization' of losses in Yugoslavia. The various means by which losses have been covered are presented in figure 6.3, which shows that 80 per cent to 95 per cent of enterprise losses in the 1980–7 period were covered through the resources of other enterprises, socio-political communities and banks; only in 1988 did this percentage decline, to 62.6 per cent. The largest part of losses was covered through rehabilitation credit, although a substantial part was also covered through non-reimbursable funds and the writing off of claims. As a percentage of commercial bank loans, the writing off of loans increased from 0.1 per cent in 1983 to 3.1 per cent in 1988 (OECD 1990, p. 37). In this respect, instead of 'hardening', the budget constraint seems to have become even softer during the 1980s: rehabilitation credits, by means of which over 80 per cent of total losses were covered in 1980, declined to 50 per cent by 1987 and to 24 per cent in 1988, whereas non-reimbursable funds increased from 15 per cent in 1980 to 31 per cent in 1987 and 38.5 per cent in 1988.

In Yugoslavia, the coverage of losses is explicitly foreseen by law. All firms are obliged to set aside a certain percentage (usually 1–2 per cent) of their net income for a republican solidarity fund, but such contributions are limited to profitable firms only (Vodopivec 1988). Even in the most recent 1989 Law on Financial Operations,[14] which has imposed more stringent conditions on enterprises operating at a loss,[15] it is stated

Table 6.3. *Enterprises for which the initiation of bankruptcy procedures was required in 1990*

	30 June			31 December	
	Number of firms	Workers involved	Procedures initiated by 30 June	Number of firms	Workers involved
TOTAL	582	321,117	n.a.	1,659	754,898
Bosnia and Herzegovina	84	72,503	10	283	206,052
Croatia	107	61,397	20[a]	299	141,737
Kosovo	78	33,467	n.a.	136	60,449
Macedonia	41	7,915	5	121	20,162
Montenegro	36	23,120	n.a.	63	29,374
Serbia proper	172	97,682	2[b]	513	221,859
Slovenia	31	11,716	1	95	24,594
Voivodina	33	13,317	n.a.	149	50,672

[a]Only in Zagreb, where there were around forty requests for the initiation of bankruptcy procedures.
[b]Only in Belgrade, where there were around seventy requests.
Source: Ekonomska politika 2,027, 4 February 1991, and 2,000, 30 July 1990.

that 'losses shall be covered from available reserve resources, reserve resources of other legal entities, or resources of other funds formed for the purpose of loss coverage, subsidies, writing off of claims by creditors and the distribution of before-tax income, and at the expense of permanent sources of funds through a correction of value' (Article 23).

It is not only enterprise losses that are legally socialized; bank losses are also covered through various means. Before 1989, the banking law required banks to evidence all non-cashed liabilities in the course of sixty days, and to 'regulate' them by refinancing, by writing them off, or by booking them as 'dubious' – requirements which effectively enabled banks not to evidence losses (see Grličkov 1987b). It was only in 1987 – in connection with the financial scandal regarding false promissory notes of the Bosnian Agrokomerc enterprise – that the first commercial bank was closed in Yugoslavia.

The most spectacular example of financial indiscipline and soft budget constraints in Yugoslavia in recent years came with the January 1991 scandal over serious violations of monetary regulations by the single republican national banks. In order to finance the budget deficit, wage increases and other expenditures, republican national banks had spent a part of their obligatory reserves, and had surpassed the permissible limits on credit expansion, without even notifying the National Bank of Yugoslavia. Although the violations were most serious in Serbia, they occurred in all the republics (although sometimes this was not officially reported).

Proliferation of inter-enterprise credits. Restrictive monetary policies applied since the early 1980s in Yugoslavia have been seriously undermined by the rapid growth of alternative channels of finance, primarily various forms of inter-enterprise credit, such as letters of credit and promissory notes.[16] These were frequently issued without effective financial backing (as in the most notable example of the Agrokomerc) and their use and abuse grew out of control, adding a large quantity of quasi-money to overall liquidity, virtually outside the reach of monetary policy. It could be argued that inter-enterprise credits cancel out when they are consolidated within the enterprise sector. However, an increase in inter-enterprise credits can be a net claim on resources and is a form of quasi-money which is difficult to subject to central control, unless strict rules are established or penal interest rates on arrears are imposed by law. By 1985, inter-enterprise credits amounted to more than 55 per cent of enterprise liabilities (OECD 1987a, p. 57),[17] and, as a percentage of total bank credit, increased from 33.8 per cent in 1980 to 44.8 per cent in 1988 (OECD 1990, p. 37).[18]

Promissory notes, as one of the most frequently used forms of inter-enterprise credit, accounted for by far the largest part of all securities in Yugoslavia in the 1977–88 period (40–60 per cent), while the main issuers of all types of securities were, in fact, enterprises. Only in 1989, following the introduction of major controls and restrictions on the issuing of promissory notes, did their share decline, to 7.4 per cent of all securities in 1989 and further to 4.1 per cent in 1990 (see table 6A.4 in the appendix).

Time and cost overruns. Table 6.4 provides data on time and cost overruns for a sample of 125 investment projects in industry and agriculture, all in Serbia, undertaken in the 1979–82 period through the Associated Belgrade Bank (Čelenković *et al.* 1984).

The data presented reveal that the average delay in project completion, compared with planned time, was around 50 per cent. Of the 122 completed projects,[19] 82 per cent exceeded the planned time of

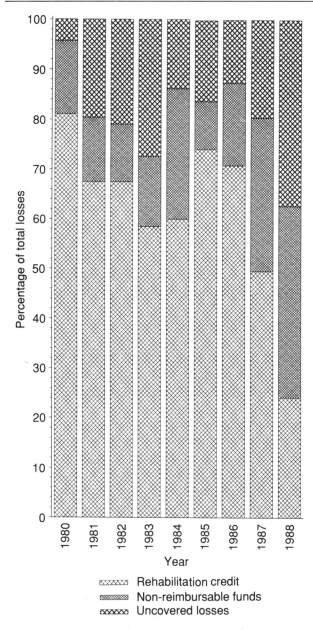

Figure 6.3 Coverage of losses in Yugoslavia, 1980–1988

completion, only 14 per cent were finished on time, and 4.1 per cent were completed before time. The analysis of cost overruns shows that 87.5 per cent of investment projects exceeded their estimated planned cost, by around 50 per cent of the planned value. As to the financing of cost overruns, enterprises participated with a relatively small amount (22 per cent of total), the bulk being financed through bank credit (over 50 per cent).

Another empirical study undertaken by the Associated Belgrade Bank provides similar data, analysing in addition the sectoral distribution of delays and cost overruns of investment projects (Ostojić et al. 1985).[20] The study shows that projects undertaken in sectors which were priority sectors for the 1980–5 period had longer time overdues and cost overruns than projects in non-priority sectors. Of total loans for financing cost overruns, by far the largest part was assigned to projects in priority sectors (70 per cent to 90 per cent in 1979–83). The study therefore clearly confirms a high level of protection of priority sectors and credit rationing in their favour.

Non-market allocation of investment resources. The procedures involved in investment project appraisal in Yugoslavia can serve as a good example in illustrating the infrequent use of market criteria and the influence of political structures (and considerations) in the microeconomic sphere. Prior to 1965, investors had to prepare investment projects according to unified instructions provided by the social investment funds, whereas project appraisal was done by specialized agencies. After 1965, these functions were transferred to banks, as one of the principal agents of investment policy, and banks were 'free' to choose their own criteria for project selection (see below).

This resulted in very heterogeneous banking practices for project selection, and economic criteria based on project profitability were seldom applied. As noted by Tyson, 'it is rare that any project is abandoned, because there are no accepted criteria to distinguish good from bad projects . . . the criteria used varied from project to project, region to region, and time to time' (1983, pp. 301–2). Moreover, the system of priority investments introduced after 1976 envisaged the setting aside of investment resources for priority sector development, supported by selective credits for priority sectors. The selective credit mechanism meant that priority sector projects were not exposed to realistic pricing of capital, and were not subject to the same methods of appraisal as projects in non-priority sectors (World Bank 1983, pp. 286–7). The system encouraged investment in priority sectors,

Table 6.4. *Time and cost overruns in a sample of 125 investment projects in Yugoslavia, 1979–1982*

	Length of overrun	Number of projects	As percentage of total
Time overruns			
Total			
planned time: 3,590 months	Less than 12 months	46	37.7
Total			
realized time: 4,878 months	13–24 months	31	25.4
Overdue: 1,775 months	25–36 months	14	11.5
	More than 36 months	9	7.3
	Completed in planned time	17	14.0
	Completed before time	5	4.1
	TOTAL	122	100.0

	Investment project		Estimated planned cost	Cost overrun	Cost overrun as percentage of estimated cost
	Number	Percentage	(in billions of dinars)		
Cost overrun					
Without					
cost overrun	29	12.5	2.355	—	—
With					
cost overrun	96	87.5	16.515	8.280	50.1
TOTAL	125	100.0	18.870	8.280	43.9

	Billions of dinars	Percentage of total
Financing of cost overrun		
Bank loans	4.276	51.6
Investors' sources	1.830	22.1
Pooled resources	0.811	9.8
Other firms' sources	0.941	11.4
Foreign sources	0.144	1.7
Other	0.278	3.4
TOTAL	8.280	100.0

Source: Čelenković *et al.* (1984), pp. 16, 71, 82.

irrespective of effective returns, rather than in projects promising the highest yield. Some of the selective credits were not even used for the purposes for which they were intended: enterprises in priority sectors often tried to obtain the maximum amount of credit, in order to lend it on to other enterprises in the grey market (OECD 1987a, p. 49).

That the economic profitability of investment in Yugoslavia was usually subordinated to more general economic objectives is confirmed by some of the existing methodologies of project appraisal.[21] All of these methodologies have the same general features: they contain an excessive number of criteria that ought to be met simultaneously. Besides including 'micro' criteria concerning the financial efficiency of a project, based on standard criteria of project selection (net present value, internal rate of return, etc.), these methodologies also include a number of 'macro' criteria concerning the socio-economic efficiency of an investment project, such as its effect on exports, foreign exchange, domestic sources of energy, raw materials and equipment, employment, and sources of finance; and its contribution to regional development, pollution reduction, and to the pooling of labour and resources. Social cost-benefit considerations clearly prevail over profitability criteria. The methodology of the Association of Belgrade Banks (Udruženje bankarskih organizacija Beograd 1985), for example, contains a total of twenty-one criteria that should be taken into account, of which only the first three refer to the economic profitability of an investment.

Since no adequate institutional mechanism existed to encourage efficiency in investment selection (no uniform methodology at the national level, no mandatory evaluation of investment projects), a social compact was concluded in December 1985.[22] The compact provided for the elaboration of a uniform methodology for project appraisal, which was to be institutionalized as obligatory through a self-management agreement on its application signed by all Yugoslav banks. However, the compact also stipulated that approval for projects had to be obtained from the Federal Institute of Social Planning, which was required to give its opinion on whether the project was consistent with the economic policy established by the social plan.

The uniform methodology, completed by the middle of 1986, was widely criticized for its excessive length (over 600 pages), its failure to cover important aspects, its inconsistency (for example, between the methodological part and the operative part), and its duplication of prescriptions. A revised version was ready by the middle of 1987 (Bendeković et al. 1987), but this methodology does not differ much from the methodologies described above: it similarly includes both market (financial) criteria (internal rate of return, net present value, etc.), and a number of socio-economic criteria designed to allow evaluation of a project's contribution to broader objectives of socio-economic development (relating to savings, balance of payments, employment, foreign market competitiveness, under-utilization of resources, technology, and even the effect of a project 'on the economic and military-strategic independence of the country'). Besides the individual discount rate, a social discount rate which takes into account the social preferences of the community, must also be applied. The analysis clearly illustrates how the Yugoslav political authorities use extra-market processes to direct the investment activities of enterprises, as well as the supremacy of social over individual interests.

In conclusion, while Furubotn and Pejovich's theory is based on assumptions which in part correspond to an idealized capitalist environment (a perfect capital market, perfect labour mobility, project appraisal according to criteria used by a capitalist firm), in Yugoslavia severe capital market distortions have prevailed, labour force mobility has been limited, and investment criteria have not been those typically used in market economies. By contrast, several of Kornai's hypotheses do seem to be confirmed by evidence from Yugoslavia, in particular the presence of soft budget constraints through concessionary forms of finance and the socialization of losses as an alternative to bankruptcy; time and cost overruns of investment projects; proliferation of interfirm credits; and the use of non-market criteria in the allocation of investment resources. Further evidence in support of these assertions is presented in the next chapter.

Appendix

Table 6A.1. *Investment in 'owned' and 'non-owned' assets in Yugoslavia, 1966–1985*

	1966	1967	1968	1969	1970	1971	1972	1973	1974	1975	1976	1977	1978	1979	1980	1981	1982	1983	1984	1985
Investment in owned assets																				
Maximum interest rates on household savings[a]	6	7	7	7.5	7.5	7.5	7.5	10	10	10	10	10	10	10	10	10	20	28	55	60
Inflation	23	7	5	8	11	16	17	20	21	24	12	15	14	20	30	41	32	41	53	74
Real rate of return (maximum)[b]	−13.8	0.0	1.9	−0.5	−3.2	−7.3	−8.1	−8.3	−9.1	−11.3	−1.8	−4.3	−3.5	−8.3	−15.4	−22.0	−9.1	−9.2	1.3	−8.0
Investment in non-owned assets																				
Maximum interest rates on bank loans	8	8	10	8	8	8	12	12	12	12	12	10	11.5	11.5	12	12	21	38	63	64
Inflation[c]	11	2	0	3	9	15	11	13	29	22	6	10	8	13	27	45	25	32	57	82
Real cost of borrowed funds (maximum)[b]	−2.7	5.9	10.0	4.9	−0.9	−6.1	0.9	−0.9	−13.2	−8.2	5.7	0.0	3.2	−1.3	−11.8	−22.8	−3.2	4.5	3.8	−9.9
Capital returns																				
Profit rate I[d]	24.4	23.5	24.3	30.0	32.6	25.2	30.8	30.9	38.0	25.5	25.1	24.3	25.5	26.0	27.0	25.7	21.9	22.7	23.5	21.9
Profit rate II[e]	12.3	11.5	11.8	11.7	13.5	12.1	14.5	14.5	19.4	12.3	10.5	10.5	11.1	11.4	13.3	12.6	11.3	11.2	11.6	9.7
Average returns[f]	36	34	35	28	28	28	53	53	48	23	24	27	31	31	30	29	27	26	27	n.a.
Labour turnover[g]	2.3	1.9	1.7	1.7	1.8	1.7	1.6	1.5	1.0	1.3	1.2	1.2	1.3	1.3	1.2	1.2	1.1	1.0	1.1	1.1

aCost of living annual percentage increase.

bCalculated as [(1+interest rate/1+inflation rate) −1] × 100.

cIndustrial producer prices annual percentage increase.

d[(Gross revenue − material costs − net personal incomes − depreciation)/historical value of capital]×100 (includes all taxes and contributions, contractual and legal obligations, and expenditure on various services, which are paid out of current profits). This category is what in Yugoslav terminology is called *višak proizvoda* (surplus value).

e[(Depreciation + allocation to funds)/historical value of capital]×100.

fRealized returns on 100 Dinars of utilized resources (SDK data).

gFluctuation of workers in productive sectors is calculated by the SZS on a monthly basis, from a sample covering 80 per cent of workers in OALs, working communities and other organizations. Workers' fluctuation is the ratio between the number of workers left, and the number of workers at the beginning of the month increased by the number of newly admitted workers during that month.

Sources: Interest rates: NBY *Bilten Narodne Banke Jugoslavije*, various issues, Table 'Pregled kamatnih stopa'.

Inflation rates: SZS, *SGJ*, various years, Table 'Indeksi cena'.

Profit rates: SZS, *SGJ*, various years, calculated from Table 'Osnovni podaci o organizacijama udruženog rada društvenog sektora'.

Labour turnover: SZS, *SGJ*, various years, Table 'Fluktuacija radnika prema granama delatnosti'.

Table 6A.2. Organizational changes of Yugoslav enterprises, 1976–1989

	1976–8			1979–80			1981–2			1983–4		
	Number of enter-prises	Percentage of enterprises	Percentage of ceased enterprises	Number of enter-prises	Percentage of enterprises	Percentage of ceased enterprises	Number of enter-prises	Percentage of enterprises	Percentage of ceased enterprises	Number of enter-prises	Percentage of enterprises	Percentage of ceased enterprises
TOTAL	13,770	100.0		9,403	100.0		6,048	100.0		5,721	100.0	
Ceased, total	2,721	19.8	100.0	1,993	21.2	100.0	1,671	27.6	100.0	2,030	35.5	100.0
Liquidation	262	1.9	9.6	442	4.7	22.2	345	5.7	20.7	283	4.9	13.9
By will of members	266	1.9	9.8	281	3.0	14.1	264	4.3	15.8	274	4.8	13.5
Mergers	950	6.9	34.9	600	6.4	30.1	530	8.8	31.7	781	13.7	38.5
Affiliations	687	5.0	25.2	424	4.5	21.3	405	6.7	24.2	603	10.5	29.7
Divisions	556	4.1	20.4	246	2.6	12.3	127	2.1	7.6	89	1.6	4.4
Newly-established	8,183	59.4		4,965	52.8		2,877	47.6		1,687	29.5	
Status changes	1,978	14.4		1,230	13.1		919	15.2		929	16.2	
Activity changes	888	6.4		1,215	12.9		581	9.6		1,075	18.8	

	1986			1987			1988			1989		
TOTAL	4,087	100.0		4,384	100.0		4,695	100.0		12,620	100.0	
Ceased, total	1,655	40.5	100.0	1,988	45.3	100.0	2,210	47.1	100.0	4,809	38.1	100.0
Liquidation	34	0.8	2.1	23	0.5	1.2	60	1.3	2.7	41	0.3	0.85
Bankruptcy	28	0.7	1.7	20	0.5	1.0	52	1.1	2.3	41	0.3	0.85
Closures	48	1.2	2.9	42	0.9	2.1	48	1.0	2.2	276	2.2	5.7
Reorganization	1,545	37.8	93.3	1,903	43.4	95.7	2,050	43.7	92.8	4,451	35.3	92.6
Newly-established	706	17.3		701	16.0		769	16.4		4,014	31.8	
Status changes	627	15.3		750	17.1		847	18.0		2,375	18.8	
Constituted	79	1.9		59	1.3		87	1.9		63	0.5	
Initiation of liquidation procedures	34	0.8		39	0.9		29	0.6		20	0.2	
Initiation of bankruptcy procedures	35	0.9		59	1.3		100	2.1		43	0.3	
Reorganization	479	11.7		593	13.6		631	13.4		2,249	17.8	
Activity changes	1,099	26.9		945	21.6		869	18.5		1,422	11.3	

Note: Enterprises refer to organizations of associated labour in the productive sector. The figures are reported differently for the two periods 1976–84 and 1986–9 because prior to 1986, a different methodology was applied by the SZS. Organizational changes started being reported in the SGJ only in 1987, within which bankruptcies are included as a separate item.

Source: 1976–84: SZS (1986), p. 31.
1986–9: SZS, SGJ, various years. Table 'Organizacione promene u privredi prema delatnosti organizacije – zajednice' (in SGJ 1990, Table 103-2).

Table 6A.3. *Coverage of enterprise losses in Yugoslavia, 1980–1988 (by year of coverage)*

	\multicolumn{9}{c}{Billions of current Dinars}									\multicolumn{9}{c}{Ratios of total losses (in per cent)}								
	1980	1981	1982	1983	1984	1985	1986	1987	1988	1980	1981	1982	1983	1984	1985	1986	1987	1988
Total losses (covered and uncovered)	16.4	20.9	28.6	47.7	87.1	99.8	241.8	458.2	1117.0	100	100	100	100	100	100	100	100	100
Loss covered from:																		
Non-reimbursable funds	2.4	2.7	3.3	6.7	22.8	9.6	40.0	141.8	430.8	14.6	12.9	11.5	14.0	26.2	9.6	16.5	30.9	38.5
• of BOALs	0.4	0.7	1.5	1.5	6.1	3.4	17.0	35.1	75.1	2.4	3.4	5.2	3.1	7.0	3.4	7.0	7.7	6.7
• common reserve funds	0.2	0.3	0.8	0.3	1.4	0.5	2.4	21.5	—	1.2	1.4	2.8	0.6	1.6	0.5	1.0	4.7	—
• socio-political communities	1.6	1.4	0.7	4.6	14.6	4.5	9.4	38.1	256.0	9.8	6.7	2.4	9.6	16.8	4.5	3.9	8.3	22.9
• claims written off	0.2	0.3	0.3	0.3	0.7	1.2	11.2	47.1	99.7	1.2	1.4	1.0	0.6	0.8	1.2	4.6	10.3	8.9
Rehabilitation credit	13.3	14.1	19.3	27.9	52.3	73.9	171.3	226.9	269.5	81.1	67.5	67.5	58.5	60.0	74.0	70.8	49.5	24.1
• of BOALs	1.5	2.3	2.6	5.6	11.0	30.9	58.3	93.7	93.9	9.2	11.0	9.1	11.7	12.6	31.0	24.1	20.4	8.4
• common reserve funds	6.5	7.1	11.4	12.9	25.1	12.6	12.6	0.0	—	39.6	34.0	39.9	27.0	28.8	12.6	5.2	0.0	—
• banks	3.5	3.8	4.2	6.6	12.9	23.7	95.2	113.4	166.1	21.3	18.2	14.7	13.8	14.8	23.7	39.4	24.7	14.9
• socio-political communities	1.8	0.9	1.1	2.8	3.3	6.7	5.2	19.8	9.5	11.0	4.3	3.8	5.9	3.8	6.7	2.2	4.3	0.8
Loss still uncovered at end of year	0.7	4.1	6.0	13.1	12.0	16.3	30.5	89.5	416.7	4.3	19.6	21.0	27.5	13.8	16.4	12.6	19.5	37.3

The table reports losses according to year of coverage, referring to losses as shown in the financial reports at the end of the previous year. BOALs are basic organizations of associated labour. Socio-political communities include the federation and socio-political communities at the republican/regional and the communal level.

Source: Data of the Federal Accounting Office (SDK); for 1980–1, calculated from Knight (1984), also on the basis of SDK data.

Table 6A.4. Securities in Yugoslavia, 1973–1990 (billions of Dinars, end-year values)

	1973	1974	1975	1976	1977	1978	1979	1980	1981	1982	1983	1984	1985	1986	1987	1988	1989	1990
Securities bought by banks, total	1.6	2.1	3.4	19.1	35.0	75.2	107.9	147.3	199.9	207.8	222.1	269.3	341.8	530.3	1,252.0	4,053.5	1,983.8	8,186.9
By type:																		
• Promissory notes	0.0	0.0	0.0	2.9	13.7	42.8	68.0	92.5	114.5	117.7	103.8	137.1	141.8	273.2	632.6	1,733.9	147.1	337.8
• Bonds	0.9	1.1	2.3	10.9	15.3	18.7	17.7	22.7	29.2	28.1	26.4	26.3	28.2	40.0	60.9	68.3	7.3	1,021.4
• Treasury bills	0.7	1.0	1.1	5.1	5.6	5.2	5.1	5.0	4.7	4.6	4.9	9.6	12.1	44.8	98.0	349.5	109.7	6,455.7
• Other	0.0	0.0	0.0	0.2	0.4	8.5	17.1	27.1	51.5	57.4	87.0	96.3	159.7	172.3	460.5	1,901.8	1,719.7	372.0
By sector:																		
• Productive OALs	—	—	—	—	17.1	50.8	82.3	113.6	158.7	165.0	181.1	224.9	295.6	425.3	1,032.3	3,587.1	1,812.4	788.1
• Federation	—	—	—	—	9.6	13.1	11.0	16.5	24.0	23.9	23.6	23.3	25.7	34.4	52.7	54.6	5.8	5.2
• Other socio-political communities	—	—	—	—	1.3	2.2	3.1	3.4	3.1	2.5	1.6	1.2	1.2	4.0	5.0	6.7	0.8	888.3
• Other sectors	—	—	—	—	7.0	9.1	11.5	13.8	14.1	16.4	15.8	19.9	19.3	66.6	162.0	405.1	164.8	6,505.3
Securities issued by banks, total	3.4	4.1	4.7	9.6	15.6	17.2	85.8	110.0	137.6	161.6	161.0	206.3	268.8	551.3	655.9	1,262.0	383.5	7,955.9
By type:																		
• Bonds	—	—	—	—	9.9	11.7	80.3	104.4	132.4	155.4	155.1	196.2	254.6	505.4	553.0	875.5	205.5	1,106.0
• Treasury bills	—	—	—	—	5.6	5.2	5.1	5.0	4.6	4.6	4.9	9.6	12.0	44.7	97.9	352.2	130.3	5,222.9
• Other	—	—	—	—	0.1	0.3	0.4	0.6	0.6	1.6	1.0	0.5	2.2	1.2	5.0	34.3	47.7	1,627.0
By sector:																		
• Productive OALs	1.7	1.7	1.8	3.0	6.8	5.5	73.9	98.7	127.4	152.6	153.1	195.2	255.6	505.4	557.8	908.3	224.6	2,284.1
• Socio-political communities	0.6	0.9	1.1	0.9	1.8	3.9	3.9	3.5	3.1	2.5	1.5	0.4	0.0	0.0	0.0	0.0	0.0	6.0
•Other sectors	1.1	1.5	1.8	5.7	7.0	7.8	8.0	7.8	7.1	6.5	6.4	10.7	13.2	45.9	98.1	353.7	158.9	5,665.8

The table reports securities of all issuers (holders) that undertake their transactions concerning securities through banks. *Promissory notes* include domestic promissory notes in foreign currency, Dinar discounted promissory notes, and rediscounted promissory notes. *Bonds* include short-term bonds of socio-political communities and other issuers, subscribed from reserve funds and giro accounts. *Treasury bills* are NBY treasury bills, subscribed by basic and associated banks. *Other securities* include various types of certificates for the pooling of resources, both in Dinars and foreign currency. Banks include the NBY, commercial and associated banks, and other financial institutions.
Source: NBY, *Bilten Narodne Banke Jugoslavije*, various issues, Table 'Hartije od vrednosti', and data obtained directly from the NBY.

7   Econometric tests of Yugoslav investment behaviour

Furubotn and Pejovich's theory will now be compared with Kornai's theory in order to assess, using econometric methods, which of the two theories offers a better analysis of investment in Yugoslavia. The two theories are first considered separately, evaluating the role of the alternative groups of variables proposed by each of the two theories as being crucial for explaining savings deposits, investment and self-financed investment. The theories are then evaluated jointly, applying the complete parameter-encompassing procedure (unrestricted-restricted model).

Testing Furubotn and Pejovich's theory

The most explicit statement made by Furubotn and Pejovich on the determinants of savings, investment and self-financed investment in a Yugoslav-type LMF is found in their 1973 (p. 281) article: 'We find that (1) the shorter the collective's planning horizon, (2) the higher the rate s [interest paid on savings deposits], (3) the lower the rate i [cost of bank credit], and (4) the lower the marginal productivity of capital in the firm, the less attractive are non-owned assets in comparison with owned assets and the less likely is self-finance activity.' The theory therefore maintains that savings deposits, investment, and self-financed investment are determined by the planning horizon, the interest rate on savings deposits, the cost of bank credit, and capital returns, the first three variables being the dependent, and the last four being the explanatory variables.[1]

In testing the theory on Yugoslavia, in the lack of enterprise level statistics, aggregate data has been used for the above seven variables: savings deposits of households (SD); investment in fixed assets of the social sector (INV); investment in fixed assets financed by social sector enterprises (SFI); interest rate on savings deposits of households (IR);

Table 7.1. *Correlation matrix – Furubotn and Pejovich's theory (1967–84)*

	SD	INV	SFI	IR	LR	H	PF
SD	1.000						
INV	0.949	1.000					
SFI	0.929	0.951	1.000				
IR	−0.337	−0.452	−0.461	1.000			
LR	−0.334	−0.459	−0.403	0.959	1.000		
H	0.663	0.625	0.783	−0.425	−0.308	1.000	
PF	−0.178	−0.306	−0.359	−0.096	−0.147	−0.174	1.000

lending rate on bank loans to enterprises (*LR*); capital returns represented by the profit rate (*PF*), defined as social sector firms' gross value added minus depreciation and minus personal incomes, divided by the historical value of capital; and a proxy for the time horizon (*H*), calculated from data on labour fluctuation, on the assumption that the time horizon is inversely related to labour turnover.[2] All variables have been deflated and hence are in real terms. The period being examined is 1966–84, but investment and self-financed investment data refer to the 1967–84 period, since changes in the methodology used in reporting statistics did not permit the inclusion of 1966 (for further details on all variables, see the appendix to this chapter).

The following procedure was applied. First, in order to get a first insight into the relationship between these seven variables, correlation coefficients were calculated, and their significance tested. Second, a series of single regression equations was estimated. Finally, two simultaneous equation models were estimated.

Correlation

The correlation matrix between the seven variables reflecting Furubotn and Pejovich's theory, for the 1967–84 period, is presented in table 7.1.

The corresponding *t* values, which measure the significance of correlation coefficients, reveal that all of the above coefficients are statistically significant.[3] Quite surprisingly, there is higher correlation among variables considered dependent by the theory (*SD, INV, SFI*), than between each of these and the explanatory variables. The only variable that is highly correlated with *SD, INV,* and *SFI* is the time horizon variable (*H*).[4] The correlation coefficients between *SD, INV, SFI* and the other three variables are generally low. As to the relationship among explanatory variables, only the two interest rates seem highly correlated.

The general model

Three single equations were first estimated using the method of ordinary least squares (OLS):

Savings deposits equation:[5]

$$SD = b_1 IR + b_2 LR + b_3 H + b_4 PF + b_5 + u \tag{1.1}$$
$$b_1 > 0, b_2 < 0, b_3 < 0, b_4 < 0$$

IR: interest rate on savings deposits
LR: lending rate on credits to firms
H: a proxy for the time horizon
PF: profit rate
u: error term

The investment equation:[6]

$$INV = b_1 IR + b_2 LR + b_3 H + b_4 PF + b_5 + u \tag{1.2}$$
$$b_1 < 0, b_2 \leqq 0, b_3 > 0, b_4 > 0$$

INV: investment in fixed assets (social sector). All other variables are the same as those in (1.1).

The self-financed investment equation:[7]

$$SFI = b_1 IR + b_2 LR + b_3 H + b_4 PF + b_5 + u \tag{1.3}$$
$$b_1 < 0, b_2 > 0, b_3 > 0, b_4 > 0$$

SFI: self-financed investment in fixed assets (social sector). All other variables are the same as those in (1.1) and (1.2).

RESULTS:

OLS Period: 1966–84   (1.1)

Dep. variable: SD				R2: 0.620	R2C: 0.511
	Indep. variables	Estd. coeff.	Std. dev.	t	BC%
b_1	IR	1.644	1.100	1.49	33.0
b_2	LR	−1.694	1.034	1.64	35.9
b_3	H	23.616	5.136	4.60	27.3
b_4	PF	−0.284	0.432	0.66	3.7
b_5	Constant	−2,288.496	505.614	4.53	0.0

Std. error: 7.245 MAPE: 16.90 DW: 0.953 RH0(1): 0.52

OLS Period: 1967–84   (1.2)

Dep. variable: INV				R2: 0.601	R2C: 0.478
	Indep. variables	Estd. coeff.	Std. dev.	t	BC%
b_1	IR	4.008	2.840	1.41	31.6
b_2	LR	−4.824	2.569	1.88	40.2
b_3	H	50.015	17.609	2.84	19.1
b_4	PF	−1.726	1.080	1.60	9.2
b_5	Constant	−4,806.978	1,737.728	2.77	0.0

Std. error: 17.559 MAPE: 15.43 DW: 1.045 RH0(1): 0.46

OLS Period: 1967–84   (1.3)

Dep. variable: SFI				R2: 0.724	R2C: 0.639
	Indep. variables	Estd. coeff.	Std. dev.	t	BC%
b_1	IR	0.826	1.236	0.67	19.8
b_2	LR	−1.194	1.118	1.07	30.2
b_3	H	30.831	7.661	4.02	35.8
b_4	PF	−0.882	0.470	1.88	14.2
b_5	Constant	−2,978.088	756.053	3.94	0.0

Std. error: 7.639 MAPE: 14.63 DW: 0.937 RH0(1): 0.51

Details concerning reported statistics are given in the appendix to this chapter.

The results are similar for all three equations. The relatively low corrected coefficients of determination (R2C) indicate that the fit is not very good. The Durbin-Watson statistics (DW) and the high first-order autocorrelation coefficient of the residuals (RH0(1)) indicate that there may be a problem of positive autocorrelation of residuals. Since the DW in all three equations lies in the inconclusive region, the Durbin-Watson Exact Test (DWE) was applied; this confirmed positive autocorrelation in all three equations.[8]

Since autocorrelation of residuals suggests misspecification of the equations and produces inefficient regression estimates and misleading t statistics, in order to discover which type of specification bias was present a series of tests was performed: for normality of residuals, presence of outliers, heteroscedasticity, linearity of variables, correctness of the functional form and of the model specification (NORMAL, OUTLIE, HETERO, HARVEY, RBOW, DIFF, IMT).[9] The three regressions passed all of the above tests (see appendix to this chapter), suggesting that misspecification derives primarily from the omission of relevant variables and/or inclusion of irrelevant ones.

Improving the model

Several attempts were made to improve the model. First, in order to correct for autocorrelation, instead of OLS, the Cochrane–Ocrutt (CO) method was applied in estimating equations 1.1, 1.2, and 1.3, both by including and excluding the first observation. This, however, did not yield satisfactory results, since serial correlation remained a problem.[10] Second, since the two interest rates, IR and LR, are highly correlated (correlation coefficient of 0.959), a remedial measure was applied to remove the problem of collinearity, by a different parametrization of the interest rates. IR was retained, while LR has replaced by a new variable DIR representing the absolute difference between IR and LR ($DIR=IR-LR$). However, in all three equations, the results were very similar to those previously obtained (identical R2, R2C, and DW, and similar t statistics). Third, since the dependent variable is taken to be the level of self-financed investment, which is closely related to the level of total investment and can thus be expected to rise when total investment rises, as an alternative we used the ratio of self-financed investment to total investment as the dependent variable – but the results were not very different. Finally, although Furubotn and Pejovich (1973) very explicitly list IR, LR, H and PF as the crucial determinants of SD, INV, and SFI, additional explanatory variables were added to the original three equations.

First, besides considering the *cost* of credit, captured by the variable *LR*, it may be equally important to consider the *level* of credit availability. Therefore, a variable on credits from banks and various funds (*CR*) extended to enterprises was added to the original three equations:

1 Savings equation: (1.1) + $b_5 CR$ $b_5 > 0$ (1.4)

2 Investment equation: (1.2) + $b_5 CR$ $b_5 \leqq 0$ (1.5)

3 Self-financed equation: (1.3) + $b_5 CR$ $b_5 < 0$ (1.6)[11]

RESULTS:

OLS Period: 1966–84   (1.4)

Dep. variable: *SD*   R2: 0.715   R2C: 0.605

	Indep. variables	Estd. coeff.	Std. dev.	t	BC%
b_1	IR	2.361	1.048	2.25	36.1
b_2	LR	−2.294	0.974	2.36	37.0
b_3	H	17.758	5.414	3.28	15.7
b_4	PF	−0.026	0.408	0.06	0.3
b_5	CR	0.149	0.072	2.08	11.0
b_6	Constant	−1,735.291	527.089	3.29	0.0

Std. error: 6.516   MAPE: 16.25   DW: 0.995   RH0(1): 0.49

DW Exact: Prob. 0.0%

OLS   Period: 1967–84   (1.5)

Dep. variable: *INV*   R2: 0.741   R2C: 0.633

	Indep. variables	Estd. coeff.	Std. dev.	t	BC%
b_1	IR	6.603	2.593	2.55	35.9
b_2	LR	−6.855	2.299	2.98	39.4
b_3	H	40.151	15.277	2.63	10.6
b_4	PF	−0.841	0.971	0.87	3.1
b_5	CR	0.426	0.168	2.54	11.0
b_6	Constant	−3,906.357	1,500.518	2.60	0.0

Std. error: 14.733   MAPE: 12.41   DW: 1.316   RH0(1): 0.32

DW Exact: Prob. 0.38%

OLS   Period: 1967–84   (1.6)

Dep. variable: *SFI*   R2: 0.878   R2C: 0.828

	Indep. variables	Estd. coeff.	Std. dev.	t	BC%
b_1	IR	2.254	0.929	2.43	30.9
b_2	LR	-2.311	0.823	2.81	33.4
b_3	H	25.406	5.472	4.64	16.9
b_4	PF	-0.396	0.348	1.14	3.7
b_5	CR	0.234	0.060	3.90	15.2
b_6	Constant	-2,482.750	537.503	4.62	0.0

Std. error: 5.278   MAPE: 9.09   DW: 1.275   RH0(1): 0.35

DW Exact: Prob. 0.27%

Although adding the variable *CR* improves the fit of all three equations (which was to be expected), it did not eliminate the problem of autocorrelation, confirmed to be present in all three equations by the DWE.[12] Consequently, the t statistics, although high for most of the variables, are not precise and do not permit any definite conclusions.[13]

Next, although all variables were deflated, this might not have been sufficient to remove the influence of time on the dependent variables. Hence a trend variable was added to the original three equations:

1 Savings equation: (1.1) + b_5T $b_5>0$ (1.7)

2 Investment equation: (1.2) + b_5T $b_5>0$ (1.8)

3 Self-financed equation: (1.3) + b_5T $b_5>0$ (1.9)[14]

RESULTS:

OLS Period: 1966–84   (1.7)

Dep. variable: *SD*   R2: 0.742   R2C: 0.643

	Indep. variables	Estd. coeff.	Std. dev.	t	BC%
b_1	IR	2.680	1.030	2.60	37.1
b_2	LR	-2.436	0.934	2.61	35.6
b_3	H	-0.394	10.645	0.04	0.3
b_4	PF	0.354	0.451	0.79	3.2
b_5	T	1.881	0.759	2.48	23.8
b_6	Constant	-76.464	992.450	0.08	0.0

Std. error: 6.197   MAPE: 13.21   DW: 1.048   RH0(1): 0.47

DW Exact: Prob. 0.03%

OLS   Period: 1967–84   (1.8)

Dep. variable: INV R2: 0.722   R2C: 0.606

	Indep. variables	Estd. coeff.	Std. dev.	t	BC%
b_1	IR	6.277	2.661	2.36	36.2
b_2	LR	−6.462	2.345	2.76	39.4
b_3	H	−5.593	28.770	0.19	1.6
b_4	PF	−0.298	1.128	0.26	1.2
b_5	T	4.273	1.872	2.28	21.6
b_6	Constant	323.415	2,707.834	0.12	0.0

Std. error: 15.260   MAPE: 13.60   DW: 1.293   RH0(1): 0.33

DW Exact: Prob. 0.33%

OLS   Period: 1967–84   (1.9)

Dep. variable: SFI R2: 0.876   R2C: 0.825

	Indep. variables	Estd. coeff.	Std. dev.	t	BC%
b_1	IR	2.159	0.928	2.33	32.0
b_2	LR	−2.156	0.818	2.63	33.7
b_3	H	−1.828	10.037	0.18	1.3
b_4	PF	−0.044	0.394	0.11	0.4
b_5	T	2.509	0.653	3.84	32.6
b_6	Constant	35.052	944.699	0.04	0.0

Std. error: 5.324   MAPE: 9.24   DW: 1.176   RH0(1): 0.39

DW Exact: Prob. 0.10%

Since, in these equations, autocorrelation was not eliminated, a further attempt was made to improve Furubotn and Pejovich's model using single regressions by including a variable reflecting the change in economic policies in Yugoslavia from 1980 onwards: the change was represented by a dummy variable, *DA*, which is 0 until 1979 and 1 thereafter:

1 Savings equation: $(1.1) + b_5 DA$ $b_5 < 0$ (1.10)

2 Investment equation: $(1.2) + b_5 DA$ $b_5 < 0$ (1.11)

3 Self-financed equation: $(1.3) + b_5 DA$ $b_5 < 0$ (1.12)[15]

RESULTS:

OLS Period: 1966–84   (1.10)

Dep. variable: SD			R2: 0.642	R2C: 0.511

	Indep. variables	Estd. coeff.	Std. dev.	t	BC%
b_1	IR	1.014	1.273	0.80	22.1
b_2	LR	−1.223	1.140	1.07	28.1
b_3	H	26.374	5.852	4.51	33.2
b_4	PF	−0.498	0.484	1.03	7.1
b_5	DA	−5.922	6.002	0.99	9.5
b_6	Constant	−2,555.106	573.724	4.45	0.0

Std. error: 7.252   MAPE: 17.05   DW: 0.953   RH0(1): 0.52

DW Exact: Prob. 0.0%

OLS   Period: 1967–84   (1.11)

Dep. variable: INV			R2: 0.607	R2C: 0.444

	Indep. variables	Estd. coeff.	Std. dev.	t	BC%
b_1	IR	3.223	3.415	0.94	26.6
b_2	LR	−4.248	2.947	1.44	37.1
b_3	H	52.372	18.924	2.77	21.0
b_4	PF	−1.987	1.258	1.58	11.1
b_5	DA	−6.781	15.146	0.45	4.2
b_6	Constant	−5,033.029	1,863.485	2.70	0.0

Std. error: 18.125   MAPE: 15.41   DW: 1.052   RH0(1): 0.46

DW Exact: Prob. 0.04%

OLS   Period: 1967–84   (1.12)

Dep. variable: SFI			R2: 0.724	R2C: 0.610

	Indep. variables	Estd. coeff.	Std. dev.	t	BC%
b_1	IR	0.932	1.497	0.62	21.2
b_2	LR	−1.271	1.292	0.98	30.6
b_3	H	30.514	8.296	3.68	33.7
b_4	PF	−0.847	0.552	1.54	13.0
b_5	DA	0.913	6.639	0.14	1.6
b_6	Constant	−2,947.641	816.863	3.61	0.0

Std. error: 7.945   MAPE: 14.56   DW: 0.9375   RH0(1): 0.51

DW Exact: Prob. 0.01%

Similar conclusions can be drawn for both groups of regressions (1.7, 1.8, 1.9, and 1.10, 1.11, 1.12). Although in some cases the R2C is higher, suggesting a better fit, the problem of autocorrelation has not been eliminated (confirmed by the DWE test), thus producing misleading t statistics and inefficient coefficient estimates. Therefore, as before, little can be concluded about the significance of each of these variables in determining savings deposits, investment and self-financed investment in Yugoslavia. Our attempts to improve the original model did not produce better results, more supportive of the theory, but have in addition provided evidence that the model is very sensitive to minor changes.[16]

A simultaneous equation model

The theory examines the choice of workers to invest in savings accounts or in the firm's capital stock, thus postulating that savings deposits and self-financed investment are mutually dependent, moving in opposite directions. A simultaneous equation model may, therefore, reflect the theory more appropriately; two such models were estimated using two-stage least squares (TSLS).

The first simultaneous equation model was based on the original three equations (1.1, 1.2, 1.3):

$$SD = a_1 SFI + a_2 IR + a_3 + u_1 \tag{1.13a}$$
$$a_1 < 0, a_2 > 0$$

$$SFI = b_1 SD + b_2 LR + b_3 H + b_4 PF + b_5 + u_2 \tag{1.13b}$$
$$b_1 < 0, b_2 > 0, b_3 > 0, b_4 > 0$$

In each of the equations, only those variables which are expected directly to influence the dependent variable were included. Thus in 1.13a, savings deposits are directly influenced by the interest rate and by self-financed investment, whereas all other explanatory variables influence it indirectly, through self-financed investment, and therefore these variables are excluded from 1.13a, but included in 1.13b.

RESULTS:

TSLS Period: 1967–84   (1.13a)

	Dep. variable: SD				R2: 0.872
	Indep. variables	Estd. coeff.	Std. dev.	t	BC%
a_1	SFI	0.651	0.102	6.39	93.7
a_2	IR	0.092	0.181	0.51	6.3
a_3	Constant	5.149	3.584	1.44	0.0

Std. error: 3.821   MAPE: 10.47   DW: 0.469   RH0(1): 0.73

ARSIM: value of test statistic 1.056

TSLS   Period: 1967–84   (1.13b)

	Dep. variable: SFI				R2: 0.913
	Indep. variables	Estd. coeff.	Std. dev.	t	BC%
b_1	SD	0.486	0.417	1.17	30.0
b_2	LR	−0.355	0.206	1.72	14.6
b_3	H	18.977	9.003	2.11	35.7
b_4	PF	−0.752	0.286	2.63	19.7
b_5	Constant	−1,828.526	875.430	2.09	0.0

Std. error: 4.393   MAPE: 8.56   DW: 1.054   RH0(1): 0.46

ARSIM: value of test statistic 1.053

Although the model produces a better fit than the one obtained with single regressions (a higher R2), the ARSIM test statistics in both regressions suggest that the null hypothesis (H0) that autocorrelation is present cannot be rejected.[17]

In the alternative simultaneous equation model, the variable on credits to firms (CR) has been added to the second, SFI equation:

$$SD = a_1 SFI + a_2 IR + a_3 + u_1 \tag{1.14a}$$
$$a_1 < 0, a_2 > 0$$

$$SFI = b_1 SD + b_2 LR + b_3 H + b_4 PF + b_5 CR + b_6 + u_2 \tag{1.14b}$$
$$b_1 < 0, b_2 > 0, b_3 > 0, b_4 > 0, b_5 > 0$$

RESULTS:

TSLS Period: 1967–84 (1.14a)

Dep. variable: *SD*   R2: 0.873

	Indep. variables	Estd. coeff.	Std. dev.	t	BC%
a_1	SFI	0.661	0.089	7.46	93.2
a_2	IR	0.101	0.173	0.58	6.8
a_3	Constant	4.841	3.180	1.52	0.0

Std. error: 3.789   MAPE: 10.45   DW: 0.464   RH0(1): 0.74

ARSIM: value of test statistic 1.082

TSLS   Period: 1967–84 (1.14b)

Dep. variable: *SFI*   R2: 0.991

	Indep. variables	Estd. coeff.	Std. dev.	t	BC%
b_1	SD	0.842	0.094	8.95	49.0
b_2	LR	−0.216	0.062	3.48	8.4
b_3	H	8.006	2.036	3.93	14.3
b_4	PF	−0.453	0.095	4.78	11.2
b_5	CR	0.098	0.017	5.63	17.1
b_6	Constant	−777.531	199.059	3.91	0.0

Std. error: 1.443   MAPE: 2.87   DW: 2.340   RH0(1): −0.23

ARSIM: value of test statistic 2.333

The savings equation again suggests that there may be auto-correlation,[18] but the self-financed investment equation provides good overall results: the R2 is higher than in 1.13b, there is no auto-correlation of residuals,[19] and all variables are highly significant at the 1 per cent level. Nevertheless, looking at the signs of the estimated coefficients, four out of five are contrary to what is postulated by Furubotn and Pejovich's theory (for variables *SD, LR, PF,* and *CR*). Self-financed investment seems highly influenced by savings deposits, but *positively* so;[20] the lower the lending rate and the lower are profits, quite contradictorily, the higher will be self-finance; and the availability of credits given to firms, instead of decreasing self-financing, increases it.[21] Therefore, the equation confirms only the influence of *H* on self-financed investment, whereas the wrong signs of the coefficients for the remaining variables obviously indicate that the model does not fulfil one of the most important conditions for accepting it: congruence with theory.[22] This was to be expected, since real interest rates, having been negative in Yugoslavia over most of the sample period under consideration, did little (as we saw in chapter 6) to constrain investment demand in the expected manner.

Testing Kornai's theory

Several hypotheses based on Kornai's (1980) theory on the socialist economy will now be quantified and tested on Yugoslav data, in order to determine whether, in the field of investment, Yugoslavia is indeed primarily a socialist economy.

Since the household sector in a socialist economy faces a 'hard' budget constraint, variables influencing savings deposits should depend on standard economic aggregates. However, while Kornai speaks of motives for household savings, he doesn't specify which economic aggregates are likely to influence them; he is only explicit in stating that the interest rate is not among these. Hence we have made our own assumptions, considering savings deposits to be a function of disposable household income (INC), gross material product (GMP), and changes in government economic policy (represented by the dummy variable DA, which is 0 until 1979 and 1 thereafter).

Kornai's hypotheses on investment have been quantified in the following way (for further details, see the appendix to this chapter):

Expansion drive. One of the main determinants of investment in a socialist economy, according to Kornai's theory, is 'expansion drive', which can be approximated by the priority given to investment growth as compared to consumption growth. This priority is represented by the variable ED, which was calculated as the absolute difference between the investment growth index and the GMP growth index (base year 1966) of the social sector. Expansion drive is present whenever investment in fixed assets grows more rapidly than GMP, and therefore whenever investment growth is realized at the expense of consumption.[23]

'Irresistibility' of growth. Kornai's assertion that in a socialist economy enterprises must grow – something which leads to continuous growth of the productive forces (1980, pp. 191–4, 202) – is represented by the variable FXA<1>, fixed assets of the social sector of the economy

lagged by one year (increasing capital stock as compared to the previous year).[24]

No failure of investment projects. According to Kornai, what is important is to get approval for the starting of an investment, since a true investment failure (in the financial sense) never occurs (1980, pp. 194–8, 523). This hypothesis is approximated by a variable on the estimated value of unfinished fixed investment projects, or work in progress (*WIP*). In the absence of failure of unprofitable projects, investment projects which have been initiated are expected to put pressure on investment: the higher is *WIP*, the higher effective investment is likely to be.

Investment planning. Official expectations regarding investment behaviour – one of the factors which explains investment tension in a socialist economy (Kornai 1980, p. 210) – have been represented by a variable measuring the planned annual rate of growth of investment in fixed assets (*PINV*), as provided for in government one-year plans ('economic resolutions').

Growth priority. Investment tension is strengthened if central economic policy itself forces the fastest possible rate of economic growth (Kornai 1980, pp. 208–9). The influence of growth policies is represented by a variable measuring the planned annual rate of growth of GMP (*PGMP*), again as provided for in government economic resolutions.

Tolerance limit. The upward swing of investment growth will last as long as the process does not hit one of the 'tolerance limits' (Kornai 1980, pp. 211–14). In Yugoslavia, the tolerance limit (worsening of the balance of payments position) was hit at the end of 1979, which brought about a radical change in official policies from 1980 onwards: restrictions were introduced on all forms of consumption, and especially on investment, in order to reduce the balance of payments deficit. Restrictive policies are represented by a dummy variable *DA*, which is 0 until 1979 and 1 thereafter.

The above hypotheses were tested using a procedure similar to the one used before. First, correlation coefficients between variables were calculated, and their significance tested. Second, a series of single regression equations were estimated. Since *SD* and *SFI* are not

Table 7.2. *Correlation matrix – savings (1966–1984)*

	SD	INC	GMP	DA
SD	1.000			
INC	0.858	1.000		
GMP	0.818	0.660	1.000	
DA	0.253	0.193	0.734	1.000

considered to be mutually dependent, there was no need to estimate a simultaneous equation model.

Correlation

Two separate correlation matrices are presented, one for variables assumed to determine savings in Yugoslavia (table 7.2), and another for those reflecting Kornai's theory of investment and self-financed investment (table 7.3).

The correlation matrix for savings deposits and the variables assumed to influence them shows that whereas SD is highly correlated with GMP and INC, it is not correlated with DA (although a low correlation coefficient does not yet mean that in conjunction with other variables, DA will not prove significant).

In table 7.3, the correlation coefficients between the dependent variables and the explanatory variables are generally high, except for those between INV and DA and between SFI and ED. As to the relationship between the explanatory variables, it is clear that multi-collinearity may pose a serious problem, since some of these variables are highly collinear (especially FXA<1> with DA and PGMP; WIP with PINV; PINV with PGMP). The t test for the significance of the correlation coefficients showed that all were significant at the 5 per cent level, except one.[25]

The general model

Three single equations were first estimated using OLS. As before, in the savings equation for 1966–84, and in the investment and self-financed equations for 1967–84, aggregate data were used.

Table 7.3. *Correlation matrix – Kornai's theory (1967–1984)*

	INV	SFI	FXA<1>	ED	WIP	PINV	PGMP	DA
INV	1.000							
SFI	0.951	1.000						
FXA<1>	0.699	0.876	1.000					
ED	0.601	0.333	−0.145	1.000				
WIP	0.974	0.874	0.556	0.720	1.000			
PINV	0.968	0.924	0.694	0.554	0.951	1.000		
PGMP	0.800	0.936	0.981	0.005	0.677	0.804	1.000	
DA	0.340	0.537	0.878	−0.431	0.206	0.419	0.762	1.000

Savings deposits

$$SD = b_1 INC + b_2 GMP + b_3 DA + b_4 + u \qquad (2.1)$$
$$b_1 > 0, b_2 > 0, b_3 < 0 [26]$$

INC: Household disposable income
GMP: Gross material product
DA: Dummy, reflecting changes in government policies from 1980 onwards.

Investment

$$INV = b_1 ED + b_2 FXA<1> + b_3 WIP + b_4 PINV$$
$$+ b_5 PGMP + b_6 DA + b_7 + u \qquad (2.2)$$
$$b_1 > 0, b_2 > 0, b_3 > 0, b_4 > 0, b_5 > 0, b_6 < 0 [27]$$

All explanatory variables in this equation reflect Kornai's hypotheses: *ED* (expansion drive); *FXA<1>* (growth of productive forces); *WIP* (no investment failure); *PINV* (investment planning); *PGMP* (growth priority); and *DA* (tolerance limit).

Self-financed investment. Since Kornai suggests that expansion drive, the principal determinant of investment in a socialist economy, is present at all levels (1980, p. 193) investment financed by firms, representing a part of total investment, should depend on factors similar to those that determine total investment. Hence the same variables as those in the *INV* equation were included.[28]

$$SFI = b_1 ED + b_2 FXA<1> + b_3 WIP + b_4 PINV$$
$$+ b_5 PGMP + b_6 DA + b_7 + u \qquad (2.3)$$
$$b_1 > 0, b_2 > 0, b_3 > 0, b_4 > 0, b_5 > 0, b_6 < 0$$

RESULTS:
OLS Period: 1966–84   (2.1)

Dep. variable: SD			R2: 0.957	R2C: 0.949
Indep. variables	Estd. coeff.	Std. dev.	t	BC%
b_1 INC	0.025	0.008	3.01	13.5
b_2 GMP	0.142	0.016	8.63	55.9
b_3 DA	−13.476	2.192	6.15	30.5
b_4 Constant	−15.062	3.132	4.81	0.0

Std. error: 2.349   MAPE: 6.90   DW: 1.983   RHO(1): −0.05

Tests: NORMAL, OUTLIE, HETERO, DIFF, F; see appendix.

The statistics in the savings regression are quite satisfactory: the fit is good, there is no serial correlation (confirmed by the DWE probability of 23.09 per cent), the t statistics reveal that all three variables are highly significant (at the 1 per cent level),[29] and the model passed all of the performed tests. Hence the regression supports our theoretical postulations: savings deposits in Yugoslavia were positively influenced by the rise in both disposable income and GMP, and negatively influenced by the restrictive policies of the 1980s.

OLS Period: 1967–84   (2.2)

Dep. variable: INV			R2: 0.999	R2C: 0.999
Indep. variables	Estd. coeff.	Std. dev.	t	BC%
b_1 ED	0.343	0.028	12.37	34.1
b_2 $FXA<1>$	0.028	0.009	3.19	17.9
b_3 WIP	0.058	0.019	3.07	11.3
b_4 $PINV$	−0.005	0.049	0.10	0.4
b_5 $PGMP$	0.162	0.034	4.77	32.5
b_6 DA	−2.830	1.117	2.53	3.7
b_7 Constant	−2.365	2.559	0.92	0.0

Std. error: 0.836   MAPE: 0.86   DW: 2.540   RHO(1): −0.34

Tests: NORMAL, OUTLIE, HETERO, RBOW, DIFF, F; see appendix.

The investment regression offers substantial support for Kornai's hypotheses. Not only is the fit very good, but there is no auto-correlation,[30] and the t statistics reveal that five out of six explanatory variables are highly significant (four at the 1 per cent level, and one at the 5 per cent level of significance).[31] However, the *PINV* variable is not significant; the possibility that it actually does not affect *INV* will be investigated in the next section. The model passed all of the performed tests.

OLS Period: 1967–84   (2.3)

Dep. variable: *SFI*				R2: 0.996	R2C: 0.994
	Indep. variables	Estd. coeff.	Std. dev.	t	BC%
b_1	ED	0.063	0.033	1.90	11.3
b_2	FXA<1>	0.040	0.011	3.74	45.3
b_3	WIP	0.030	0.023	1.32	10.5
b_4	PINV	0.054	0.059	0.92	7.1
b_5	PGMP	0.036	0.040	0.90	13.2
b_6	DA	−5.359	1.325	4.04	12.6
b_7	Constant	−5.848	3.037	1.93	0.0

Std. error: 0.993   MAPE: 2.01   DW: 2.850   RH0(1): −0.57

Tests: NORMAL, OUTLIE, HETERO, RBWO, DIFF, IMT, F; see appendix.

The self-financed regression again suggests a good fit, there was no autocorrelation of residuals,[32] and the t statistics reveal that *FXA<1>* and *DA* are significant at the 1 per cent level, and that *ED* is significant at the 10 per cent level.[33] However, the remaining three variables, *WIP*, *PINV* and *PGMP*, did not prove significant; whether this was due to a high level of multicollinearity will be checked in the next section. The model passed all of the tests applied.

Improving the model

Investment. The investment equation was re-estimated by drop-ping *PINV*, the variable which was previously not significant.

RESULTS:

OLS Period: 1967–84   (2.4)

Dep. variable: INV			R2: 0.999	R2C: 0.999
Indep. variables	Estd. coeff.	Std. dev.	t	BC%
b_1 ED	0.342	0.025	13.53	34.3
b_2 FXA<1>	0.029	0.007	4.10	18.4
b_3 WIP	0.058	0.017	3.43	11.3
b_4 PGMP	0.159	0.025	6.46	32.3
b_5 DA	−2.894	0.888	3.26	3.8
b_6 Constant	−2.247	2.193	1.02	0.0

Std. error: 0.801   MAPE: 0.86   DW: 2.531   RH0(1): −0.33

Tests: NORMAL, OUTLIE, HETERO, RBOW, DIFF, F; see appendix.

The results reveal that R2 and R2C remain unchanged, and hence dropping PINV is probably justified. All variables are now highly significant (at the 1 per cent level, for thirteen degrees of freedom, $t>3.012$), and there is no autocorrelation of residuals.[34] The model passed all of the applied tests.

Self-financed investment. In choosing which variables to include in the model, we were guided not only by the t statistics in equation 2.3, but also by the level of correlation between variables. Thus in addition to the highly significant variables in equation 2.3 (*FXA<1>*, *DA*), in choosing between two collinear variables, *ED* and *WIP*, *ED* was included because it proved more significant in 2.3. In choosing between the other two highly collinear variables, *PINV* and *PGMP*, *PINV* was included because it proved more significant in 2.3.[35]

RESULTS:

OLS Period: 1967–84   (2.5)

Dep. variable: *SFI*			R2: 0.995	R2C: 0.994	
	Indep. variables	Estd. coeff.	Std. dev.	t	BC%
b_1	ED	0.083	0.022	3.74	14.2
b_2	FXA<1>	0.052	0.003	15.66	56.5
b_3	PINV	0.124	0.037	3.30	15.5
b_4	DA	−6.168	1.250	4.94	13.8
b_5	Constant	−1.314	1.319	1.00	0.0

Std. error: 1.021   MAPE: 2.11   DW: 2.442   RH0(1): −0.33

Tests: NORMAL, OUTLIE, HETERO, F, DIFF; see appendix.

The results reveal that although R2 is a bit lower than in 2.3 (0.995 as compared to 0.996), R2C remains the same, and hence dropping *WIP* and *PGMP* was probably justified. All variables are now highly significant (at the 1 per cent level, for fourteen degrees of freedom, $t > 2.977$), there is no autocorrelation of residuals,[36] and the model passed all of the tests applied.

Kornai's theory: a final evaluation

Finally, we wanted to check whether the low t values for single variables which were dropped in the second stage, really are a sign of no (low) influence of these variables on the dependent variable, or whether this is due to multicollinearity.

In the original *INV* equation (2.2), the insignificant variable was *PINV*. The F test was applied to the estimated coefficient (H0: $b_4 = 0$), and the test seemed to indicate that *PINV* is not significant (probability of 91.97 per cent that H0 is correct). However, regressing *PINV* on *INV*, a very high R2 is obtained (R2 = 0.937) which suggests that 94 per cent of the variations in *INV* can actually be explained by this single variable *PINV*.[37] Recalling that *PINV* was highly correlated with *WIP* and *PGMP* (correlation coefficients were 0.951 and 0.804 respectively), the low t statistics for *PINV* in the general model (2.2) were probably due to multicollinearity, and not to the small impact of *PINV* on *INV*.

In the original *SFI* equation (2.3), the insignificant variables were *WIP*, *PINV*, and *PGMP*. The F test was applied to each of the estimated coefficients (H0: $b_3 = 0$; H0: $b_4 = 0$; H0: $b_5 = 0$, for *WIP*, *PINV*, and *PGMP* respectively), and this seemed to confirm that these variables are not significant (the probability that H0 is correct was 21.44 per cent, 37.89 per cent and 38.82 per cent respectively). However, regressing each of these variables separately on *SFI*, high coefficients of determination are obtained[38] ($SFI=b_1$ *WIP* $+ b_2$, R2=0.765; $SFI=b_1$ *PINV* $+ b_2$, R2=0.854; $SFI=b_1$ *PGMP* $+ b_2$, R2=0.876), which again suggests that each of these variables has a substantial influence on *SFI*. Recalling that these three variables were highly correlated (correlation coefficient between *WIP* and *PINV* was 0.951, and between *PGMP* and *PINV* 0.804), it can again be concluded that the low *t* statistics for these three variables in the original model are probably again due to multi-collinearity, and not to the small influence of *WIP*, *PINV*, and *PGMP* on self-financed investment.

Joint testing of the theories

An alternative way of confronting the two theories is to use the complete parameter-encompassing procedure: combine both sets of variables in a single regression equation (the 'unrestricted' model), and then apply the F test to test the significance of each of the two subsets of regression coefficients. If the null hypothesis being tested is accepted, the correct model will be the restricted model (restricted by the zero coefficients). This should reveal which of the two subsets (theories) helps to explain more of the variation in the dependent variables.

Two alternative null hypotheses have been tested in order to see whether the joint effect of the first/second subset of regression coefficients on the dependent variable is equal to zero:[39]

First theory: H0(1): $b_{11}=b_{12}= \ldots b_{1n}=0$
Second theory: H0(2): $b_{21}=b_{22}= \ldots b_{2n}=0$.

This procedure was applied to three regressions in which the explanatory variables are a combination of the two theories. They have been estimated without the constant in order to test the 'net' influence of the first against the second group of variables.

Savings deposits. In the savings deposits equation, all variables from Furubotn and Pejovich's theory and the alternative hypothesis have been included.

OLS Period: 1966–84   (3.1)

Dep. variable: *SD*   R2: 0.998   R2C: 0.998

	Indep. variables	Estd. coeff.	Std. dev.	t	BC%
b_{11}	IR	0.638	0.335	1.90	15.8
b_{12}	LR	−0.314	0.319	0.98	8.2
b_{13}	H	−0.141	0.045	3.16	0.2
b_{14}	PF	0.070	0.122	0.58	1.1
b_{21}	INC	0.036	0.009	4.13	15.8
b_{22}	GMP	0.129	0.015	8.43	41.0
b_{23}	DA	−9.738	2.067	4.71	17.8

Std. error: 1.846   MAPE: 4.93   DW: 2.036   RH0(1): −0.03

Results of the F test:
   Probability that H0(1) ($b_{11}=b_{12}=b_{13}=b_{14}=0$) is correct: 0.03 per cent.
   Probability that H0(2) ($b_{21}=b_{22}=b_{23}=0$) is correct: 0.00 per cent.

In the savings regression, we therefore reject both H0(1) and H0(2): both groups of variables seem to influence *SD*. Nevertheless, the lower probability of H0(2) (rejecting it at 100 per cent) suggests that the second group influences the dependent variable more than the first group of variables. Moreover, since there is no autocorrelation,[40] additional conclusions can be drawn from *t* statistics and the beta coefficients. The overall significance of the second group of variables is clearly higher than that of the first group, and 74.6 per cent of the variation in *SD* can be explained by changes in the variables proposed by the alternative theory.

   Investment. In the investment equation, as a representation of the second theory (Kornai's) the same number of explanatory variables were included as for the first theory (the ones which previously proved most significant).

OLS Period: 1967–84   (3.2)

Dep. variable: INV R2: 1.000   R2C: 1.000

	Indep. variables	Estd. coeff.	Std. dev.	t	BC%
b_{11}	IR	0.131	0.249	0.52	2.2
b_{12}	LR	−0.092	0.223	0.41	1.7
b_{13}	H	−0.016	0.058	0.27	0.0
b_{14}	PF	0.099	0.143	0.69	1.1
b_{21}	ED	0.377	0.080	4.73	37.0
b_{22}	FXA<1>	0.029	0.029	1.00	18.2
b_{23}	WIP	0.043	0.042	1.03	8.3
b_{24}	PGMP	0.158	0.075	2.10	31.5

Std. error: 1.129   MAPE: 1.06   DW: 2.097   RHO(1): −0.09

Results of the F test:
   Probability that H0(1) ($b_{11}=b_{12}=b_{13}=b_{14}=0$) is correct: 83.99 per cent.
   Probability that H0(2) ($b_{21}=b_{22}=b_{23}=b_{24}=0$) is correct: 0.00 per cent.

   Therefore, since H0(1) is accepted and H0(2) is rejected, the investment regression offers direct support for Kornai's theory. Since there is no autocorrelation of residuals (DWH: probability of 83.63 per cent), additional support can be derived from t statistics and the beta coefficients. The variables reflecting Kornai's theory are as a group clearly more significant than Furubotn and Pejovich's variables, explaining around 94.0 per cent of the variation in INV.

   Self-financed investment. Again, as a representation of the second theory, the same number of explanatory variables have been included as for the first theory (the most significant ones).

OLS Period: 1967–84   (3.3)

Dep. variable: *SFI*   R2: 1.000   R2C: 1.000

	Indep. variables	Estd. coeff.	Std. dev.	t	BC%
b_{11}	IR	0.061	0.226	0.27	1.7
b_{12}	LR	−0.094	0.209	0.45	2.7
b_{13}	H	−0.033	0.026	1.24	0.0
b_{14}	PF	0.089	0.085	1.06	1.6
b_{21}	ED	0.104	0.030	3.50	16.5
b_{22}	FXA<1>	0.056	0.005	12.38	56.3
b_{23}	PINV	0.080	0.053	1.52	9.3
b_{24}	DA	−5.683	1.451	3.92	11.8

Std. error: 1.065   MAPE: 2.10   DW: 2.786   RH0(1): −0.50

Results of the F test:
   Probability that H0(1) ($b_{11}=b_{12}=b_{13}=b_{14}=0$) is correct: 59.86 per cent.
   Probability that H0(2) ($b_{21}=b_{22}=b_{23}=b_{24}=0$) is correct: 0.00 per cent.

Since H0(1) is accepted and H0(2) is rejected, Kornai's theory is again directly supported. Since there is no autocorrelation of residuals,[41] additional support can be derived from *t* statistics and the beta coefficients. The variables reflecting Kornai's theory are as a group clearly more significant than Furubotn and Pejovich's variables, explaining around 93.9 per cent of variation in *SFI*.

Concluding remarks

   In the separate tests of the two theories, all regressions based on Furubotn and Pejovich's theory suggested either misspecification (autocorrelation of residuals), or non-congruence with the theory (wrong signs of the estimated coefficients). Since the presence of autocorrelation implies imprecise *t* statistics on the significance of the variables, and inefficient estimates of the coefficients, the initial analysis suggested, at best, that no definite conclusions could be drawn about the confirmation of the theory on Yugoslav data. In testing Kornai's theory, on the other hand, good overall results were obtained. In joint testing of the two theories, additional evidence was obtained which seemed to indicate that Kornai's theory finds more support in empirical evidence from Yugoslavia than Furubotn and Pejovich's theory. The main implication of the analysis is that the investment behaviour of Yugoslav firms, in spite of decentralization, self-management and increasing use of the market after 1965, is being determined primarily by the socialist features of the economy.

Nevertheless, the limitations of the above analysis are several. The first is the use of aggregate data to test Furubotn and Pejovich's theory, which is fundamentally microeconomic in nature; nevertheless, the theory does maintain that underinvestment at the firm level will have similar implications for the economy as a whole. The second is the small number of observations. However, quarterly data on some of the variables do not exist; extending the period by including data prior to 1966 would not have been justified; and at the time the regressions were run, data beyond 1984 were not yet available. The third limitation is the approximation of several variables, such as the time horizon, the profit rate (ideally, data on the marginal productivity of capital should have been used), and most of Kornai's variables, since they are a simplification of the actual hypotheses (especially expansion drive). The translation of Kornai's theory into a testable model was not simple, precisely because of the specific features of socialist economies, in which different agents react not only and not primarily to market signals, but also to non-market signals, which are difficult to measure and quantify.

A further objection could be made to the use of lagged fixed assets, which may misrepresent the theory, since self-financed investment is measured gross of depreciation. This implies that at least part of the correlation between self-financed investment and fixed assets would be due to the replacement expenditure required to cover depreciation of fixed assets; thus the larger fixed assets are one year, the higher is the level of depreciation and hence replacement investment the following year. However, in Yugoslav statistics the distinction between self-financed gross and net investment is not made, so the problem could not be avoided.

Last but not least, self-financed investment reflects the proportion of investment in fixed assets financed by enterprise resources, which are not an entirely voluntary component of enterprise savings. An alternative set of figures could have been used (for example, depreciation above the legally prescribed rates, which is completely voluntary). However, not only is such depreciation an underestimation of actual voluntary self-finance in Yugoslavia, but such an alternative model would not have provided us with the answers we were seeking. It might have offered an explanation of what determines depreciation in Yugoslavia, but not overall investment or self-financed investment. What we were primarily interested in was to evaluate the role of the alternative variables of the two theories in determining investment in Yugoslavia, irrespective of whether a smaller or larger part of it is imposed on firms through external regulations.

This may again imply that Furubotn and Pejovich's theory, which assumes voluntary investment decisions, cannot be refuted. Nevertheless, our analysis does suggest that the variables considered crucial by Furubotn and Pejovich have had a limited role to play in determining investment decisions in Yugoslavia, and hence confirms our previous conclusion that the theory is not fully applicable to the Yugoslav economy.

Appendix: econometrics – data and statistics

Data sources

Deflation. Since the Yugoslav economy has been characterized by high and rising inflation, all data in current Dinars have been transformed into constant 1972 Dinars; current Dinar values were deflated by the cost of living index (base year 1972), provided in Savezni zavod za statistiku (SZS), *Statistički godišnjak Jugoslavije – SGJ*, various years, table 'Indeksi cena' (table 112-1 in *SGJ* 1985). The year 1972 was chosen as the basis because it is the year usually used by the Federal Statistical Institute in its statistical yearbooks when reporting statistics in constant prices.

Variables. SD: Savings deposits of households (excluding foreign currency), in 1972 Dinars.
Calculated from SZS, *SGJ*, various years, table 'Primanja i izdavanja u gotovom novcu, novčana sredstava i krediti stanovništva' (table 102-32 in *SGJ* 1985) in current Dinars, deflated by the cost of living index (1972=100). Although allowed to have foreign currency accounts, households were not able to freely buy foreign currency, and hence foreign currency deposits are excluded.
INV: Investment in fixed assets of the social sector, in 1972 Dinars.
Calculated from SZS, *SGJ*, various years, table 'Bruto investicije u osnovne fondove, društveni sektor' (table 110-1 in *SGJ* 1985) in current Dinars, deflated by the cost of living index (1972=100).
SFI: Investment in fixed assets financed by enterprises of the social sector, in 1972 Dinars.
Calculated from SZS, *SGJ*, various years, table 'Izvršene isplate za investicije po osnovnim oblicima finansiranja' (table 110-2 in *SGJ* 1985)

in current Dinars, deflated by the cost of living index (1972=100). Investment is gross of depreciation.

IR: Real interest rate on savings deposits of households (maximum). Calculated from National Bank of Yugoslavia (NBY), *Bilten Narodne Banke Jugoslavije*, various issues, table 'Kamatne stope'. Nominal interest rates on time deposits of households (end-year) were deflated by the annual percentage increase of the cost of living index (*CLI*) according to the formula:

$$IR = [\frac{(1+NIR)}{(1+CLI)} - 1] \times 100$$

LR: Real lending rate of bank loans extended to firms (maximum). Calculated from NBY, *Bilten Narodne Banke Jugoslavije*, various issues, table 'Kamatne stope'. Nominal interest rate on loans to enterprises (end-year) were deflated by the annual percentage increase of the cost of living increase (*CLI*), according to the formula:

$$LR = [\frac{(1+NLR)}{(1+CLI)} - 1] \times 100$$

H: A proxy for the time horizon of the average Yugoslav worker. Calculated from the indicator on the average monthly fluctuation of workers (labour turnover) in the productive sectors, provided in SZS, *SGJ*, various years, table 'Fluktuacija radnika prema granama delatnosti' (table 105-12 in *SGJ* 1985), in per cent:

$$FW = \frac{WL}{WT+WN} \text{ where}$$

FW: fluctuation of workers
WL: number of workers leaving during a month
WT: total number of workers at the beginning of a month
WN: newly admitted workers during a month

The time horizon proxy can be represented as $H=1-FW$. The lower the fluctuation of workers, the longer the time horizon of the average worker. (*FW* could have been used directly, but since *H* and *FW* are inversely related, this would have provoked confusion in expected signs.)

PF: Profit rate (in per cent) of social sector enterprises in Yugoslavia. Calculated from SZS, *SGJ*, various years, table 'Osnovni podaci o organizacijama udruženog rada društvenog sektora' (table 113-1 in *SGJ* 1985), according to the formula:

$$PF = \frac{GMP - depreciation - personal\ incomes \times 100}{Historical\ value\ of\ capital}$$

DIR: Absolute difference between the real interest rate on savings deposits and the real lending rate for enterprises, i.e.

$$DIR = IR - LR$$

CR: Total credits (bank loans and loans from funds of socio-political communities) extended to enterprises of the social sector, in 1972 Dinars.
Calculated from SZS, *SGJ*, various years, table 'Novčana sredstva i krediti organizacija udruženog rada u privredi' (table 111-5 in *SGJ* 1985) in current Dinars, deflated by the cost of living index (1972= 100).

T: Trend variable, which takes the values 1–19 in 1966–84.

DA: Dummy variable, which takes the value of 0 until 1979, and 1 thereafter. It reflects the change in economic policies of the Yugoslav government from 1980 onwards.

INC: Total disposable income of households, in 1972 Dinars.
Calculated from SZS, *SGJ*, various years, table 'Primanja i izdavanja stanovništva u gotovom novcu, novčana sredstva i krediti stanovništva' (table 102-32 in *SGJ* 1985) in current Dinars, deflated by the cost of living index (1972=100).

GMP: Gross material product, in 1972 Dinars, as provided by the SZS, *SGJ*, various years, table 'Društveni proizvod u cenama 1972' (table 102-10 in *SGJ* 1985).

ED: Kornai's 'expansion drive', represented as the difference between the investment growth index in the social sector (*INVi*, base year 1966=100) and social sector GMP growth index (*SGMPi*, base year 1966=100):

$$ED = INVi - SGMPi$$

Calculated from SZS, *SGJ*, various years, table 'Bruto investicije u osnovne fondove, društveni sektor' (table 110-1 in *SGJ* 1985), in current Dinars, deflated by the cost of living index; and table 'Društveni proizvod u cenama 1972' (table 107-1 in *SGJ* 1985).

FXA<1>: Fixed assets of the social sector of the economy, in 1972 Dinars, as provided by the SZS, *SGJ*, various years, table 'Osnovna sredstva privrede društvenog sektora u cenama 1972' (table 102-12 in *SGJ* 1985), lagged for one year.

WIP: Work in progress, i.e. fixed investment projects in course, in 1972 Dinars.

Calculated from SZS, *SGJ*, various years, table 'Predračunska vrednost investicija u osnovne fondove' (table 110-5 in *SGJ* 1985) in current Dinars, deflated by the cost of living index (1972=100).

PINV: Planned growth of investment in fixed assets, in 1972 Dinars.

Calculated from the planned annual rate of growth of investment in fixed assets in per cent (*PGRI*), as provided by annual economic resolutions (one-year plans), and the actual level of real investment in fixed assets in previous year:

$$PINV(t) = INV(t-1) + [(PGRI(t) \times INV(t-1)]$$

PGMP: Planned growth of social sector GMP, in 1972 Dinars.

Calculated from the planned annual rate of growth of GMP in per cent (PGMP), as provided by annual economic resolutions (one-year plans), and the actual level of real GMP in previous year:

$$PGMP(t) = GMP(t-1) + [(PGMP(t) \times GMP(t-1)]$$

Statistical methods

The IAS System was used, an econometric software package for the analysis of time series data (Sonnberger *et al.* 1986).

Standard statistics. The standard way of reporting regressions in the IAS System is the one used in the text (except that the estimated coefficients and the standard deviations have been rounded to three decimals).

$R2$ is the coefficient of determination, and $R2C$ is the corrected coefficient of determination. For regressions without an intercept, $R2$ and $R2C$ are computed using a special option (R) which takes into account the non-inclusion of the intercept.

BC are the so-called beta-coefficients, which measure the percentage change in the dependent variable explainable by the change in the explanatory variable.

DW is the Durbin-Watson statistic, testing for the presence of serial autocorrelation of the residuals. Whenever DW lies in the inconclusive region, or whenever the standard DW tables are not applicable, as in the case of regressions without an intercept, the Durbin-Watson Exact Test

(DWE) can be used to obtain the exact probability that the Durbin-Watson statistics takes a value less than or equal to the sample outcome. The null hypothesis on no autocorrelation is rejected whenever the probability is less than the assumed percentage level of the Durbin-Watson test. Thus at the 5 per cent level of significance, if we are testing for positive autocorrelation, its presence will be confirmed if DWE gives a probability lower than 5 per cent; if we are testing for negative autocorrelation, its presence will be confirmed if DWE gives a probability higher than 95 per cent. In case a lagged variable is included among the explanatory variables, Durbin's h statistics can be used for testing for autocorrelation by applying the DWH Test.

RH0(1) is the first order autocorrelation coefficient of the regression residuals.

STD. ERROR: standard error of the regression.

MAPE is the mean absolute percentage error of the regression, defined as

$$\text{MAPE} = 100 \left(1/T \sum_{t=1}^{T} u_t/y_t \right),$$

where u is the estimated residual of the regression, $u = y - xb$.

Tests. NORMAL: Jarque-Bera test for normality. H0: residuals are normally distributed.

HARVEY: Harvey-Collier test for functional misspecification. H0: equation linear in variable X.

RBOW: Utts test for correctness of the functional form. H0: model is correct.

DIFF: Plosser-Schwert-White test for correctness of the model specification. H0: standard assumptions of OLS regression apply.

IMT: White and Hall's test for correctness of the model specification. H0: standard assumptions of OLS regression apply.

HETERO: Pagan-Hall-Trivedi test for specific heteroscedasticity. H0: variance of residuals is constant.

F test: Tests whether single parameters in a regression are equal to certain values.

All of the above tests give the probability value that the null hypothesis is correct. Whenever this probability is higher than 5 per cent, the null hypothesis can be accepted at the 5 per cent level of significance.

OUTLIE: Cook-Weisberg test for the presence of outliers. The test gives the maximum t value of the outlier coefficients, which should be lower than the critical value (reported in tables) in order to conclude that there are no outliers.

ARSIM: Harvey-Phillips test for autocorrelation. The test detects first-order autocorrelation of the regression disturbances of a single equation in a simultaneous equation model. H0: residuals of the equation are uncorrelated. The test reports the value of test statistics, which should then be checked in the DW tables.

AR: Breusch-Pagan and Godfrey's test. Tests for the presence of higher-order autocorrelation of residuals.

Results of tests performed

Equation Test	1.1	1.2	1.3	2.1	2.2	2.3	2.4	2.5
NORMAL (prob.)	19.84	20.87	26.79	64.09	76.17	45.51	75.68	64.68
OUTLIE (*t* value)	2.49	2.28	2.36	2.45	2.16	2.14	2.19	1.92
HETERO (prob.)	26.04	25.22	54.38	23.72	11.70	75.91	11.32	50.63
HARVEY (prob.)								
Variable 1	91.74	74.62	63.24	—	—	—	—	—
Variable 2	81.45	13.14	12.87	—	—	—	—	—
Variable 3	24.97	32.02	35.75	—	—	—	—	—
Variable 4	18.08	38.40	65.10	—	—	—	—	—
RBOW (prob.)	75.79	87.52	91.08	—	95.75	47.06	91.58	—
DIFF (prob.)	17.29	14.60	24.30	33.91	56.81	41.03	42.55	28.41
IMT (prob.)	—	—	99.99	—	—	52.80	—	—

F TEST
Equation 2.2: H0: $b_4=0$, probability that the H0 is correct: 91.97 per cent.
Equation 2.3: H0: $b_3=0$, $b_4=0$, $b_5=0$, probability that the H0 is correct: 21.44 per cent, 37.89 per cent and 38.82 per cent respectively.

Part III

Pressure for more radical reforms in Yugoslavia

8   Early attempts at introducing investment incentives

In the period before 1965, when the system of mobilizing and allocating investment resources was centrally directed through state investment funds, there was no need for investment incentives at the enterprise level. Following the 1965 reform, decentralization and the desire to introduce a market-oriented system required the creation of new mechanisms which would provide built-in incentives for the enterprise to invest and allocate capital efficiently. Such a requirement led to the elaboration of new concepts by one of the leading politicians of the time, Edvard Kardelj, and to their implementation during the 1970s through a series of new financial instruments.

The views of Edvard Kardelj

Among the various problems that emerged after the 1965 economic reform was that of the increasing concentration of economic power in banks, and the related problem of 'autonomous' financial capital. These problems were perceived by the Yugoslav authorities as being directly in conflict with self-management, because they were thought to imply rental income for privileged classes and the deprivation of workers of a part of the income they had produced. Consequently, the economic reform of the 1970s was intended to enable enterprises to appropriate a larger part of income, while reducing the role of banks by introducing new methods of mobilizing savings that would not necessarily require the banks' intermediation.

A lively debate at the end of the 1960s apparently resulted in the victory of economic reasoning over ideology. Investment in capital and entrepreneurship were to be recognized as functions that ought to be rewarded. It was Edvard Kardelj who proposed and elaborated the new system of workers' remuneration, which was to be based not only on their 'live' (current) labour, but also on their 'past' (embodied) labour.

Kardelj preferred to use the term 'past labour' instead of 'social capital', 'accumulation', or 'means of enlarged reproduction',[1] in order to emphasize that such remuneration would not be linked to capital but to labour: workers contribute directly to the increase of capital through their investment decisions, and therefore they ought to be rewarded by receiving a part of income on this basis (see Kardelj 1978, pp. 52–3). The scheme was thus intended as an incentive for workers to invest, both in their own and in other enterprises.

Kardelj's proposal at first provoked severe opposition. The most dogmatic ideologists identified the very notion of past labour with the concept of private shareholding, a capitalist category totally in conflict with Marxism, socialism, and self-management.[2] Their main argument was that since, in line with the Marxist theory of value, it is only live labour that produces new value, live labour must remain the exclusive basis for rewarding workers. A remuneration scheme that includes the contribution of past labour (capital) would imply earning income on the basis of investing capital and not on the basis of work done, and hence remuneration on the basis of property.

Kardelj strongly criticized such views, regarding them as a mis-interpretation of Marx. Although live labour is the only creator of value, a part of surplus value created by live labour (profit on capital, bank profit and rent), while not producing new value, does represent value, and it has a specific use value, since more efficient management of social capital creates more favourable conditions for the increase of live labour's productivity (1978, pp. 55–6). Rewarding past labour cannot be interpreted as being independent of workers' live labour, but on the contrary – 'it is clear that you need to open the tap of a cask in order to produce a flow of wine' (1971a, p. 139). The essential point was to see to it that workers did not fill the cask of social property with their work, while someone else opened the tap. Hence, 'It is not a question of whether past labour produces value or not, but a question of who disposes of income' (1971a, p. 141).

Kardelj recalled that Marx did not identify state ownership with social ownership, but considered social property as also enabling a form of individual property: 'Social property is . . . the common property of all working men, and therefore also the personal property of each individual worker in the scope and form in which it ensures him the right to work with social means' (1978, p. 24). Workers dispose of means of production collectively, but enjoy the fruits of their labour individually. Social property is not the monopolistic right of any indi-vidual subject (the state, the working collective, the individual worker), but the property of everybody and nobody, i.e. it is both collective and personal. This is the only way that social property could really 'belong' to all members of society (1972, p. 318; 1978, pp. 11, 23). Nevertheless, social property is not to be interpreted as a no-property category, since 'as long as appropriation exists, property will continue to exist' (1972, p. 293).

The post-1965 alienation of past labour related to 'group-ownership' tendencies had, according to Kardelj, represented a form of managerial capitalism. Rewarding workers' past labour would be the only way of properly implementing self-management (1971a, p. 137). Workers should be rewarded for good management of social capital, but should also bear the consequences deriving from its bad management (1978, p. 141).

Kardelj therefore regarded the system he was proposing as a way of avoiding the negative effects of both state ownership and 'group' ownership; but he was also very explicit in emphasizing that the scheme would be fundamentally different from private shareholding. Indeed, he firmly rejected proposals for citizens' shares in socially-owned enterprises.[3] Private shares imply a permanent right to exploit someone else's labour, while the proposed system would be based on the right of a worker deriving from his own work, thus definitely eliminating the old relationship between the worker as hired labour, and the owner or manager of capital (1978, p. 53). The personal incomes of workers would not be linked to the amount or cost of invested capital, because this would result in the division of social capital into shares, but would depend on results achieved, i.e. the returns of an investment – and this in order to make the worker aware that his material position depended on his choice to save. Workers would not receive this part of their income as proprietors, but as managers of social capital, and would thus be encouraged to manage capital rationally (1978, pp. 68, 133–5).

However, while Kardelj was critical of shareholding, he proposed at the same time that possible methods of rewarding past labour could include shares and bonds (although he remained vague, suggesting this was 'a secondary problem', for which 'concrete solutions must be found'; 1971a, p. 140); he also stressed the need for a market for such securities. Since Kardelj's ideas concerning the issuing of workers' bonds had 'provoked a real affair' (to use his own words), Kardelj insisted that what the worker would receive on the basis of such a receipt would be a minimum of an incentive character. Hence, 'it is absurd to identify a worker that consumes these means in the form of personal income with a capitalist that appropriates them on the basis of a share due to private capital' (1978, p. 70).

The principal merit of Kardelj's writings on past labour lies in his insistence that being rewarded for investment decisions is not only compatible with socialism, but is one of the necessary requirements for capital to be used rationally. Nevertheless, Kardelj's writings are not always sufficiently consistent. One of the central points that gives rise to confusion is the relationship between 'social' and 'individual', whether referring to property, income, past labour, or other categories.

Thus Kardelj contemporaneously speaks of property 'of the whole society'; of social property as a form of personal property; and occasionally, in spite of all his criticism of 'group-ownership', seems to consider the enterprise as the main subject of property rights.[4] Similarly, Kardelj emphasizes the social character of income: income is in social property, it belongs to all workers and to each of them individually, for it is the result of the labour of the whole of society, the result of social productivity (1978, pp. 36–44). The same type of ambiguity is also present in his references to past labour: Kardelj does not make a clear distinction between 'social past labour' and 'individual past labour', as his definitions are often imprecise, ambiguous, and even contradictory.[5]

Kardelj fails to distinguish between enterprises' initial capital endowment received from the state when social property was introduced – which could be considered as 'social property', the result of 'social past labour', thus ensuring a part of income that is 'social' – and successive increments of capital arising from 'individual past labour', for which workers ought to be rewarded depending on the income realized by the individual enterprise. In this sense, Kardelj was not explicit enough in emphasizing the individual basis of the scheme: if the scheme was to be effective, the subject of property could not be the whole of society, realized income that was to serve as the basis for determining workers' past labour had to be income of the individual enterprise, and past labour rewards had to be linked to the individual worker's contribution.

Kardelj is also ambiguous concerning the relationship between his scheme and socialist objectives. A way of avoiding tendencies towards private property relations would be to implement simultaneously not only the principle of distribution according to work (both current and past), but also the principle of workers' solidarity (1978, p. 141). In order to incorporate his scheme into a mechanism of planning and coordination, Kardelj proposed that rewards for workers' past labour 'would every year be set by the social plan' (1978, p. 65), and that 'a worker does not have the right, through his personal income, to appropriate a part of social capital . . . since self-management agreements and social compacts should regulate distribution relations' (1978, p. 141).

In conclusion, Kardelj encountered some difficulties in incorporating his individually-based system of workers' remuneration of past labour into a more general framework that took into account social interests, socialist objectives, and a planning mechanism.

Implementation of financial innovation

The economic reform implemented during the 1970s resulted in the adoption of new mechanisms designed to stimulate investment both within and outside the enterprise, together with the introduction of a variety of new financial instruments.

Incentives within the firm

The new system of remuneration based on rewards for past labour was to become the main instrument for encouraging workers to invest. The 1976 Associated Labour Act (ALA) and other documents adopted during the 1970s explicitly recognize past labour as a criterion determining the level of personal income.[6] However, legal provisions concerning past labour were very general: they clearly stated only that past labour was to be rewarded, without indicating how an individual's contribution to capital increase was to be measured, or according to what criteria.[7] Details concerning past labour rewards were to be specified in enterprises' self-management acts, which are firm-specific.[8] Without precisely defined methods of rewarding past labour, it is not surprising that in everyday practice the scheme was implemented in a rather simplistic way.

The common feature is that past labour rewards are usually determined in proportion to seniority. For each year of employment, usually starting with the second year, a worker is given an additional percentage (around 0.5 per cent) of his personal income.[9] Since such a reward is usually linked to the total number of years a worker has been employed in the social sector, the scheme in no way encourages efficient management of capital (and investment) of the enterprise where the worker is employed. In addition to past labour rewards, an indemnity in cash is usually paid to workers upon retirement. However, this method of rewarding workers cannot constitute adequate compensation for their investment decisions either, for the amount involved is small, and is in no way related to investment or successful entrepreneurship.[10]

Several Yugoslav economists have criticized the way the scheme has been implemented in practice, claiming that it represents a mis-interpretation of the original idea advanced by Kardelj. In fact, Kardelj himself complained that the scheme did not have a positive impact on workers' motivation to invest, since bonuses related to seniority were considered more as an instrument of social policy, than as an economic right of a worker linked to his investment decisions (1971b, p. 248).

Since implementation of the past labour scheme did not result, as expected, in its further elaboration in practice, there was felt to be a need for further legislation. After long discussions and seven versions of a law on past labour,[11] in 1982 the Law on Expanded Reproduction and Past Labour (LERPL) was finally adopted. In spite of its containing twenty-four articles specifically relating to past labour, the law fails to clarify some of the crucial issues.

The procedure for determining the amount of income to be devoted to past labour rewards is rather complicated (Articles 60–9). This part of income is determined on the basis not only of eight obligatory indicators for evaluating business performance (as prescribed in Article 141 of the ALA), but also on the basis of three other criteria. As well as there being many of them, the indicators are mutually inconsistent; already the ones contained in the ALA have been demonstrated to be conflicting (see Babić, 1982). What is surprising is that the part of income set aside for past labour rewards need not necessarily be used in the enterprise that has realized it, nor need it be used exclusively to reward past labour.

Furthermore, the law does not ensure that an individual worker will be rewarded according to the quantity and quality of past labour he *personally* has contributed, since the incentive has more a collective, than an individual character (see Articles 70–83).[12] As compared to the ALA, the only innovation introduced by the law seems to be that it explicitly states that the right to past labour can also be claimed after a worker's termination of employment (probably in order to legalize what was effectively being done in practice).

The system of rewarding past labour was changed further in 1987. In the new 1987 law on income, an attempt has been made to define the part of income to be devoted to past labour rewards more accurately, by linking it to obtained profitability of an enterprise, profitability being defined as the ratio of accumulation (net savings) to average utilized business assets (see Mates 1987). Instead of being calculated as the ratio of accumulation to *total* business assets of an enterprise, the profitability rate ought to have taken into account only returns from own capital (Dumezić 1986). In addition, an efficient system of rewarding past labour must consider not only the profitability of invested resources, but also the absolute increase in the value of the enterprise's net assets.

Although in the new system it has been recognized that the seniority criterion is not satisfactory, past labour rewards are simply the positive difference between gross personal incomes and personal incomes for current labour, to be distributed in every enterprise that allocates a part of net income to accumulation (Bogetić 1987). Thus the emphasis has been shifted from rewards for past investment, to rewards for current accumulation. Since a minimum allocation to accumulation is a legal requirement, this seems to imply that past labour rewards will be distributed in all enterprises; even if an enterprise allocates a minimum to accumulation, and incurs losses from investing these resources, it will nevertheless reward its workers, instead of penalizing them.

Diversification of financial instruments

The economic reform of the 1970s introduced a variety of new instruments designed to increase the mobilization of external savings, including different types of securities. The organization of an effective market for securities was also recommended in all five-year social plans from 1970 onwards. The present analysis will primarily consider the long-term financial instruments an enterprise can use for financing investment.[13]

Pooling of labour and resources. At the enterprise level, one of the possible ways in which the firm can participate in the so-called 'pooling of labour and resources' is for it to invest in another enterprise. In such a case, what is effectively pooled is the investing enterprise's financial resources with the labour and resources of the enterprise invested in.

Once the pooling of labour and resources has been stipulated through the signing of a self-management agreement, the participants are supposed to jointly share income and risk, and influence the business and development policy of the firm being invested in (ALA, Articles 64–5). However, legal provisions are very unfavourable to the investing enterprise.[14] First, although the investing enterprise is supposed to have a right to both repayment of its capital and a compensation, the enterprise invested in is given priority in income distribution.[15] Second, the possibility of a permanent share in the income of the enterprise invested in is explicitly excluded.[16] Third, contrary to the envisaged 'joint bearing of risk', it is the investing enterprise that bears all the risk: once the time limit of the contract has expired, it has no further rights to recover invested capital, while the enterprise invested in is guaranteed, in advance, even a part of income for accumulation. Finally, it is even envisaged that the investing enterprise may renounce its right to the restitution of pooled resources.[17]

It is therefore hardly surprising that this method of pooling resources has had a very limited role in stimulating direct investment in other firms. Prašnikar (1983) found that in a sample of Yugoslav firms, only about 1 per cent of total investment by enterprises consisted of direct investment in other firms in 1975–8 (though the proportion rose to 7.8 per cent in 1979) (see table 5A.9, appendix to chapter 5). In 1984, only 13.2 per cent of enterprises' total long-term investments consisted of investment in other enterprises (SZS 1986, p. 43). In 1981, long-term bank credits to enterprises were eleven times higher than long-term pooled resources among enterprises, while the ratio of, on the one hand, enterprises' short-term obligations on the basis of pooled resources, and on the other, bonds, bank credits, and direct credits, was 1:1.5:10:20 respectively (Mramor 1984, pp. 82, 86).

The LERPL of 1982 merely elaborates the legal provisions already contained in the ALA. It confirms the temporary character of a contract concluded by two enterprises, and adds an additional element protecting the enterprise invested in. The only exception to the rule that the partnership ends when the time limit of the agreement has expired, is 'when the time limit is exceeded owing to the fault of the enterprise invested in' (Article 39). Therefore, if an enterprise in which capital is invested through a joint project encounters difficulties in realizing that project, it can prolong the duration of the contract and hence effectively postpone its obligations towards the investing enterprise (instead of being in some way penalized).

Ostojić (1984) has examined these problems in detail. His empirical analysis has shown that most Yugoslav enterprises tend to reinvest savings in themselves. Even when joint projects are undertaken with other firms, resources invested are usually given on credit, and not on the basis of the joint risk-bearing arrangement described above. The absence of a cost for the use of social capital, together with deficiencies in the accounting, distribution and fiscal systems, have led to very low mobility of capital between firms and regions, and to its inefficient allocation.

Pooling resources in a bank. Another method of pooling resources is in the formation of a bank. As emphasized earlier, during the 1970s banks were transformed into 'service agencies' of enterprises, operating under the direct control of their founder members. A bank can be founded by enterprises and self-managed communities of interest (prior to 1977, also by socio-political communities), which sign a self-management agreement concerning the bank's foundation (ALA, Article 16). The founders of a bank *may* contribute a proportion of the initial capital, but since 1977 this has no longer been obligatory. Founder members guarantee all the obligations of a bank with their own resources, and are thus jointly liable for the bank's operations. Decisions are made not by the workers in a bank, but by the bank's members, each of whom, irrespective of the amount of invested capital, has an equal say at the general assembly.[18] After operating costs have been covered and resources set aside to pay personal incomes to the bank's staff, all new income is distributed among the founder members, both depositors and borrowers, for it is considered that both borrowing and lending contribute to the bank's income. Income is distributed in proportion to the 'contribution' made by these organizations, to be determined in a self-management agreement (ALA, Article 89).

For the different methods of pooling of resources, the 1971 Law on Securities provides for the use of certificates of pooled resources, which entitle the bearer to participate in both profits and management. These certificates have a minimum redemption period of ten years, and can be issued by an enterprise, a bank, or an insurance company, being transferable to other enterprises, banks, and socio-political communities. Certificates issued by an enterprise can be subscribed only by another enterprise or a foreign firm; those issued by a bank can be held by enterprises, communities of interest, and socio-political communities; and those issued by an insurance company can also be subscribed by banks, in addition to the other kinds of organization mentioned above.[19]

Bonds. Fixed-interest bonds issued by socio-political communities and by enterprises had already been legally introduced into the Yugoslav economy during the 1960s, but those issued by enterprises were few, and were only on an experimental basis.[20] The 1971 Law on Securities allowed enterprises, socio-political communities, and communities of interest to issue not only bonds at a fixed rate of interest (which could be higher than the legally limited rate on bank credits), but also profit-related bonds, which yield interest directly linked to enterprise performance. The redemption period of bonds cannot be shorter than two years.

The 1971 law also relaxed the conditions under which issues might be made. An enterprise has to have a certain minimum amount of capital in its business and reserve fund, and the total nominal value of bonds issued must not exceed the value of the enterprise's business and reserve fund. However, if an enterprise cannot fulfil these conditions, it can still issue bonds provided that another enterprise, bank, or socio-political community is willing to offer the necessary guarantees. Unlike certificates on pooled resources, which can be subscribed only by a limited number of institutions, bonds can be bought by practically all types of organization and also by households.

During the 1980s, bonds accounted for a declining share of all securities issued in Yugoslavia, falling from 15.4 per cent in 1980 to only 0.4 per cent in 1989 (though rising again to 12.5 per cent in 1990; see figure 8.1). Enterprises issued bonds infrequently, for they preferred short-term instruments, primarily promissory notes, which until 1989 accounted for by far the largest proportion of all securities pertaining to the enterprise sector.[21] Socio-political communities have issued bonds far more often than enterprises, but most of these bonds have effectively been issued on behalf of enterprises, as part of the mechanism for ensuring obligatory funds for investment in less developed regions.[22] Some recent examples of successful bond issues by enterprises include Elektroprivreda, which issued bonds at a fixed interest rate slightly higher than the bank interest rate, and Crvena Zastava, which issued bonds for its latest 'Florida' car at an interest rate lower than the bank interest rate, but granting subscribers priority in delivery.

COALs. The laws introduced during the 1970s envisaged different ways of channelling private savings of individuals to intermediate forms of enterprise that are based on a combination of private capital and the self-management system. The first of these forms is the 'contractual organization of associated labour' (COAL), in which an individual pools his labour and privately-owned resources with the labour of other workers on a self-management basis. The individual receives compensation for invested resources, participates in profits, and has the right to run, as a manager, the business of a COAL. Private capital in a COAL can be contributed by more than one individual.

Although the ALA provides for the participation of different organizations with their socially-owned assets in the establishment of a COAL (Article 306), in practice COALs have more often been financed

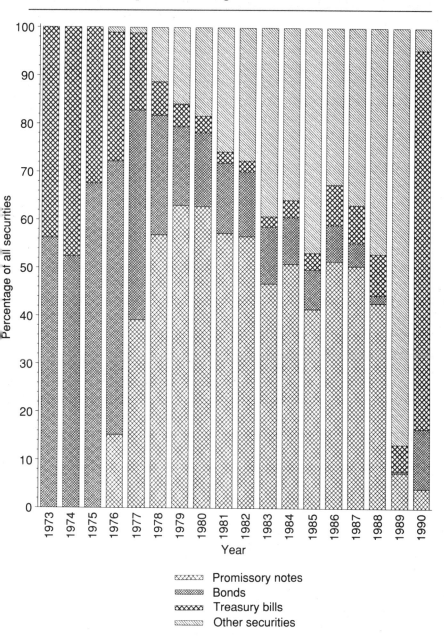

Figure 8.1 Securities in Yugoslavia bought by banks, 1973–1990

by private capital alone.[23] Two features distinguish a COAL from a small-scale private sector firm. First, there is no limit on the number of workers that can be employed in a COAL, and hence COALs are often much larger than enterprises operating in the private sector. Second, COALs must respect certain rules which apply to normal social-sector enterprises, and these rules may have served to inhibit the development of COALs. Thus workers' personal incomes take precedence in income distribution (the proportion which the manager receives by virtue of ownership, over and above his personal income, is a residual); and the capital maintenance requirement must be respected (ALA, Articles 311–12). Furthermore, the manager's rights on account of ownership are not clearly defined, being determined, rather, by the contract that establishes the COAL (ALA, Article 312). Finally, the COAL was envisaged as a transitional form of enterprise, to be gradually transformed into the standard socially-owned firm; thus workers have the right to buy owners out over time, by paying the historical cost of capital investment.[24] This would only be fair if workers were committed to buy shares at the time of foundation; otherwise workers exercise an *ex post* free option, which gives them a share in success without exposing them to the risk of failure.

Evidence on COALs reveals that from twenty-three in 1976, their number grew to 249 in 1985 and further to 412 in 1988; in 1989, however, their number fell to 389, this figure representing 0.3 per cent of the total number of organizations in Yugoslavia (all forms included) (see SZS, *SGJ* 1990, table 103-1).

Individual private savings. The second instrument for mobilizing private savings allows firms to raise capital from citizens (ALA, Article 91). A citizen who invests his savings in a socially-owned enterprise has the right to recover his capital, and to receive a compensation in the form of interest or other benefits. If his investment is used for creating new jobs, a labour relationship with the citizen may be established. The LERPL of 1982 further specified what was intended by 'other benefits' – employment, housing and training, or use of the enterprise's services – while also making clear what such benefits could *not* include – namely, that an individual might receive them indefinitely, that he might participate in management, or that he might receive a share of income, other than interest (Article 46).

Private investment by citizens was regulated by a special law adopted in 1986.[25] The law both encourages and restrains private investment. On the one hand, instead of taking up employment himself, the investor may by this means obtain employment for a member of his family. On the other hand, the investor has a right to repayment of his capital only after three years have elapsed – a condition which thus reduces the liquidity of his investment.

The above analysis suggests that none of the legislation on financial instruments in Yugoslavia has been sufficiently motivating. Potential investors ought to have been assured fuller control over invested capital (even at the expense of self-management rights of workers in decision-making), for example by being offered joint participation in management alongside workers. These arrangements all allowed individuals/institutions contributing capital to participate in profits on a temporary basis only; a solution could have been found by providing for the automatic renewal of contracts with external providers of capital, thus allowing a 'hidden' form of shareholding. Such schemes could have been interpreted as a temporary (renewable) right to income based on the use of socially-owned resources, rather than as a perma-nent right to income from ownership. They might thus have been acceptable from an ideological point of view, while significantly increasing incentives to invest.

Workers' views

It is also of interest to examine how workers feel about the notion of past labour. A sociological study based on interviews with some 3,500 workers from Croatia and Slovenia sought to ascertain their views on four specific issues: criteria for rewarding past labour, its con-crete forms, the character of such a right, and its time dimension (Županov 1977).

Table 8.1 reveals that less precise criteria for rewarding past labour – such as personal income and total years of employment – were given priority. In order to explain such attitudes, additional questions relating to the more precise criteria of individual workers' investments were asked. A relative majority thought that these criteria would not be in conformity with the law, which may be the reason why they had not considered them.

With regard to ways of realizing the right to past labour, sixteen different forms were grouped into one of three categories, depending on what role they envisaged for past labour rewards: the entrepreneurial (as compensation for postponed consumption); self-managed (as compensation for managing social capital); and security-oriented (securing workers' socio-economic welfare). Table 8.2 reveals

Table 8.1. *Criteria for rewarding past labour*

Criteria	Percentage of positive answers		Rank	
	Croatia	Slovenia	Croatia	Slovenia
Investment of own capital (workers' personal loans)	18.9	22.8	5	4
Rewards for innovation	28.4	21.1	4	5
Total personal income	70.5	69.5	1	1
Years of employment in the firm	40.7	42.5	3	3
Total years of employment	61.4	52.2	2	2

Source: Županov (1977), p. 150.

that the most favoured methods of rewarding past labour were those linked to seniority in a specific firm (E), the firm's productivity (J), help in resolving housing problems (O), and job protection (P).

A third group of questions concerned the character of the right to past labour rewards: whether it was felt to be a worker's subjective right, or a moral right based on solidarity; and whether it was a property right. In reply to the first question, a majority considered past labour rewards to be a subjective right of each individual. Concerning the second question, workers thought that past labour rights should not be linked to membership in an enterprise; they thought that if a worker were dismissed for economic reasons, he should continue to enjoy such a right, though if he were dismissed for misconduct, his right to past labour rewards should cease. Only around 15 per cent of workers thought that the right to past labour rewards should be transferable, although a majority (around 60 per cent in both republics) thought that it should be inheritable by members of the worker's family.

Workers were also asked what they thought should be the minimum length of employment required in order to acquire the right to past labour rewards; in Croatia 51.5 per cent, and in Slovenia 45 per cent of workers thought five years was sufficient. Replying to the question whether the right to past labour ought to be recognized retrospectively, 50 per cent of Croatian, and 39 per cent of Slovenian workers replied positively.

The results of the survey reveal certain social constraints on the introduction of workers' shareholding in Yugoslavia, for it seems that the Yugoslav worker is risk-averse and is not willing to accept fully the role of entrepreneur, preferring instead the present 'implicit' contract with

Table 8.2. *Methods of rewarding past labour*

Orientation	Form	Percentage of positive answers	
		Croatia	Slovenia
Entrepreneurial	A Worker invests in the firm, receives a personal income and a profit share	68.2	75.3
	B Worker puts his savings at firm's disposal, receives interest in advance	51.4	58.6
	F Worker receives a special reward linked to contribution to past labour while employed in the firm	58.7	55.3
	J Worker's personal income linked to enterprise productivity	80.3	89.0
Self-managed	K Worker's personal income linked to average sectoral productivity in the republic	48.3	40.6
	L Worker's personal income linked to average productivity in the commune	37.7	29.4
	M Worker's personal income linked to average productivity in the republic	40.0	32.0
	N Worker's personal income linked to average productivity of Yugoslavia	38.2	23.4
Security oriented	C All workers receive equal rewards linked to firm's business results	49.8	47.5
	D Worker receives a special reward linked to total employment	72.8	68.0
	E Worker receives a special reward linked to seniority in his firm	72.8	76.5
	G Worker receives a pension depending on seniority in his firm	51.4	52.6
	H All workers receive same pensions	23.3	18.9
	I Workers performing similar jobs receive equal pensions	61.5	62.1
	O Workers helped to resolve housing problems	88.4	88.5
	P Workers' job protection	72.8	81.3

Source: Županov (1977), pp. 152–3.

the state, which assures benefits irrespective of the worker's personal contribution. This is attested to by the fact that workers prefer less precise criteria for rewarding past labour, by their negative attitude towards investing personal savings, by answers concerning methods of rewarding past labour – three out of the four most-preferred methods belong to the 'security'-oriented category (rather than the entrepreneurial one) – and by their attitude towards the right to past labour rewards, which they felt ought to be non-transferable and not linked to membership, though inheritable.

Moreover, workers in Yugoslavia may be happy with the way things are: the solutions effectively adopted in practice do not diverge much from the expressed desires of this group of workers, for the most preferred criteria – personal incomes and total seniority – are precisely the ones that are applied in practice; while of the four most preferred methods of rewarding past labour, three can be said to be applied in practice (personal income linked to collective productivity, job protection, and help in resolving housing problems).

The missing elements

Financial innovation in Yugoslavia since the early 1970s has not been very successful in introducing the build-in investment incentives that are necessary for the development of a market-oriented system, in which enterprises make autonomous investment decisions primarily according to market criteria. Rewarding past labour has not greatly increased the motivation of enterprises to invest, nor has the diversification of financial instruments proved sufficient to increase inter-enterprise and inter-regional mobility of capital or to substitute bank credits by more direct forms of investment finance.

In order for securities to play the role they usually play in a capitalist economy, a developed securities market is necessary, including a secondary market for securities. In Yugoslavia, the absence of such a market, which would have ensured immediate liquidity of resources placed in securities, is probably one of the principal reasons why, with the exception of promissory notes, securities in Yugoslavia have not been used to a greater extent.

The reasons why a secondary market for securities has not been set up are of a broader nature, and are directly linked to the cautious and limited use of the market in general. The role of the market has always been more important for final demand than for production factors. Fully-fledged capital and labour markets have never been entirely accepted, mainly for ideological reasons (see R. Uvalić 1964; Schrenk *et al.* 1979). The belief expressed in the early 1960s, that a capital market is inconsistent with the principles of socialism,[26] continued to be held widely in Yugoslavia until recently. Given such an attitude, only a 'specific' capital market, one adapted to the needs of a self-managed socialist economy (and hence a highly regulated market) was to be developed. Ćirović (1976, p. 85) gives an illustrative explanation of the official attitude towards capital markets with reference to securities:[27]

> The introduction of a securities market is not a purely technical issue, since . . . it enables speculative operations on the market, . . . financial losses for some and financial gains for others, leading to a redistribution of financial income. This is directly in conflict with the self-managed economic system, which aims to develop a system of distribution based on labour contributions. A complete market for securities would require the introduction of a flexible interest rate, formed exclusively on the basis of demand and supply of financial assets . . . In such a system, associated labour would not be able consciously to regulate the level of the interest rate, but the market interest rate, formed 'behind the back of commodity producers', would be the main parameter. Hence the interest rate would dominate (rule over) enterprises . . . This is the principal reason why the Yugoslav economic system has not accepted the introduction of a securities market . . .

Given that such attitudes prevailed, it is clear that the new financial instruments could not have proved successful.

The setting up of a secondary market for securities also requires an adequate banking system, one which can successfully organize and undertake operations on such a market. A secondary market for securities might have developed if banks had been prepared to buy as well as sell securities, but banks could only issue securities under very special circumstances. Moreover, despite all banking reforms, Yugoslav banks have never been assigned the role of autonomous financial intermediaries. This is because commercial banks in Yugoslavia, at least until the very recent reforms, were never conceived of as independent, profit-making institutions – apart, possibly, from the period immediately following the 1965 economic reform. Rather, banks were to be merely 'service' agencies of the founder enterprises, and in line with such a concept, banks' capital was limited by law. In addition, given that the political authorities influence enterprise decision-making in various formal and informal ways, their indirect influence on banks' policies has also remained substantial. Since a bank in Yugoslavia has no capital of its own and cannot freely decide on the use of its funds – for it is under the pressure of both the founder enterprises and the political structures – it could not have played an important role in placing capital in the most profitable ventures. And without an independent banking system, a capital market could not have developed.

All of the new mechanisms and financial instruments introduced during the 1970s in Yugoslavia bear some similarities to shareholding, suggesting that such an arrangement was necessary in a socialist economy too. However, since other important limitations have persisted, these new financial instruments were in practice no more than hybrid forms of shareholding.

Had Kardelj's scheme of rewarding past labour been implemented in such a way as to link past labour rewards more directly to capital returns, or ideally, to the absolute increase in the value of net assets of an enterprise, the scheme could have contained some elements of shareholding. Workers would have been rewarded for investing retained earnings in capital stock, and hence a worker, just like a shareholder, would have been able to count on a personal return on a part of the equity of the enterprise, while the firm would have been able to obtain additional capital in a way similar to the issuing of shares.

In this sense, a better application of Kardelj's scheme might have improved incentives to invest – though it would still not have eliminated the disincentive arising from the capital maintenance requirement (in spite of the partial ineffectiveness of the requirement in practice in Yugoslavia; see chapter 3). Moreover, an important limitation concerning the possibility of converting shares into liquid assets would remain: the collective would not be able to cash in past labour rights, as workers are not permitted to liquidate the enterprise voluntarily and distribute the proceeds; and neither would the individual worker be able to cash in these rights, as he could not transfer them to other individuals. Therefore, past labour rewards, at best, could have taken the form of non-transferable, non-marketable dividends.

The second group of mechanisms, intended to encourage investment outside the enterprise, also had some similarities with shareholding. Had the scheme of investing in other enterprises allowed a permanent sharing of income by the two enterprises, and had the joint bearing of risk been ensured, the instrument could have represented a form of shareholding of one socially-owned enterprise in another. The pooling of financial resources in a bank resembles shareholding, insofar as it ensures the participation of member enterprises in profits and management, and the joint bearing of risk; but it differs fundamentally from shareholding inasmuch as it gives such rights and obligations to all members, irrespective of the amount of capital invested. The individual who invests his capital in a COAL can be compared to a shareholder, as he receives a part of profits on account of property, but such participation is only temporary. The scheme for mobilizing private savings by socially-owned enterprises, as envisaged by the ALA, effectively puts the citizen in the position of a shareholder, although the LERPL of 1982 took care to exclude such a possibility.

As to financial instruments, the certificate of pooled resources comes closest to shares; but in spite of being a long-term security, the certificate is also redeemable at its face value, which excludes large capital gains; and in addition, it cannot be subscribed by households. Moreover, although all of the instruments discussed above bear some similarities with shareholding, they have not succeeded in playing one of the essential roles that equity shares play, or ought to play, in the capitalist economy, namely that of providing a pricing mechanism by which enterprises value themselves.

It could be argued that because the mechanisms we have analysed have not functioned in such a way as to substitute successfully the role of state intervention, there remains a need for state involvement in investment decision-making in Yugoslavia. However, without all the restrictions on liquidity of instruments and on appropriability of gains, these mechanisms might have been more successful to the point of eliminating, or at least reducing, the need of continuous state involvement in enterprise affairs.

Nevertheless, the setting up of a complete market for securities, together with an independent banking system and more stimulative legislation, would probably not have been sufficient to ensure an efficient system of investment mobilization and allocation in Yugoslavia – nor perhaps even possible – without departing from other systemic features of the traditional socialist economy. The crucial missing element was freedom for the individual enterprise to operate as an autonomous economic agent. This has never been possible in Yugoslavia because of political tutelage, ensured by the essentially unchanged property regime. A permanent right to income from ownership posed insurmountable ideological barriers even in a reformed, highly decentralized, socialist economy. Such an attitude seems to be changing only very recently, as evidenced by the property reforms which are discussed in the next chapter.

9 Current property reforms

Towards private property: the debates of the 1980s

Investment reforms in Yugoslavia have not produced fundamental changes in enterprise behaviour, because other elements of
the system have remained essentially unchanged – in particular, the
property regime, as probably the most constant feature of the Yugoslav
system over the last forty years (Bonin and Putterman 1987, p. 105).

The property issue came to the fore of academic and public discussions in Yugoslavia in the mid-1980s. From the debates, a generally
favourable attitude towards the diversification of property rights
emerged. The concept of social property, which for years had been
taken for granted as one of the fundamental features of the Yugoslav
economy (in spite of endless academic discussions about its real meaning),[1] was for the first time openly criticized. There was also a revival of
interest in traditional financial instruments; in particular a lively debate
on shareholding developed. Although many of the initial proposals
sought ways of introducing shareholding without affecting the
socialist features of the economy – and in some cases, without affecting
the existing framework of social property – they have stimulated
discussion and thus have prepared the ground for successive, more
radical, reforms of the property regime.

Workers' 'shareholding'

One of the contributions that revived the debate on workers'
shareholding in recent years was by S. Babić. Babić (1983) argued that
there is no reason why shareholding by producers should be explicitly
prohibited, since the law does not prohibit ownership of income-
generating assets (e.g. citizens' savings accounts). In order to increase
an entrepreneur's motivation to invest as well as the mobility of

capital, Babić advanced two proposals: first, the introduction of a scarcity-reflecting charge for the use of social capital (thus ensuring the social character of property); and second, 'shareholding entrepreneurship', i.e. the possibility for the collective entrepreneur to recover the principal of an investment and receive a dividend on invested capital. Resources obtained through the capital charge would be left at the disposal of the enterprise, but specifically for investment purposes. As long as the entrepreneur can recover the principal of an investment with a cumulated yield, he will be indifferent between investment in his own or another enterprise.

While Babić's proposal would probably increase capital mobility, it would not eliminate the essence of the underinvestment problem. A minimum savings constraint, as in the existing system, would be imposed on firms through the capital charge, and hence the investment decision would hardly reflect a voluntary choice. Moreover, Babić disregarded the disincentive effects of the capital maintenance requirement. If the firm is obliged to maintain the value of capital, Babić's 'shareholding entrepreneurship' *per se* would not ensure the full recovery of an investment. Despite the existence of partial relief from this requirement in Yugoslavia, the obligation still applies to a part of capital; under Babić's scheme, a firm would not be able to recover the principal of an investment in capital which is effectively being maintained.

Milovanović (1986) has developed a theoretical model of workers' past labour rewards.[2] Among the assumptions required for an equilibrium solution is the existence of a capital market, and of a charge for the use of social capital. The model shows that under free capital market conditions, optimal remuneration of past labour is possible; and that an economy without a capital market is inferior, as compared to an economy having such a market, since it will have lower consumption per worker in all time periods. Milovanović also makes a concrete proposal concerning how to introduce workers' shares in a socialist economy (1986, pp. 116–17). He suggests that the state issues initial shares for a total value of social capital, and distributes them to the population. What would then follow is the trading of shares on an organized market. Workers would in general own shares in their own firms, but could also buy shares in other firms. Such ownership would not give the worker any management rights, which would remain the prerogative of the workers employed in the firm in question, and would only guarantee a dividend depending on the firm's profits. A shareholder would not have to renounce his shares on retirement; only after a worker's death would his rights cease. Shares would not be transferable to heirs, but would go into a state fund from which each eighteen-year-old citizen would be given a certain number of shares. In this way social resources would become 'social' in a real sense, while workers would become permanently interested in investment.[3]

Milovanović's proposal is appealing, although it fails to elaborate several issues. How would shares be valued on the market, and would they reflect the net worth of an enterprise? What would be the incentive for outside shareholders to buy non-voting shares? How would a possible divergence of interests between workers and outside shareholders be resolved? What would govern the initial distribution of shares to the population? Would new shares, corresponding to the increment in social capital, be equally accessible to all; or would workers employed in the enterprise issuing new shares be given priority, in order to ensure that the majority of shares remained in the hands of workers employed? Otherwise, the underinvestment problem would not be resolved: workers could vote for consumption rather than investment, while the outside shareholder, having no vote, would be powerless to press for more investment. Finally, either shares are fully transferable and can always be sold and bought, thus negating the idea of losing all at death, or they are not, in which case there would be little incentive to buy them, and their price would not reflect the underlying earning capacity, and therefore value, of assets.

Another economist in favour of shareholding is T. Nikolić, who argues (1986) that workers' shareholding has definite advantages over the credit relations that have led to the present high level of indebtedness of the economy. As co-owners of social capital, workers would have an interest in the latter's increase for two reasons: because past labour dividends would be directly linked to realized profits, and because the value of their personal property (i.e. their shares) would depend on the efficiency with which social capital was used. The introduction of workers' shareholding would not only prevent inefficient investment by political bureaucracy, but would remove the 'enigma' concerning the imprecise definition of social property, as each individual subject would have to take risks and responsibilities. Social capital would increase to an extent which would depend directly on the creation of domestic savings, and hence further indebtedness would be prevented.[4] Workers' shareholding would not represent the negation of social property, since it is directly Marxist. When describing cooperative factories, Marx spoke of the worker as having two functions: as the owner of his own means of production, he is a capitalist and receives profit, and as a worker, he is hired labour and receives a wage. Nikolić does not, however, discuss the problem of how to reconcile social property with property rights and workers' share capital. In fact, he finds a compromise by using a highly ambiguous term: 'workers' shareholding social property'.

A concrete solution to this problem is offered by Labus (1987), who proposes a clear distinction between macro and micro interests and responsibilities regarding property. Such responsibilities would be divided between working collectives and state organs. In order to prevent 'group ownership' tendencies, a price for the use of capital would be reintroduced.

At the other extreme, several economists have attacked such proposals, mainly on ideological grounds, evaluating workers' shareholding as a step backwards, leading to privatization and the negation of socialism. Korać (1986, p. 188) has gone as far as to calculate the effect of the introduction of workers' shareholding in terms of capital losses: social capital, instead of increasing six times over the next forty years, would only increase 1.8 times. Korać's calculations are based on the simplified assumption that workers would distribute the larger part (two thirds) of accumulation in the form of dividends, that would thereafter be spent on personal consumption, thus considerably decreasing the average accumulation rate of the economy. However, Korać offers no valid arguments in support of his assumption. If workers are co-owners of capital, such a high level of distribution would not be in their long-term interest. Even if a large part of profits were distributed, mechanisms could be found to mobilize workers' savings for productive purposes, thus preventing a lowering of the accumulation rate. But even if all profits are reinvested and there are no dividends, with an efficient capital market the value of the shares will increase by at least the amount of investment (as long as the present value of investment is positive); shareholders can always 'declare their own dividends' by selling a fraction of their shares which corresponds to the growth of their value generated by the reinvestment of all profits.

Similarly, Štambuk is against workers' shares, acritically opting for the status quo solution: the only way to motivate workers to produce efficiently, according to the author, 'is by enforcing a property form through which the individual and class interests of the direct producers are expressed in a most efficient way, and this can only be social property' (1988, p. 19).

Bajt (1988a, pp. 6–7) has expressed doubts about the positive effects of workers' shareholding in the enterprise of employment. Workers would need to be allowed to sell their shares (otherwise motivation would be absent), but this could seriously undermine the whole social sector and transform the Yugoslav system into a capitalist economy. The principal problem of the Yugoslav economy, according to Bajt, is not the lack of savings, but of entrepreneurship.

Shareholding by external capital providers

The second group of proposals advanced in recent years concern incentives for an enterprise to invest outside the firm. B. Kovač proposed a division of the economy into three sectors: social, private, and mixed. The social sector would be given a transition period of five to six years, during which conditions for the survival of firms would be tightened, and enterprises not surviving would be liquidated, while competition would be stimulated by the establishment of a mixed sector with diversified property forms in which shareholding was allowed (see Round table discussion (RTD) 1986).

Other economists were sceptical about the possibility of introducing shareholding even on a limited scale, for a variety of reasons: ideo- logical barriers (Mencinger); the possible negative consequences on socially-owned enterprises of increasing competition (Inić); an absence of public confidence in the state, without which a shareholding system cannot function properly (Jerovšek); incompatibility between a stock market and the present system in which the government 'freezes' and 'unfreezes' the entire economy every three months (Labus); and fear of a loss of control by the government which, while easily giving orders to 200 enterprise managers, could obviously not control two million shareholders (Labus) (RTD 1986). Bajt (1988a, 1988b) emphasized the high level of inefficiency of the Yugoslav economy, expressing doubts about whether shareholding could function at all under existing con- ditions: recent liquidity problems of Yugoslav enterprises have shown that they are often not even able to pay interest on bank loans, and hence would be even less capable of paying (higher) dividends.

However, the principal argument that has worried Yugoslav economists was that shareholding would be in conflict with self- management. Labus (in RTD 1986) argued that no one would be willing to invest in a firm's shares unless such investment brought some form of influence over the firm's management. Unless such control were assured, shareholding capital would remain at very low levels – yet such control would be in conflict with self-management. Instead of shareholding, Labus considered that bonds, which do not imply participation in management, would have a better chance of being successfully implemented.

Others, however, considered that the conflict between shareholding and self-management could be resolved. Božović suggested joint participation in management by both workers and capital providers (see Lakićević 1987b). Nikolić and Raić proposed the establishment of an assembly of shareholders within enterprise workers' councils, which would have certain rights concerning the election of managerial bodies and the economic policy of the firm (see Nikolić 1986).

Alongside academic discussions, property began to be discussed in the mid-1980s at the official level also. Although the 1982 Stabilization Programme, the main policy document of the reforms of the 1980s, did not specifically treat the issue of property, since at that time social property was not in question, with the worsening of the economic crisis, problems related to property began to be examined officially by the Party, the government, and other political bodies.[5] At a February 1987 meeting of the Central Committee of the League of Communists (CCLCY), it was proposed that individuals (even foreigners) be allowed to privately own means of production (apart from those in the small-scale private sector); while at a March meeting it was suggested that 'the economic and social situation requires that other forms of property, besides social, are developed within the framework of our socio-economic system' (see Lakićević 1987a). This resulted in a document on property being prepared for the Presidency of the CCLCY, which considered how to encourage private investment on a wider scale, especially on the part of Yugoslavs employed abroad. In another government document it was proposed to increase the rights of enterprises investing in other firms (see Lakićević 1987b). The issue of workers' shares in socially-owned enterprises was also discussed at the official level; in particular, employee share-ownership was one of the proposals in 1988 of the Serbian Commission for reform implementation.[6]

The diversification of property was therefore accepted as a general orientation, but without any fundamental change in the existing system of social property. This was the official position of the Yugoslav authorities, which prevailed at least until 1988. It was felt that to allow forms of shareholding on a limited scale would not be a serious threat to the socialist features of the economy, as long as the socially owned enterprise remained the dominant form. This resulted in the intro-duction of specific measures and legislation designed to encourage small-scale private enterprises (duty-free imports of equipment and other measures meant to stimulate private investment, especially by Yugoslavs returning from abroad; special credits reserved for small-scale enterprises, although limited in extent; simplification of bureaucratic procedures necessary for the setting up of private firms). Nevertheless, there was a great deal of resistance even towards changes in this direction; for example, the draft law on enterprises with foreign capital, which was designed to attract savings of Yugoslavs employed abroad, was at first rejected on the grounds that Yugoslav emigrants' exclusive rights to invest in such enterprises would put them in a privileged position with respect to workers employed inside Yugoslavia. The history of economic reforms in socialist countries teaches us, in fact, that the road from initial proposals to their elaboration and implementation is a long one.

The 1988 change in the target model

A decisive change in the official attitude took place in Yugoslavia in 1988, away from the socialist self-management model, towards private ownership and a mixed market economy. Since November 1988, thirty-nine amendments to the Federal Constitution have been adopted, together with over twenty separate laws, among which the most radical departure from past policy objectives regards property.

Constitutional amendments designed to encourage small-scale private and mixed property enterprises have been adopted (see amendments no. 21 and 22). Investment in Yugoslav firms, banks, and other organizations was opened up to foreigners (constitutional amendment no. 15), while the 1988 Foreign Investment Law offered major protection of foreign partners' ownership and management rights, and abolished the limits on the amount of foreign capital. Foreign investment is now permitted in all types of enterprise, participation in decision-making is in accordance with the share of capital contributed, and the list of sectors in which foreigners can invest has been significantly enlarged. In agriculture, the adoption of constitutional amendment no. 23 finally raised the limits on individual holdings from 10–15 hectares to 30 hectares per family (or more in mountainous regions). Currently laws on the privatization of socially-owned housing and on the reprivatization of property confiscated after the Second World War are being elaborated.

While these measures designed to facilitate growth of the private sector were important, the main problem in Yugoslavia today is primarily the low level of efficiency of the social sector of the economy, which at the end of 1989 still accounted for 86.3 per cent of GMP. The fundamental problem of restructuring the social sector began to be tackled in 1988 through a series of important laws.

The first step was taken in December 1988, when the Law on Enterprises was adopted,[7] virtually replacing the 1976 Associated Labour Act, which had once been regarded as the workers' 'Bible' because of the apparently extensive rights it gave them. The law introduced the diversification of both property types and legal forms of enterprises. Besides the already existing types of property (social, private and cooperative), the law introduced mixed property based on a combination of private and socially-owned capital, as well as a variety of new legal forms of enterprise: joint-stock and limited liability companies, limited partnerships, companies with unlimited joint liability, and public enterprises.

In the field of self-management, the general direction in the Law on Enterprises is to limit self-management rights and replace the collective responsibility of workers by the individual responsibility of managers/directors and capital owners. The law has introduced collective bargaining agreements, concluded between the representatives of the government, of enterprises and trade unions. In mixed ownership companies, the law has limited the rights of workers' councils, the main self-management organ, now reduced to monitoring and consulting (and no longer decision making). In private enterprises, the law gives full decision-making rights to shareholders proportional to capital invested. Basic organizations of associated labour have been abolished, thus returning to the old concept of enterprises.

Significant legislative changes were also introduced in the banking system (at least on paper). As early as 1986, voting power in banks, previously equal for all members, was made proportional to the funds invested (confirmed by constitutional amendment no. 13 of 1988). The establishment of a bank must now be authorized by the NBY, and no longer by the local socio-political community, and other changes have been introduced in order to further enhance the supervisory powers of the NBY. Socio-political communities will now be held responsible for all the consequences of rules imposed by them on banks.

Changes of the banking system introduced in 1989 provide for the transformation of banks from non-profit institutions into joint-stock and limited liability banks, thereby introducing the legal category of mixed banks with no limits imposed on foreign investment.[8] Shareholders now have full property rights, including the right to management, and such a right is directly linked to the amount of capital invested. Besides enterprises and self-managed communities of interest, as under the previous system, shareholders can also be socio-political communities, citizens, foreign investors and banks. A detailed process of rehabilitation and liquidation has been defined for banks in difficulties.[9]

The 1989 Law on Securities has for the first time formally introduced equity shares in the Yugoslav legal system, along with other types of securities existing since 1971 (bonds, certificates, treasury bills and commercial notes).[10] A special government commission ought to authorize the issuing of securities, except in the cases of newly-established shareholding companies or securities issues by socio-political communities. Another important law was also adopted in 1989 – the Law on the Money Market and the Capital Market – which provides for the establishment of such markets by banks and other financial institutions, with the task of performing financial inter-mediation: the money market in liquid assets and the capital market in securities.[11]

Finally, the 1989 Law on the Circulation and Disposal of Social Capital allows workers' councils to sell social capital to domestic and foreign buyers (both firms and individuals) through auctions. The law provides that all proceeds from sales should go to Republican Funds and be used for development purposes, the whole process being super-vised by a specialized agency.[12]

All of these laws were important steps in the right direction. However, the Law on Enterprises, despite allowing different forms of private property, left social sector property intact; while the Law on the Circulation and Disposal of Social Capital has been interpreted as tacit nationalization, officially creating state property within Republican Funds, thus recognizing that the seller (and hence real owner) of capital in Yugoslavia is the state. This interpretation is seemingly justified by the constitutional ruling that property literally belongs to no one, but on reflection can be rejected, because property formerly owned by the state has never officially been transferred to other physical or legal persons, and therefore must have remained with the state.

Due primarily to a lack of enthusiasm on the part of workers, by June 1990 no sales under the law had actually taken place (see Milanović 1990), although in the meantime other provisions of the law were implemented (for example, legislation on the institutions envisaged by the law has been adopted).[13]

The 1990 privatization programme

The decisive step for privatization was taken in July 1990, in Prime Minister Ante Marković's economic package for the second half of the year. Along with stabilization policies similar to those applied in the first half of 1990, the core of the package consisted precisely of privatization. The main instruments of privatization are 'internal shares' – initially not tradable on the stock exchange – regulated in two federal laws adopted in August 1990. The first is the Law on Social Capital, which has virtually replaced the 1989 Law on the Circulation and Disposal of Social Capital.[14] The second is the Law on Personal Incomes, which envisages that, in addition to basic wages, enterprises give internal shares to their workers as part of regular earnings.[15]

Internal shares are offered for sale at a discount of 30 per cent to enterprise workers, to citizens and to pension funds; but workers – presently employed, or subject to at least two years' service, and retired workers – have the right to a further discount of 1 per cent for each year of employment, up to a maximum of 70 per cent of the nominal value of shares. Internal shares give the right to participate in after-tax profits and in management. Shares need not be paid for immediately, though the entire payment has to be made within ten years. Once an internal share has been fully paid for, it becomes a normal share, tradable on the stock exchange. Internal shares can be issued for the purposes both of raising new capital and of selling an enterprise. Such issues must be accompanied by the transformation of the enterprise into a joint-stock or limited liability company, as well as the reduction of the value of social capital by the approved discount. The first round of share offers was to have taken place within one year of the law's enactment (i.e. by August 1991).

Several limits are imposed on internal share issues: on the total value, which must not exceed six times an enterprise's annual wage bill;[16] on the amount sold to each of the three categories (workers, citizens, and pension funds), where the maximum is set at three times the annual wage bill; and on the value that can be subscribed by an individual worker, set at three times his annual personal income.[17] That part of social capital which is not subscribed through internal share issues, determined by the above global limit, will be offered for sale to domestic and foreign enterprises or individuals through public auctions. If an enterprise issues internal shares for the purpose of raising new capital, it does so on the basis of the book value of assets (although the basis can also be the estimated value of assets if the management board so decides). The price of an enterprise sold at auction will be set by the market; otherwise, the value of assets must be determined by an authorized agency.

Specific functions regarding privatization are assigned to different institutions. The management board of the enterprise takes most of the initial decisions: on the issuing of shares, on the transformation of the enterprise into a new legal form, on its sale, and on other issues not defined by the law, such as the value of internal shares that are to be issued to categories other than workers. Republican Funds are the main institutions receiving and investing proceeds from sales (unlike the German privatization agency, the *Treuhandanstalt*, which is specifically forbidden to make further investments, and is a self-liquidating agency). Republican Funds can invest up to 5 per cent of their total resources in enterprises, although proceeds from the sale of a given enterprise can be reinvested entirely in that enterprise. A part of the proceeds from a sale can also be used to make a one-off payment to workers in the form of securities of either the Fund or the enterprise, unless workers have already taken advantage of their right to a discount on internal shares.[18] Republican Agencies which function as public enterprises perform all expert and consultative functions concerning the sale of enterprises; they nominate the organization in charge of estimating the value of an enterprise, give their opinion on the sale, and authorize sales to take place other than through auction. Officials of the Federal Government are to determine the methodology for calculating the various discounts and limits.

The proceeds from sales go primarily to the Republican Funds, but can also go to a complex organization, i.e. an association of enterprises,[19] or, if a part of a firm is sold and is organized as a new legal entity, to the parent enterprise. If shares are issued for the purpose of raising new capital, the proceeds belong to the issuing enterprise.

The Law on Social Capital is so far the most serious attempt to change the existing property regime in Yugoslavia. The introduction of equity shares implies a radical change in public opinion, since until recently, instruments ensuring a permanent right to income on the basis of ownership had been strenuously opposed. The law allows a wide diffusion of property rights, taking into account the interests of the various social groups – the state, workers, and citizens – and hence represents a fair compromise between more extreme models of privatization. Moreover, since workers are the most privileged category – and thus are intended to become the principal owners – this should reinforce incentives precisely where they are most needed, namely within firms. The law should also help resolve some of the most pressing stabilization problems: it is to reduce inflationary pressures (by withdrawing part of the liquidity in circulation) and the present liquidity problems of many Yugoslav firms (by giving them access to new capital).

At the same time, this type of privatization is likely to be a very slow process. It does not ensure the transformation of all anonymous social capital – over which no legal entity at present has property rights – into private capital.[20] The law is also ambiguous concerning a number of crucial issues, including the valuation of enterprise assets and the definition of social property. The redistribution of property rights is therefore unlikely to proceed without difficulties, especially as regards the rights of socio-political communities.[21] Furthermore, demand by workers for internal shares is likely to be low, for a series of reasons: the liquidity constraint (low purchasing power) imposed by wage freezes, many loss-making enterprises, workers' risk-aversion, deficiencies in balance sheet accounting, and the absence of secondary trading in stock markets. Some of these problems are also likely to deter investment by external shareholders.

Implementation problems

Although the federal law offers a general framework for privatization, a lively debate has in the mean time developed on how to proceed with its implementation. The dilemmas are similar to those in other former socialist economies: whether to implement privatization gradually, or as fast as possible; 'from above' or 'from below'; by distributing property freely to all citizens, or through the sale of assets; by offering privileged conditions primarily to employees, or also to other categories. Thus several republics are in the process of drawing up their own privatization laws. Regulations introduced by the Slovenian and Croatian governments in October 1990 suspended implementation of the federal law (internal share issues), until Republican Agencies were officially set up and other relevant legislation adopted,[22] a postponement which had effectively frozen the privatization process in these two republics.

The Slovenian government has drawn up its privatization programme in great detail, set out in several separate laws, which in the spring of 1991 were still being debated by the Slovenian Assembly.[23] The debate on privatization, which started in the summer of 1990, has been extremely intense and highly political, reflecting the different views of the newly-elected political parties. Beginning with an initial proposal which was not very different from the federal privatization law (see Mencinger 1990), through the debate on whether social property should first be nationalized or should be privatized right away, the government presented a first draft privatization law on 11 October 1990. Since the draft law was not accepted by the Slovenian Assembly in November 1990, on 14 February 1991 a second draft law was presented, which in April 1991 was still under discussion. Given that this draft law was strongly criticized by Jeffrey Sachs, a consultant to the Slovenian government (such criticism led the Minister of the Slovenian economy, Jože Mencinger, to resign), it is probable that yet another version of the law will appear.

According to existing proposals, Slovenia has opted for a model of decentralized privatization without prior nationalization. The whole process is to be controlled by specialized institutions (the Development Fund and the Privatization Agency), and is to be based on the sale of assets. Some of the basic elements of the Slovenian privatization programme are similar to provisions contained in the federal law,[24] although many aspects have been modified or developed in much greater detail. Initially, stricter conditions governing the issue of shares to workers were proposed,[25] while those for Slovenian citizens were more generous; the more recent proposal, however, has raised the discount for workers (although it sets a maximum of 50 per cent). Privatization can be undertaken autonomously by enterprises, with the help of the Privatization Agency, or directly by the Agency. Among the various methods of autonomous privatization, particular emphasis is placed on 'internal privatization', i.e. employee-leveraged buy-outs (inspired by the system of ESOPs in Western countries). Certain sectors (energy, telecommunication, communal services, housing, agriculture, banks and insurance companies, which account for around 45 per cent of the Slovenian economy) are to be excluded from privatization. Proceeds from sales would normally go into the Development Fund, which would manage them in the name of the Slovenian Republic, while consultative functions would be performed by foreign experts through the Agency for Privatization. The valuation of enterprise assets is to be based on their 'corrected' book value, thus enabling more realistic valuation. In the long run, it is planned to privatize 1,200 companies employing 540,000 workers (Simoneti 1991). Parallel to privatization, a denationalization law is also being prepared, which concerns claims of Yugoslav citizens for property nationalized during 1945–58.

The criticism to which the Slovenian proposal has recently been subject mainly concerns 'internal' privatization. It is feared that labour/management buy-outs will result in full control of enterprises – obtained at a very low price – by their management. Mencinger has been accused of having stuck too closely to Marković's federal law (see *Vreme*, 29 April 1991, p. 13).

Within the Croatian government, the debate over privatization became so heated in late September 1990 that it led one of its ministers, Dražen Kalodjera, to resign. Kalodjera was proposing to proceed with privatization as fast as possible without prior nationalization, by distributing 80 per cent of property to the state, workers, and creditors (banks) according to their contribution to the creation of existing capital; the rest would be offered for sale on the market, the proceeds going to the state. All shares would be immediately tradable on the stock exchange, but a sales tax progressively diminishing over time would be imposed in order to discourage their immediate sale (Kalodjera 1990).[26] The main opponent of Kalodjera's proposal was the then Vice-President of the Croatian government, Mate Babić. Babić warned of the 'big dangers of simple robbery' that privatization could lead to, and seemed to advocate nationalization.[27] However, Babić has in the mean time also left the Croatian government (in November 1990).

A draft privatization law for Croatia was finally drawn up in January 1991, similar in several respects to the Slovenian law. It envisaged a smaller discount on internal shares sold to workers (a maximum of 30 per cent) and pension funds (20 per cent), and assured certain rights to ex-owners who had lost their property through nationalization. Proceeds from sales would go either to the Restructuring Agency or the Republican Fund. A more realistic valuation of assets was also envisaged. Banks and other financial institutions and insurance companies were to be excluded from privatization (see *Ekonomska politika* no. 2028, 11 February 1991, p. 14).

The Croatian proposal has since been modified in several important aspects, with the adoption, in February 1991, of the Law on the Transformation of Social Enterprises (see *Ekonomska politika* no. 2039/40, 29 April 1991). Although enterprises can decide freely whether they wish to be transformed into private, public, cooperative or mixed property, the process of transformation must be completed by 30 June 1992 at the latest. All firms that have not transformed their property status by this date will automatically become the property of the Croatian Development Fund. Internal shares are no longer envisaged; all shares are to be sold on the stock exchange, although workers will have the right to a discount (set at a maximum rate of 20 per cent). Since the law is ambiguous on many issues concerning the process of transformation, it is feared that the Development Fund will become the main beneficiary in mid-1992, and thus that the 'privatization' programme will effectively have resulted in massive nationalization.[28]

These privatization laws in Slovenia and Croatia have been interpreted as tacit nationalization, as a tendency of both governments to first renationalize (partly or fully) social property in order to proceed with privatization later, to implement it gradually, and initially on a limited scale. According to unofficial sources, republican governments do not seem ready to give up their previous direct influence on enterprises, their implicit property rights and the tutelage system, but wish instead to reinforce their political control of the economy.

In the other republics, although no official regulations have been adopted to prevent application of the federal privatization programme, implementation has been slowed down by other informal means, such as various bureaucratic obstacles concerning enterprise registration in court registers. In Serbia there is still resistance to privatization and the abolition of 'social property',[29] but other parties in opposition to the ruling Socialist (ex-Communist) Party – parties officially represented in the Serbian Assembly since the December 1990 elections – are generally in favour of privatization.[30] The Serbian government began work on its privatization law only in early 1991. Although its contents are still being debated, it seems that social property will not be abolished completely. As in Slovenia and Croatia, the conditions governing the sale of shares to workers are less generous than permitted under federal law; and the Republican Fund would also play an important role, becoming the owner of all property for which no potential buyers can be found (see *Ekonomska politika* no. 2039/2040, 29 April 1991).

The federal government has in the mean time taken measures to facilitate and speed up privatization. The Law on the Registration of Enterprises in Court Registers, adopted in November 1990, substantially eases the registration procedure by eliminating a number of bureaucratic formalities.[31] The federal government has also taken steps to popularize privatization, for a lack of information within firms is thought to be one of the major reasons for its limited application; thus 'Buy your own enterprise', a video reporting recent privatization experiences in Yugoslavia, was prepared and offered to enterprises in December 1990.

The federal government has also, in the spring of 1991, prepared amendments to the 1990 privatization law, proposing important changes designed to speed up privatization. All limits on internal share issues have been abolished; the only restriction is that a certain percentage of internal shares will have to be offered to outsiders. Dividends on internal shares will no longer depend on the extent to which they have already been paid for, but will be linked to their total nominal value. It has been proposed that the discounts on internal shares sold to workers and nationals be raised further. Finally, internal shares will also be tradable on the capital market (see interview with Vukotić in *Ekonomska politika* no. 2039/2040, 29 April 1991).

A strong countertendency to privatization has in the mean time also emerged, termed by the Yugoslav press 'illegal nationalization': it involves the transformation of complex organizations into holding companies (which have no official owner, and thus reproduce all the problems of the old system of social property), and the transformation of a number of enterprises belonging to the social sector (primarily in infrastructure, energy, post and telecommunications, public utilities, railways) into public firms. While this process has been carried furthest in Croatia (according to some estimates, 40 per cent of the Croatian economy has been nationalized in this way), it is also gaining ground in other republics; thus the Montenegrian government even wishes to nationalize sectors such as tourism and sea transport. Although, according to the Law on Enterprises, the state has no rights over public enterprises (unless it is among the shareholders), effectively public sector firms are being treated as if they were state property; this has led, for example, to the direct appointment of directors of public enterprises by the political authorities (see *Ekonomska politika* no. 2030, 25 February 1991).

Evidence on property restructuring

Despite various measures aimed at stimulating the private sector during the 1980s, its role has remained modest (see table 9.1). Private sector non-agricultural employment increased rapidly, but in 1988 accounted only for 2.5 per cent of paid employment or, if self-employed persons are included, for 6.9 per cent of total domestic employment (OECD 1990). The share of the private sector in GMP actually declined – from 14.4 per cent in 1982, to 13.7 per cent in 1989. The main reasons are considered to be fiscal disincentives and lack of financial facilities.

It is primarily since the beginning of 1990 that the existing property structure seems to have begun changing more rapidly in favour of private ownership. Although the process is moving slowly because of the problems of implementation discussed above, the fact that privatization has started implies certain irreversible changes, which are likely to have important longer-term implications.

Free distribution of securities. As provided by the Law on Personal Incomes, a part of the personal income of all Yugoslav workers employed in the social sector in July 1990 was paid out in the form of shares and bonds (or 5.4 per cent of the Yugoslav wage bill). Relatively the largest proportion was paid out in Montenegro (36.2 per cent), followed by Bosnia and Herzegovina (17.5 per cent), Serbia (18.1 per cent), Macedonia (15.9 per cent), Slovenia (5.3 per cent), and Croatia (2.4 per cent) (see *Ekonomska politika* no. 2008, 24 September 1990, p. 14). This suggests a certain correlation between independence of republican governments and respect for federal laws. Trade unions have in the mean time vigorously opposed the law, arguing that it represents 'forced employee share ownership' and automatically lowers wages. Consequently, during the second half of 1990, the newly concluded collective wage agreements seem to have resulted in suspension of the law's application – at least in some republics.

Sale of internal shares. Implementation of the Law on Social Capital has for the moment been limited to internal shares sold to employed workers. One of the first enterprises to offer shares at a discount to workers was Ohis, in Skoplje (Macedonia); the shares were for a total value of over DM 3 million, and were subscribed by some 3,500 workers. In the firm Hemofarma, based in Vrsac (Serbia), 70 per cent of employed workers subscribed the maximum permissible number of shares in their enterprise, thus contributing a substantial inflow of capital (see *Ekonomska politika* no. 2013, 29 October 1990, p. 21). In Istra, another Serbian enterprise, 33 per cent of the firm's total assets became the property of its workers as a result of internal share issues. Sintelon, from Voivodina, has already privatized 85 per cent of its capital; through internal share issues alone it has obtained $30 million. A number of other enterprises have followed these examples.[32]

The federal government estimates that by the end of 1990 some 600 enterprises throughout Yugoslavia had either already offered internal shares to workers, or had initiated the procedure for internal share issues – and hence that in only six months, around 2 to 5 per cent of social capital had been privatized. By March 1991, the number of firms making internal share offers had increased to some 700, or even 1,000 (according to the different estimates of two members of the present

Table 9.1. *Some indicators on the private sector in Yugoslavia, 1982–1989 (% shares in total GMP and paid employment)*

	1982	1983	1984	1985	1986	1987	1988	1989
GMP	14.4	14.1	14.1	13.2	13.8	13.4	13.3	13.7
Employment[a]	2.0	2.0	2.1	2.1	2.2	2.4	2.5	2.6

[a]Only workers registered with the social insurance community, thus excluding agriculture and self-employed persons.
Source: Calculated from SZS, *SGJ* 1990, 1991, tables 107-1 and 105-1.

federal government; see *Poslovni svijet*, 21 March 1991 and *Ekonomska politika* no. 2034, 25 March 1991).

Issue of other types of securities. Very remarkable changes have taken place in Yugoslavia in the structure of securities since the end of 1988, following the legislative measures restricting the use of promissory notes, providing for organizational transformation of enterprises, and changes in NBY monetary policy (see figure 9.1).

In particular, there was a remarkable increase in the relative share of NBY treasury bills in all securities bought by banks – from only 8.6 per cent in 1988, to 78.9 per cent in 1990. An increase in the relative share of bonds was also registered (from 1.7 per cent in 1988 to 12.5 per cent in 1990), together with a decline of the share of promissory notes (from 42.8 per cent to only 4.1 per cent) and of other securities (from 47 per cent to 4.5 per cent) in the two years respectively. Nevertheless, the Federal Commission for Securities authorized only fifty-one issues of bonds and shares in 1990, these to a total nominal value of 3.9 billion Dinars; two enterprises and twenty-eight banks received permission to issue shares, and twenty enterprises and one bank to issue bonds, most of these organizations being Slovenian (*Poslovni svijet*, 21 March 1991, p. 16).

New property types and enterprise forms. There is also evidence on the diversification of both property types and legal forms of enterprises, following adoption of the Law on Enterprises in December 1988. In 1989, concomitant with an increase in the number of bankruptcies (see chapter 6), there was a fivefold increase in the number of newly-established firms as compared to 1988, most of which are likely to be in the private sector (see table 6A.3, appendix to chapter 6). Property restructuring has been even more intense in 1990: in June 1990, there were 26,000 registered private firms; by 30 September 1990 their number had increased to over 50,000, and by December 1990 to almost

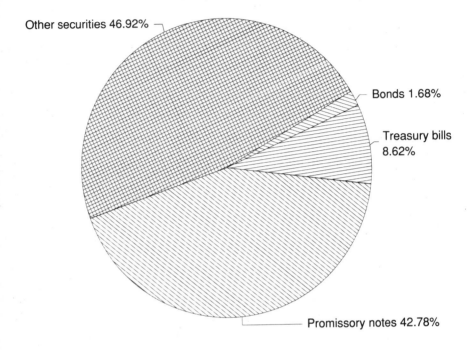

Other securities 46.92%

Bonds 1.68%

Treasury bills 8.62%

Promissory notes 42.78%

Figure 9.1a Securities in Yugoslavia bought by banks, by type, 1988

78,000. Out of 77,461 enterprises registered by December 1990, a large majority (78 per cent) were in private ownership (see table 9.2).

Too much significance should not be attributed to the above figures, however, as they suggest little about the actual role of the private sector in the Yugoslav economy. Many of the newly registered firms in the private or mixed property sectors are either very small, or have not yet started operating. Indeed, according to SDK data, of nearly 40,000 private firms registered by September 1990, only 16,490 (or 41 per cent) had actually started operating, and the share of private sector firms in the total revenue of the productive sectors of the economy was only 2.4 per cent (*Ekonomska politika* no. 2030, 25 February 1991). Thus the contribution of the social sector to GMP is still unlikely to be less than 80 per cent.

Inflow of foreign capital. In 1989, 578 foreign investment contracts were approved, which compares with a total of 371 for the whole

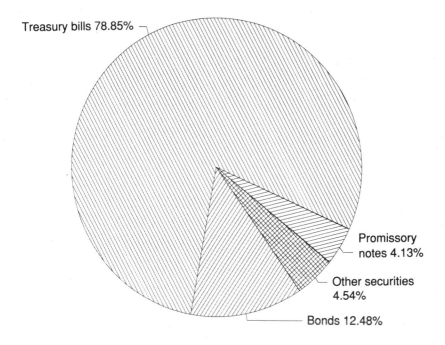

Figure 9.1b Securities in Yugoslavia bought by banks, by type, 1990

twenty-year period (1968–88) since joint ventures were first permitted.[33] The growth in the number of contracts concluded with foreign
partners was even more pronounced in 1990: between 1 January and
30 November, 2,588 contracts were concluded, with a total value of
almost DM 2 million.[34] Foreign investment has mainly been concen-
trated in the more developed republics (Slovenia, Croatia and Serbia).

Privatization of banks. Leading Yugoslav banks have been transformed into joint stock or limited liability banks, in which voting rights
of owners ought to be proportional to the amount of capital they have
contributed. However, the privatization of banks involves a number of
problems which have not yet been resolved. Since Yugoslav banks used
to be non-profit 'service' institutions, controlled by member enterprises
of which today many are loss-makers, the problem of the banking
sector's huge losses (in 1991 estimated to be around $13 billion, plus
bank exposure through guarantees) must first be resolved. A solution is

Table 9.2. *Yugoslav enterprises by property type and legal form, registered under the Law on Enterprises by December 1990*

	Number	Share in per cent
By property type		
TOTAL	77,461	100.0
Private	60,553	78.2
Social	13,370	17.2
Cooperative	2,002	2.6
Mixed	1,536	2.0
By legal form		
TOTAL	77,461	100.0
Private firms	38,069	49.2
Limited liability companies	23,602	30.5
Social firms	11,056	14.3
Cooperatives	1,967	2.5
Public companies	728	0.9
Complex organizations	501	0.7
Joint-stock companies	762	1.0
Contractual organizations	225	0.3
Financial firms	118	0.0
Enterprises for disabled persons	88	0.1
Other	345	0.4

Note: The first and second part of the table are not directly comparable because of overlapping categories.
Source: Calculated from SZS, *SGJ 1991*, table 103–1.

being sought in terms of debt-for-equity swaps and by finding additional capital in order to implement a general programme of financial restructuring. However, the proposal, made by the Yugoslav government in January 1991, to implement the programme through a series of federal measures has encountered resistance. Some republican governments are not willing to help cover the losses of other republics, and do not accept other changes which would accompany the federal programme, aimed at decreasing the autonomy of republican governments in the field of monetary policy.

Stock exchanges. Stock exchanges have officially been opened in Ljubljana, Zagreb, Belgrade, and Sarajevo, but the Zagreb and Sarajevo stock exchanges have not yet started operating. On the Belgrade stock exchange, operations are limited mainly to NBY treasury bills. The Ljubljana stock exchange is the most developed, as in 1990 a variety of securities were quoted, and a secondary market for securities is currently being set up. Even in Slovenia, however, the stock exchange 'boom' is a very recent phenomenon; in October 1990, only one enterprise was quoted on its stock exchange (Grad, a computer manufacturer in Ljubljana).

10 Specific features of the Yugoslav transition

Following the revolutionary political changes of 1989 in Eastern Europe, which have introduced multiparty democracies after decades of communist rule, all former socialist countries are currently in the process of implementing stabilization programmes and radical economic reforms as part of the transition from socialist to mixed market economies. As a result of these developments, these countries are today frequently referred to as the 'transitional economies' of Central and Eastern Europe. In some countries, such as Hungary and Poland, earlier reforms had already led to important institutional changes; in others, such as Czechoslovakia, Bulgaria and Romania, fundamental reforms started only in 1990–91.

The current aims of these formerly centrally planned economies are manifold (see Nuti 1991). The first objective is stabilization, i.e. the achievement of uniform market-clearing prices in non-hyperinflationary or excessively inflationary conditions, without distortionary subsidies and taxes, for a degree of domestic absorption consistent with the eventual service of external debt. The second, equally important, task is restructuring, i.e. the redeployment and development of productive capacity in order to adjust to domestic and international demand, which requires deindustrialization, demonopolization, extensive scrapping of inappropriate capacity, labour redundancies and the redeployment of labour, and the financial restructuring of enterprises. Finally, the most complex objective is that of implementing economic reforms required for the transition from a socialist to a mixed market economy. In contrast to political reforms, which can be implemented fairly quickly once a political consensus has been reached, and with stabilization, which can be achieved almost overnight, economic reforms (such as privatization) will require considerably more time and effort. New legislation in practically all fields needs to be elaborated, alongside the setting up of completely new institutions, changes in economic policies and other important adjustments geared to the needs of a market environment.

Yugoslavia is also in a process of transition towards a mixed market economy. Although Yugoslavia's 'transition' could be said to have started over four decades ago, the present transition is fundamentally different, for politically, Yugoslavia has also opted for a multiparty democratic system. Political reforms ought to eliminate the influence of those socialist ideological dogmas – which have for years represented a barrier to the introduction of many market-oriented policy instruments and institutions – thus facilitating the implementation of the truly radical economic reforms necessary for the creation of a mixed market economy (as is in part already evidenced by the economic reforms in course).

Whereas Yugoslavia today is pursuing objectives similar to those of the other transitional economies – stabilization, restructuring, and reform – in comparison with these countries the transition process in Yugoslavia is being both facilitated and hindered by specific factors. These features of the Yugoslav transition will now be discussed.

Yugoslavia's advantages

The most important factor facilitating the transition towards a market economy in Yugoslavia is a shorter reform agenda. Yugoslavia has had considerable experience of market-oriented reforms, and has already implemented many institutional changes which are only today being undertaken in several other transitional economies. The other two potential advantages of Yugoslavia with respect to other former socialist countries, although much more limited in scope, have emerged as a by-product of institutional changes introduced in the past. Economic reforms have required changes in economic policies, as the emergence of new problems which were non-existent in the centrally planned economy, required greater reliance on market-type instruments of regulation. At the same time, market-oriented reforms and accompanying policies have also involved some economic restructuring, although only in certain fields and limited in extent; hence in the present phase, the Yugoslav economy will require somewhat smaller-scale restructuring.

Shorter reform agenda

All past economic reforms in Yugoslavia – and in particular those in the fields of planning, prices, finance, and foreign trade – have had important implications for the functioning of the Yugoslav economy.[1]

The determination to abandon the system of centralized planning and decision-making led to the introduction of self-management at the enterprise level, parallel with the gradual devolution of powers from federal to republican and local political authorities. Supplemented as it was by self-management mechanisms of policy coordination in the 1970s, the decentralized system of planning gave more scope to enterprise decisions, thus permitting the active participation of economic agents in the overall planning process. The most recent changes introduced in 1988 have further reduced the role of planning: annual plans have been abolished; planning is no longer obligatory for a large number of organizations; and the Federal Institute of Economic Planning has been merged with the Federal Institute of Development. At the same time, the role of self-management is also being reduced through current changes in the property regime.

Price reforms and price liberalization have permitted the gradual activation of markets for many goods and services in Yugoslavia. Together with greater exposure to international prices since the mid-1960s, such changes have led to a more realistic and more flexible domestic price structure, and the elimination of many shortages.

Financial reforms have separated central banking from commercial banking, have ensured greater reliance on enterprise and bank sources of finance instead of budgetary grants, and have led to the development and diversification of financial intermediation, including both standard instruments and those adapted to the Yugoslav self-management system (different forms of 'pooling of labour and resources').

Foreign trade reforms have abolished state monopoly of foreign trade, introduced a uniform exchange rate, reduced foreign trade restrictions, and already in 1967 had created the institutional framework for the inflow of foreign capital. Further decentralization was undertaken especially after 1977, when foreign trade responsibilities were transferred to the republican governments and exporting enterprises were provided with major incentives. In the mid-1980s, a foreign exchange market was set up, organized by authorized banks in charge of purchasing and reallocating foreign currency to enterprises, together with the further liberalization of imports.

As a result of foreign trade reforms, with respect to other socialist economies Yugoslavia has been more open to the West and more highly integrated into world markets. This was reinforced by important changes in Yugoslavia's international economic relations, for after the split from the Eastern bloc in 1948, closer links with Western institutions (IMF, OECD, World Bank, EC) were established. Yugoslavia's general orientation towards Western markets has ensured a higher relative proportion of convertible currency transactions, and has reduced the problems of dual dependency on trade with both CMEA countries and the West, typical of other former socialist economies. In 1990, 63.6 per cent of Yugoslav imports and 59.8 per cent of exports represented trade with OECD countries, as compared to 24.2 per cent of imports and 28.5 per cent of exports resulting from trade with socialist countries (the balance being trade with developing countries).[2] The emphasis on convertible currency transactions has also brought about a less pronounced discrepancy between the official and the black market exchange rates than in other socialist countries, which has also been facilitated by tourism and workers' remittances from abroad, and by major access to international financial markets.

Longer experience with market-based policies

Yugoslavia has also had longer experience in the use of market-type instruments of macroeconomic regulation. Although in the past such policies were limited mainly to exchange rate adjustments and some anti-inflationary measures, since 1981 a number of new instruments of macroeconomic regulation have been applied by the Yugoslav authorities.

In the field of monetary policy, standard instruments of monetary regulation have been used in recent years by the NBY, including an active interest rate policy with the intention of abandoning negative real interest rates which in the past had permitted the redistribution of resources from households to enterprises; the use of the discount rate as an instrument of monetary control; and more frequent open-market operations. At the same time, many selective instruments typical of centrally planned economies, such as privileged credits for financing priority sectors, have been abolished.

The Yugoslav government has also led an active exchange rate policy throughout the 1980s, a policy which initially consisted of several devaluations and later, from 1983, in daily adjustments to a basket of foreign currencies. This facilitated the turnaround from a chronic current account deficit in convertible currency transactions, to a surplus from 1983 onwards.

In the field of price policies, following the limited effects of several price freezes in the first half of the 1980s, the acceptance of open instead of repressed inflation, while progressively leading the economy into hyperinflation, has nevertheless contributed to the elimination of certain problems typical of centrally planned economies. The liberalization of prices, alongside substantial drops in real wages, has contributed to the avoidance of a monetary overhang; and free prices in combination with substantial import liberalization have also facilitated the reduction of shortages.

Although the results of stabilization policies implemented throughout the 1980s have been disappointing, they have implied, in some fields, a radical change in macroeconomic management, thus contributing to the elimination of some of the systemic problems and distortions still typical today of Soviet-type economies. The experience gained in macroeconomic regulation has also facilitated more recent stabilization attempts. Thus the 'shock therapy' applied in January–June 1990 brought annual inflation down from over 1,200 per cent in 1989 to 588 per cent in 1990; it has introduced resident convertibility, facilitated by substantial foreign exchange reserves; and it has brought about a relatively smaller fall in industrial production (10 per cent in 1990) than in some other transitional economies (e.g. Poland, GDR). These positive results of the 1990 stabilization programme could have rendered present reform measures easier to implement (see Nuti 1991), had Marković's policies not lost their initial credibility in the mean time (see below).

Smaller-scale restructuring

In some fields, the Yugoslav economy will require smaller-scale restructuring. While the other former centrally planned economies are moving from over-full employment to unemployment, since the mid-1960s Yugoslavia has experienced unemployment and redeployment of labour. Although much surplus and redundant labour will still have to be released from loss-making enterprises, the process is likely to be more gradual than in other transitional economies, which until 1989 had no unemployment and indeed were characterized by chronic labour shortages (i.e. overemployment). The process of financial restructuring has also gone one step further than in other transitional economies, as in Yugoslavia there has been a larger number of bankruptcies (a total of 141 firms over the 1986–9 period), while their number in 1990 is likely to be much higher.

These advantages deriving from past reforms, economic policies applied, and some economic restructuring, suggest that the transition to a mixed market economy may be less time-consuming in Yugoslavia than in other transitional economies. The institutional and policy changes gradually introduced in Yugoslavia have effectively meant a departure from the centrally planned model in several important respects. Most importantly, however imperfect and limited in extent, in Yugoslavia today the market exists; in most other transitional economies, it will have to be built *ex nuovo*.

Yugoslavia's disadvantages

In spite of the advantages of Yugoslavia with respect to other former socialist economies, there are also a number of disadvantages which might hamper the transition process. In comparison with other Central and East European countries, the transition in Yugoslavia is being hindered by several factors: the severe political crisis, problems deriving from undefined property rights, existing features of the banking system, labour market imperfections, and unique factors determining resistance to change. Although some of these problems are similar to those encountered in other transitional economies, in the Yugoslav case they have taken on specific dimensions.

Political crisis

The credibility of federal economic policies has been substantially reduced by the present serious political crisis, characterized by continuous conflicts between the constituent parts of the Yugoslav federation, rising nationalism, moves towards republican independence – including the adoption of laws not in conformity with federal legislation, and the imposition of trade tariffs between republics[3] – and ongoing disputes over how to find a compromise between Serbian demands to preserve the federation and the attempts of other republics to institute a loose confederation or even independent states.[4] The successful implementation of the January–June 1990 stabilization programme suggested that until mid-1990 increasing regional conflicts were not a serious barrier to effective realization of federal policies, but since then the political situation has progressively deteriorated.

Given that the devolution of power to the single republics had resulted in a continuous weakening of federal control over economic policies, in January 1991 the Yugoslav Prime Minister proposed that a minimum number of state functions must be performed at the federal level if Yugoslavia is to remain united.[5] Although each of the republics had initially agreed on most of these points (lack of consensus remained concerning the financing of the Yugoslav Army, financial restructuring of banks, and social security programmes), the 'dissociation' – in February 1991 – of Slovenia and Croatia from the Yugoslav federation raised doubts about whether Marković's proposals could be implemented effectively. Moreover, with the general political atmosphere further deteriorating in the second half of 1991, as a result of the ongoing civil war and the re-emergence of the historic Serb/Croat nationalist problem in its most extreme form, the highest priority has been given to political rather than economic issues. The full independence of Slovenia and Croatia has introduced the risk of other republics following their example. Thus today, the future of Yugoslavia as a state is highly uncertain, involving a number of very delicate issues. While finding a solution for a united Yugoslavia may seem impossible, it is even more difficult to envisage its disintegration being acceptable to all republics.

Undefined property rights

While the current ownership status of firms in several transitional countries is controversial (see Portes 1990; Grosfeld 1990), the situation in Yugoslavia is even more confused. Consequently today the state, enterprises and workers all feel they have certain claims to ownership rights of enterprise assets. The delineation of property rights, as provided for by the privatization programme, may not be welcomed by various social groups. The conversion of self-management into property rights which will result from privatization is bound to reduce workers' decision-making power to the level of codetermination. For managers, private property rights will imply their being subject to direct control by shareholders, and hence with reduced security in their present positions. For republican governments, privatization will imply their being forced to give up long-established implicit property rights. However, since a number of enterprises have already started privatization on their own initiative, the main obstacle to privatization in Yugoslavia does not seem to be self-management, but other factors, primarily the fear of republican governments that they will lose their previous position of tutelage over the economy. Such fear is evidenced by the present strong tendency of the governments in several republics to nationalize large parts of the economy, and by their reluctance to implement the federal privatization programme.

The problem of undefined property rights in an atmosphere of high uncertainty, increasing nationalist conflict, and growing disintegrating tendencies, has also led to several cases of 'wild' de-mergers of subsidiaries located in Serbia from their parent companies in Croatia. These subsidiaries have subsequently been set up as new firms under different names, while the parent enterprises have in no way been compensated.[6] This process may extend to other regions, and hence risks leading to even greater disintegration and higher levels of local and regional autarky (something which was already becoming increasingly pronounced during the 1980s, with a marked decline in inter-republican trade).

Specific features of the banking system

Since Yugoslav banks were until recently directly controlled by member enterprises, including loss-making firms, the present problem of huge losses of the banking system is essentially a problem of uncovered losses of enterprise founders unable to fulfil their obligations. The crucial problem is to find new (viable) shareholders for banks. Since this problem has not yet been resolved, in spite of the fact that reforms have been announced, the actual behaviour has for the moment not changed much and continues to be characterized by monetary indiscipline. The existing banking system is directly facilitating the presence of 'soft' budget constraints in Yugoslavia.

Labour market imperfections

In the traditional centrally planned economy, even at the peak of Stalinism, the labour market has continued to function, in that relative wages, somehow or other, had to be adjusted to relative demand for and supply of skills. In Yugoslavia, however, due to different wage regulations in the single republics, and firm-specific income-shares linked to realized profits, there are no single wage rates for equivalent occupations, and labour incomes differ very considerably across enterprises, sectors, and regions (see Estrin 1983).[7] Labour income unification is therefore a further hurdle in reform implementation.

Resistance to change

Several elements which are specific to Yugoslavia seem to cause a greater resistance to change than in other transitional economies. Among the population, apart from social security and other benefits provided in all socialist countries, Yugoslavs have enjoyed major civil liberties (for example, freedom to travel abroad since the mid-1960s), which together with economic democracy through self-management seems to have caused a higher degree of popular support for the existing regime. At the policy level there is resistance to change, deriving from a higher level of consciousness of what the market may bring (Yugoslavia having experienced inflation, unemployment, income disparities and balance of payments difficulties for over a quarter of a century). These factors may in part explain why, with respect to other former socialist countries, political reforms in Yugoslavia have been implemented with a certain delay, and why multiparty elections in some republics (Serbia and Montenegro) have led to the restoration of communist power.

Main lessons to be learnt from the Yugoslav experience

Specific factors which today hinder the transition process in Yugoslavia are, paradoxically, the direct result of reforms undertaken in the past. At the same time, most of these reforms were fully in line with systemic changes needed for the introduction of a market-oriented system. Why have they not produced the desired results?

The main reason is that all past reforms were partial. The commitment to socialist ideology implied the maintenance of non-private property as the dominant form of ownership, of planning as an instrument for fulfilling broader social goals and needs, and of principles of solidarity and egalitarianism pursued through mechanisms of income redistribution. Such a commitment has effectively impeded substantial reform in many important fields, and has therefore resulted in the reproduction of practices typical of centrally planned economies.

Central planning was not replaced by an efficient system of overall macroeconomic management. Markets were allowed to operate only for goods and services, but not for production factors, since both a capital and a labour market were rejected on ideological grounds. But even in the field of product markets, prices were never completely free, for a complex system of controls was retained until 1989. Moreover, certain prices (for example of energy, raw materials, other intermediate goods, housing, transport) were kept at artificially low levels. This in turn required subsidies and income redistribution in favour of some sectors at the expense of other, thus introducing severe distortions in relative prices. Financial reforms have not assigned the banking system the role of an independent financial intermediary, and have not separated fiscal from monetary instruments – thus failing to abolish the practice of new money creation in order to accommodate deficits of the state budget, of enterprises, of commercial banks and of other institutions. In the field of foreign trade, until 1989 the economy continued to be sheltered from international competition through substantial import restrictions. The exchange rate was continuously overvalued, and the Dinar never succeeded in becoming fully convertible.

Furthermore, although the institution of social property could have implied the redistribution of property rights in favour of enterprises *vis-à-vis* the state, since the political authorities continued to be responsible for a number of fundamental issues, it was the state that was the effective owner of enterprise assets. Consequently, at the enterprise level, although self-management introduced important aspects of economic democracy – workers' participation in both decision-making and enterprise results – the primacy of social objectives and priorities implied continuous interference by local political structures in enterprise affairs, both through direct instruments (regulations concerning prices, the distribution of income, personal incomes, etc.), and indirect channels of influence (pressure from local socio-political communities concerning enterprise employment, investment and other policies). Thus enterprise autonomy and workers' self-management was effectively limited in many important fields.

At the root of these problems lay the most important missing element of past reforms in Yugoslavia – namely, the breaking down of the tutelage system. Along with reforms aimed at liberalization, decentralization and increasing reliance on the market, the state ought to have assumed a fundamentally different role, away from protection of enterprises, towards overall coordination and control; instead of *ad hoc*, unpredictable and highly selective instruments, it ought to have used indirect and generalized measures of regulation; instead of socialization of losses through redistribution, it ought to have used standard Western-type monetary, fiscal, and wage policies. The state ought to have limited its functions to those normally performed in a market economy, thus allowing enterprises to become independent economic agents bearing the full consequences of their decisions. Socialist goals could also have been pursued through such policies, while the gains in economic efficiency would probably have been substantial.

Therefore, the main lesson to be learnt from the Yugoslav experience is that one of the necessary conditions for the success of reforms in a socialist economy is the willingness to abandon the tutelage system and all of its implications. Some argue that tutelage is also present in economies based on private property; but in the socialist economic system it has particularly negative implications because it is generally and continuously applied to the whole economy (and not only to specific cases), which clearly hampers a major operation of the market.

The change in the target model evidenced by the official sanctioning of private property, the abolition of the Communist Party's political monopoly and the institution of multiparty democracy may not be sufficient, at least in the short run, to eradicate the tutelage system. This seems to be confirmed both by the Yugoslav experience – where the 1988 change in the target model has not yet produced a fundamental change in the existing regime – and by that of several other former socialist countries (for example, Poland and Hungary). The Yugoslav stabilization programme for the second half of 1990 failed to succeed not only because of problems linked to regional devolution, but because of a lack of systemic changes in behaviour at all levels – and primarily the hardening of budget constraints. While 'soft' budget constraints in Yugoslavia (and elsewhere) are the direct consequence of the system of non-private property, the radical change in the official attitude towards private property has not automatically eliminated tutelage relationships, but in certain respects has actually reinforced them.

In conclusion, systemic features inherited from the Soviet-type model render the Yugoslav economy much more similar to other former socialist economies than is usually assumed. The ultimate objectives of the transition process in Yugoslavia are similar to those of other former socialist economies, aimed at improving economic performance and efficiency and achieving sustained economic growth; similar too are the main tasks to be performed, the necessary directions of change and the problems arising during transition. In addition to the most important task of abolishing the tutelage system as the major institutional constraint limiting progress towards a market environment (Portes 1990), among the other necessary tasks common to all former socialist economies are the activation of stock exchange markets, substantial fiscal and budgetary reforms, capacity restructuring and demonopolization, financial restructuring, and full convertibility of currencies (see Nuti 1991).

Significant institutional and structural changes are therefore still needed in all transitional economies in order to transform them into mixed market economies. In the Yugoslav case, the incompleteness of the changes is due not so much to uncertainties about the target model, but to the sheer complexity of the task involved. This suggests that the completion of reforms in Yugoslavia and perhaps elsewhere will be a time-consuming and therefore gradual process. A change in the target model cannot immediately produce a fundamental change of regime.

11 An overview of conclusions

Since the early 1950s Yugoslavia has been trying to develop its own model of socialism, based on workers' self-management, extensive decentralization, social property, and an increasing use of the market mechanism. This model of self-managed market socialism has been pursued through continuous economic reforms, effectively entailing a departure from the traditional centrally planned economy in many important respects. This book has tried to illustrate how, despite all the reforms, some of the aspects of the Yugoslav economy have remained essentially unchanged with respect to the pre-self-management period, and very similar to those in other former socialist economies. The specific field of investment was chosen for illustration, for it is probably the most important area where reforms have not led to substantial changes in enterprise behaviour.

Since Yugoslavia has usually been regarded as being both a socialist and a self-managed market economy, two theoretical frameworks were considered in order to explain investment behaviour of the Yugoslav-type enterprise: one which places emphasis on self-management, and another which focuses on the distinctive features of the socialist economic system.

According to the dominant theory of the investment behaviour of the LMF – developed by Vanek, Furubotn, and Pejovich – the LMF will be less willing to invest in capital assets from retained earnings than its capitalist counterpart, for reasons connected with collective ownership of capital. Limited property rights are expected to result in a specific problem of the LMF, since workers cannot sell their jobs and future income streams, but can benefit from undertaken investment only for the duration of their employment within the given firm. Consequently, the LMF will adopt a 'truncated' time horizon, and will therefore invest less than a capitalist firm operating under similar conditions.

The underinvestment argument is weakened, however, if additional

210

factors are taken into account, as suggested by further developments of the theory. The conclusion on underinvestment cannot be generalized, for it is necessary to take into account the concrete institutional setting in which an LMF operates. In the case of Yugoslavia, this implies that the socialist characteristics of the economy need to be examined. Kornai's theory on the socialist economic system was therefore considered, which asserts the presence of systemic features in all socialist economies, these being likely to remain even after reforms aimed at introducing a more market-oriented system are implemented. Among the most important characteristics of the socialist economy are the paternalistic relationship between the state and the firm (or state tutelage); investment hunger and overinvestment drive; 'soft' budget constraints and the socialization of losses as an alternative to bankruptcies; and non-market allocation of investment resources. Kornai's theory was applied to Yugoslavia and the hypothesis advanced that, in essence, the investment process in Yugoslavia has remained very similar to that described by Kornai for socialist countries in general.

Despite major differences between the two theories – primarily in the assumed institutional framework and predictions on investment behaviour – they nevertheless have one element in common: they both consider, explicitly (Furubotn and Pejovich) or implicitly (Kornai), the negative implications of limited property rights.

Empirical evidence from Yugoslavia revealed that relatively high investment rates were maintained for most of the period after 1965. Until 1980, the Yugoslav economy was characterized by an overinvestment, rather than an underinvestment drive. Yugoslav enterprises' savings were positive and not exceptionally low, and firms financed a relatively large portion of their fixed investment from retained earnings. Nevertheless, such evidence cannot be taken as refuting the LMF theory, since the theory is based on the assumption that firms are fully free to make their own policy decisions – whereas in Yugoslavia, throughout the period, a series of external regulations substantially reduced enterprise autonomy and directly or indirectly imposed a minimum savings constraint. At the same time, the evidence does confirm one of Kornai's principal hypotheses, namely that the state retained substantial influence over enterprise decisions in Yugoslavia.

The analysis has also shown that the variables considered crucial in Furubotn and Pejovich's theory – in particular interest and lending rates – have had a limited role in determining savings and investment in Yugoslavia. The theory places all its emphasis on limited property rights, but alongside an implicit assumption that the LMF operates in a market environment. As a consequence, it disregards all the other (socialist) features of the Yugoslav economy which have played an important role in stimulating investment, such as severe capital market distortions, the underpricing of capital through negative real lending rates and capital rationing, the redistribution of income from the household to the enterprise sector, inadequate fiscal policies, and limited mobility of labour due to employment security. Therefore, Furubotn and Pejovich's theory is not really applicable to Yugoslavia.

In contrast, the evidence strongly supports the most important hypotheses advanced by Kornai for socialist economies in general. In line with Kornai's theory, the investment process in Yugoslavia continued to be characterized by capital allocation according to non-market criteria, by lack of financial discipline and the use of bankruptcy only as a last resort; by the socialization of losses and other symptoms of 'soft' budget constraints; and by frequent state intervention in current enterprise policies. Econometric tests of the two theories led to similar conclusions, namely that Kornai's theory finds greater support in Yugoslavia than Furubotn and Pejovich's theory. The main implication of the analysis is that despite decentralization, self-management and increasing use of the market after 1965, the nature of the Yugoslav system has essentially remained socialist.

This does not mean that Yugoslav policy-makers failed to attempt more radical reforms in the sphere of investment, away from the traditional socialist model. During the 1970s a number of new financial instruments were introduced with the aim of increasing investment incentives and efficiency. But in spite of intentions, financial innovation failed to create built-in incentives that were necessary for the development of a market-oriented system in which enterprises would make autonomous investment decisions primarily according to market criteria. Among the reasons for the failure of investment reforms was the inadequacy of the banking system, the absence of a secondary market for securities, and unstimulative legislation; but the most important missing element was the willingness to allow individual enterprises to operate as autonomous economic agents, by breaking up the state tutelage system. This was never possible in Yugoslavia, because of the essentially unchanged property regime.

Property became the central issue in Yugoslav economic reforms only at the end of 1988, when a change took place in the target model. Policies adopted since then – most importantly, the federal privatization programme – envisage a fundamental change in the property regime, along with a gradual suppression of self-management.

Although the federal programme has encountered difficulties in its implementation – substantial delays having been caused by the elaboration of separate republican privatization laws – property restructuring in Yugoslavia has nevertheless begun, implying certain irreversible changes which are likely to have important long-term implications.

Today, Yugoslavia is pursuing objectives similar to those of other former socialist countries, all of which are in the process of transition from a socialist to a mixed market economy, during which three main objectives ought to be realized: stabilization, restructuring, and reform. As compared to the other former socialist economies, Yugoslavia is both facilitated and hindered by specific factors. The main element facilitating Yugoslavia's transition is a shorter reform agenda, for many important institutional changes which are being undertaken in other former socialist countries only today, have already been implemented. Among the specific features hindering transition in Yugoslavia, the most serious is the political crisis regarding the future of the Yugoslav state, aggravated by the on-going civil war, as no solution acceptable to both Serbia and Croatia seems possible at the moment.

The main lesson to be learnt from the Yugoslav experience is that partial reforms of a socialist economy cannot improve the system and may in many respects be counterproductive. Because of the commitment to non-private property, planning, solidarity and other socialist values in Yugoslavia, many features of the traditional socialist economy have in fact remained, thus reproducing problems typical of the centrally planned economy of lack of economic efficiency, entrepreneurship, incentives, and discipline. Most importantly for the Yugoslav economy has been the continued subjection to state tutelage, for enterprises were not freed from external political interference. Self-management was never fully realized, for it remained subordinated to other socialist goals. The fundamental causes of the current economic crisis in Yugoslavia are therefore to be found in systemic features of socialist economies in general, rather than the specific characteristic – self-management – of the Yugoslav economy. This implies that a realistic assessment of the self-management model cannot yet be made – not even through the Yugoslav experience – since such a system has effectively never been fully implemented.

It may seem unfair to ascribe all the inefficiencies of the Yugoslav economy to socialist ideology. It has frequently been argued that some problems in Yugoslavia – such as the capital-intensive bias in investment, or extreme regionalization and fragmentation of the economy brought about by extensive decentralization – are directly attributable to self-management. Both of these (and many other) problems could have been avoided through more market-based policies – in the field of capital mobilization and allocation, taxation, firm entry and exit, foreign competition. Instead, Yugoslav policies continued to be very similar to those applied in the traditional socialist economy. Although decentralization of economic policies in Yugoslavia could indeed be interpreted as an extension of self-management to the macroeconomic level, it does not necessarily derive from self-management *per se*, since problems linked to regional devolution are today very much present in other socialist countries – for instance in the USSR and Czechoslovakia – which until 1989 had no self-management.

In spite of our main conclusion – that self-management never really had a chance of being fully implemented in Yugoslavia because of the unwillingness of the political authorities to surrender their power to the workers – self-management has nevertheless played an important role, if not for the immediate and direct consequences, for the longer-term implications. The idea of self-management could be seen as having had the function of a reformist ideal, similar to that of the social-democratic ideals in Western economies which have progressively modified and enabled a moving away from the model of unrestrained crude capitalism. In Yugoslavia, if it had not been for the decision to introduce self-management in the early 1950s, which effectively initiated (and thus facilitated) a long process of economic reforms, many institutional changes would probably not have been introduced, at least not at an early stage. In turn, such reforms have brought about a higher level of general well being to Yugoslavs as compared to citizens of other socialist countries. Notwithstanding some statistics which suggest lower GNP per capita in Yugoslavia than in several other socialist countries, Yugoslavs were for years effectively better off than other East Europeans. Economically, they lived better because the Yugoslav market was not characterized by systematic and persistent shortages, and for those products which were not available on the domestic market, they could travel abroad freely in order to buy them, using foreign currency which they could keep in private bank accounts. Politically, in spite of communist one-party rule, a decentralized political system led to more democratic procedures; political repression was less pronounced than in many other socialist countries; and whoever did not approve of the regime, was free to leave the country and live elsewhere. Finally, Yugoslavs worked in an environment which was at least apparently more democratic than in other socialist countries, because self-management, despite all its limitations, for many years did give workers the feeling that they could participate both in decision-making and in enterprise profits.

Today, both forms of participation are in retreat in Yugoslavia, whereas in many Western countries such participation has been increasing.[1] The question arises as to whether the shift of the target model from the improvement of the self-management model to a straight capitalist economy, possibly tempered by elements of the mixed economy and of the welfare state, was the only or the best course of action for Yugoslav reformers. This is a question of counterfactual and conjectural history which goes beyond the scope of this book. Until the late 1980s and especially until the general East European revolutions of 1989, it might have been possible for an alternative 'third way' to have been explored and constructed, which might have retained and developed the specific Yugoslav features of self-determination and participation. Today, for better or worse, it is too late.

Notes

1 The Yugoslav road towards market socialism

1 For a more detailed analysis, see in particular Dubey (ed.) (1975); Schrenk *et al.* (1979); Horvat (1970); Tyson (1980); Lydall (1984) and (1989); Estrin (1983); and OECD *Economic Surveys – Yugoslavia*, various issues.

2 Yugoslavia is a federal state composed of six republics (Bosnia and Herzegovina, Croatia, Macedonia, Montenegro, Serbia, and Slovenia), and two autonomous regions (Voivodina and Kosovo) within Serbia.

3 Already in 1954, 73 per cent of the total revenue of local and republican governments was derived from their own resources (Dubey (ed.) 1975, p. 35).

4 The economic problems will be discussed later; the political and social problems primarily concerned a series of nationalistic conflicts, which culminated in 1971 with the replacement of a number of leading politicians in Croatia and Serbia.

5 The reform started with a series of constitutional amendments adopted in 1971. In 1974, a new constitution was adopted, followed by other new legal documents among which the most important was the 1976 Associated Labour Act.

6 Socio-political communities are organized on a territorial basis and are established at the federal, republican/regional, and local communal levels.

7 GMP is the value added at market prices of the 'productive' sectors of the economy, thus excluding certain 'non-productive' sectors such as education, health, defence, banking, and other services. In this sense, it is similar to the concept of net material product applied in other socialist countries, but differs from such a concept because it is gross of depreciation.

8 OECD (1990), p. 19; domestic labour force is the economically active population in Yugoslavia (excluding workers temporarily employed abroad, which in 1989 numbered around 800,000).

9 Frequent switches from a system of relatively free prices to price freezes stimulated inflationary expectations, thus inducing enterprises to increase prices to levels which were higher than justified; incomes controls and

freezes had a similar effect. The objective of implementing positive real interest rates was also occasionally abandoned, as in 1985, since high interest rates were thought one of the main causes of inflation.

10 The more-developed republics, which are also the major exporters, felt negatively affected by the fixed exchange rate; the less-developed republics primarily by monetary restrictions.

11 However, even before these deviations, higher money wages than originally stipulated led to less restrictive monetary policy, to accommodate wage increases.

12 The monthly rate of inflation (retail prices) was 7.1 per cent in September and 8.1 per cent in October, and somewhat more contained in November and December 1990.

13 Calculated at the exchange rate at the end of December 1990, the trade deficit for 1990 was $4,563 million (as reported in *Ekonomska Politika* no. 2027, 4 February 1991, p. 25).

14 The new economic reform was presented in the extensive 'Long-term economic stabilization programme' consisting of seventeen separate documents; see Komisija saveznih društvenih saveta . . . (1982).

15 Kosovo has historically represented the 'heart' of Serbia, but today the large majority (over 90 per cent) of its population is ethnically Albanian.

2 The investment theory of the labour-managed firm

1 For a survey of the theoretical and empirical literature, see Bartlett and Uvalić (1986) or Bonin and Putterman (1987).

2 Of course, decision-makers in both types of firms are in reality subject to a number of other considerations, such as size, growth, status, security, political influence, and so on, but there is agreement among scholars that capitalist profits and LMF income per worker are the primary concerns.

3 It is interesting to note that some of these problems were anticipated by a Yugoslav economist – R. Uvalić (1954) – in the early 1950s, immediately after self-management had been introduced.

4 The difference between the required rates of return becomes negligible only for a fairly long time horizon; for example, assuming the principal invested is 1, for a one-year time horizon the rate of return from investment in non-owned assets, equivalent to a 5 per cent rate of interest on owned assets, will be 105 per cent, whereas for a twenty-year time horizon it will only be 8 per cent (see Sacks 1983, p. 79).

3 Extensions of the LMF investment theory

1 Notable exceptions are Zafiris (1982); Rock and Defourny (1983); Bonin (1985).

2 A somewhat different view is held by Bartlett (1986) who regards the CMR not as a disincentive, but as a savings rate constraint (a way of preventing the LMF from consuming its capital). In our view, it is both: whereas the

savings rate constraint is the main reason for imposing a CMR on the Yugoslav LMF, the CMR is also likely to provoke a disincentive to invest.

3 The rule makes the life of the asset infinite in the financial sense; see Stephen (1984).

4 This interpretation is supported by Zafiris' (1982) calculations; at the same time, it is refuted by Stephen (1984, p. 79) who argues that Vanek's under-investment force derives from the CMR. During a conversation with Vanek in Florence in July 1985, he confirmed my belief that he did not refer to the CMR.

5 According to Stephen (1984, p. 79), such an assumption 'assumes away the basic problem'; while according to Zafiris (1982, pp. 56–9) it is 'seriously misleading', because Vanek compares the *annual* returns acquired by the alternative investments – but these are not comparable because they are different in nature: investment in bank deposits, in addition to interest, returns the original capital; while investment in real assets only yields an annual return, and therefore such a return *should* exceed the rate of interest, so as to allow for depreciation.

6 In Furubotn and Pejovich (1973), specific property rights and the CMR are assumed (p. 278), but the conclusion is that 'the pure labour-managed system is an essentially unstable construction' (p. 283); or in Furubotn (1974), the Yugoslav LMF is analysed, but conclusions are generalized: '. . . there is an inherent flaw in the structure of the pure LMF' (p. 284).

7 In French cooperatives, when new assets are purchased members are some-times issued with new shares corresponding to the value of new assets, effectively guaranteeing return of the principal; in Mondragon cooperatives as much as 70 per cent of profits are allocated to individual members' accounts, which are revalued annually and redeemed fully upon retirement (see Estrin and Jones 1987).

8 This is so, for example, in an LMF consisting of a majority of young work-ers who expect to retire after thirty years: assuming that $R=6$ per cent, $A=7.2$ per cent and the differential D is only 1.2 per cent, and therefore A will not be much higher than R (as calculated by Defourny 1983, p. 209).

9 'In what may be regarded the typical case, a majority of workers . . . will not be committed to a seventeen or twenty-year planning horizon' (Furubotn and Pejovich 1973, p. 281); 'In what may be considered the typical case, the bank rate of interest (i) is almost certain to be less than the critical rate of return on non-owned assets (r^*). That is, unless the collective's planning horizon (T) is quite long' (Furubotn 1974, p. 272). The only exception is Furubotn (1980b, p. 801): the author assumes a short time horizon, but notes that 'it is still conceivable that the expected horizon will be substantial (for example $T=20$)'. Additional arguments given for a short time horizon are the preferences of retiring workers; and risk increasing with time, since new voting patterns or revised pay-off policies may be introduced (Furubotn 1974, p. 272; Furubotn 1980b, p. 801). However, these reasons do not seem

sufficient for a short time horizon to be present in an LMF. The majority of workers would have to be about to leave in order for the LMF to have a relatively short time horizon. Of course, it is plausible that older workers (with shorter time horizons) will be the more influential, but this would imply abandoning one of the basic assumptions regarding the LMF, i.e. that each worker has equal voting power. As for the second reason, the author seems to be forgetting that in an LMF, it is the workers themselves who decide these matters.

10 Alternatively, dividends could be credited to a worker's account, on which interest would be paid, and the sum returned should he leave the cooperative (similar to the scheme applied in Mondragon).

11 Unless, as proposed by Nuti (1988b), job tradability is introduced only to ensure a zero price of jobs; if the firm is obliged to hire more people as long as its jobs are demanded at a positive price, job rights would be tradable only to have an automatic check on the enterprise employment policy, but should never be so valuable as to generate active trade. On the issue of tradable workers' shares, see also Sertel (1982), and Schlicht and Von Weizsacker (1977).

12 This is an extension of Meade's (1972) initial proposal of the 'inegalitarian cooperative' where the maximization of returns per worker's share eliminates some of the drawbacks of the LMF, but not the preference of an LMF for external financing of investment. On joining the LMF, each worker is given a share L in the total surplus (S) of the firm; and shares allotted to individual workers differ, among other things, depending on the time a worker has joined the firm. The objective of the LMF will be to maximize the return per share.

13 Meade (1972) himself recognizes this drawback; see also Nuti (1988b).

14 In Yugoslavia, however, such commitment has decreased over time, and today is limited to a minority of enthusiasts.

15 Furubotn himself suggests that under labour management, high labour mobility is ruled out, but criticizes Schlicht and Von Weizsacker's approach, arguing that even if there is absolute commitment, the majority group controlling the firm will still undertake poor investment projects, since as it ages, the firm's effective planning horizon becomes shorter (Furubotn, 1979, pp. 216–29). Furubotn neglects the realistic possibility that, with time, the majority group will be renewed by younger workers, thus prolonging the LMF's time horizon.

16 Among the few exceptions are Furubotn (1979), Bonin (1985), and Conte (1980).

17 Conte (1980) is one of the very few authors that has considered this problem (in spite of the mathematical errors in the article, which Conte himself acknowledges). Conte's article has to a large extent inspired our reflections on the matter.

18 Of course, labour turnover is normally much faster; the analysis applies primarily to Yugoslavia, where labour turnover has been lower than average.

19 See Hirshleifer (1970), Nuti (1987a), Hodder (1986). Recent evidence is reported in Schall *et al.* (1978), who found that in a sample of 189 large US firms, 74 per cent used the pay-off period as an investment criterion.

20 The opportunity cost of capital may be equal to R under the following conditions: if the repayment period of an investment is shorter than the LMF's time horizon; if investment is undertaken from financial assets already committed to the firm, where funds are transferred from one use to another and no change in property takes place (Stephen 1984; Zelić 1975; Connock 1982); or if individually-held shares are introduced (in line with Meade's suggestion).

21 Bonin (1985) similarly argues that the investment decision will not be very different under external financing, since social capital, as the root of the problem, is not eliminated by external financing.

22 For a critique of some of Stephen's conclusions, see Milanović (1983).

23 Quite inconsistently, in Furubotn (1974) and (1976) the author did not apply the CMR to assets purchased by the use of borrowed funds (see Bonin 1985).

24 Similar objections are made by Zafiris (1982) who argues that the advantage of bank credit cannot be a decisive one under the CMR; if loans are ultimately repayable, bank finance also becomes self-finance in the long run. Ireland and Law (1982, p. 49) note that the theory is based on the unrealistic assumptions that banks will allow the principal to be repaid at the same rate as the rate of depreciation, and that bank finance is unlimited.

25 Ireland and Law (1982) propose a utility function which includes membership as well as income; this maximand does not require the maximization of income per worker, since the LMF may be willing to trade off lower incomes per worker for higher employment. Steinherr and Thisse (1979) and Zelić (1975) preserve the maximand of income per worker, but explicitly include a constraint that membership cannot be reduced below its initial level. Other authors, including Meade (1972) and Keren (1985), have adopted similar assumptions. Horvat (1967, 1972), inspired by the practice in Yugoslav firms, also suggests that an LMF will decrease wages, rather than dismiss fellow workers. Horvat argues that the LMF maximizes total enterprise profits above the specified personal income payments which are set in advance, and hence behaves similarly to a capitalist firm. Since profits are used for investment, investment is thus also maximized. The main difference between the LMF and the capitalist firm is that social property of capital will reduce risk and uncertainty; hence a high rate of investment will be achieved (Horvat 1972).

26 This is Furubotn and Pejovich's (1970a) initial hypothesis. Vanek also recognizes that 'it is conceivable that the LMF would see in its bigness a positive value, irrespective of what this does to the incomes of its individual members. But such megalomaniac firms . . . are not our concern' (1970, p. 304).

27 The lengthening of the LMF horizon reduces underinvestment always, i.e. also in cases 1.2, 1.3, 2.2(a), 2.2(b) and 2.2(c).

4 The investment behaviour of the socialist firm

1 For example, Kornai's notion of shortage and his perception of the pricing policy of socialist enterprises; in Yugoslavia, open (instead of repressed) inflation was accepted as a policy option as early as the mid-1960s, enabling the activation of markets for many goods and services, and thus facilitating the reduction of shortages.

2 The alternative term for state 'paternalism' frequently used in the literature is political or state 'tutelage' (see Portes 1990; Hare 1990).

3 Among Western scholars, see in particular Tyson (1983); OECD (1987a), (1988); Schrenk et al. (1979); World Bank (1983); Knight (1984).

4 Annual economic resolutions were abolished in 1989 as part of measures aimed at reducing the role of planning.

5 The most obvious example is price freezes, which have often been imposed in Yugoslavia in recent years.

6 See the 1974 Constitution of Yugoslavia, part III of Basic Principles, p. 13.

7 The abolition of the tax on social capital also implied the sanctioning of non-labour incomes and the generation of income inequality due to different capital endowments, causing many problems of allocative inefficiency. As Milenkovich commented (1971, p. 265), 'The Yugoslav principle of distribution becomes to each according to the factors of production supplied by the human agent or to which the human agent has access, as valued on the (imperfect) market'.

8 It should be stressed that Bajt has in the mean time modified his view; in *Samoupravni oblik društvene svojine* (1988a) he argues that in Yugoslavia today, the real owners of social capital, even in the economic sense, are the political structures.

9 Yugoslavia's industrial structure is thus similar to that of other East European countries (for example Hungary; see Hare 1990).

10 The concept of banks as 'service' agencies of enterprises was abandoned only in the mid-1980s. The 1989 banking law envisages their transformation into profit-making shareholding institutions.

5 Yugoslav investment and savings performance

1 Only Furubotn and Pejovich's and Kornai's theories are considered from now onwards, since Vanek's theory is not directed specifically to Yugoslavia.

2 Yugoslav statistics, however, contain an upwards accounting bias, which will be discussed later.

3 As already mentioned, GMP (or social product, in Yugoslav terminology) is the value added at market prices of productive sectors of the economy; it excludes non-productive sectors such as education, health, defence, banking, and other services. Gross investment includes investment in productive and non-productive sectors of the economy by the social and the private sector in fixed assets and increases in stocks.

4 The trade deficit was reduced from 10 per cent of GMP in 1980 to 0.9 per cent in 1988; the rapid rise in foreign indebtedness was halted in 1983 and an improvement was achieved in the current account which since 1983 has been in surplus (for transactions in convertible currencies).

5 The World Bank regularly makes adjustments for stock appreciation in Yugoslav statistics; Lydall (1989) has also made such adjustments for the 1980–6 period, while Madžar (1985, 1986) has calculated that over the whole 1953–84 period, the fictitious component created by the revaluation of stocks accounted for over 80 per cent of their nominal increment. Yugoslav GNP is regularly estimated by the OECD and the World Bank.

6 These estimates are based on National Bank of Yugoslavia (NBY) data. NBY data differ somewhat from Yugoslav national accounts provided by the Federal Institute of Statistics (Savezni Zavod za Statistiku – SZS), because the NBY records payments for investment according to flow-of-funds accounts, rather than the value of work done, as in SZS data.

7 Similar estimates are provided by the OECD, although the investment/GNP rates are somewhat higher because of a different source of data (SZS and not the NBY), and because no adjustments are apparently made for stock overvaluation.

8 See Tyson (1980); Dubey (ed.) (1975); Schrenk et al. (1979); World Bank (1983); Lydall (1984) and (1989); Bajt (1988a); Vacić (1989). The various methods used in these studies to measure allocative efficiency in Yugoslavia include aggregate and sectoral incremental capital-output ratios or alternatively, marginal and average capital-output ratios; net and gross profitability rates at the aggregate, sectoral, regional and enterprise levels.

9 Lydall (1989, pp. 83–7) gives a number of illustrative examples of such investment failures.

10 In the 1966–70 Social Plan, the very first among the principal objectives of the economic and social development of the period was said to be a 'continuous increase in the standard of living, particularly personal consumption, and a rise of the share of personal incomes in the distribution of national income'; the plan thus envisaged a decline in the accumulation/GMP ratio (see Sekretarijat za informativnu službu Savezne . . . 1966, p. 49).

11 The ratios are calculated from data on the distribution of GMP of productive enterprises in the social sector, as provided for by official Yugoslav statistics (SGJ); see table 5A.4 in the appendix to chapter 5.

12 With the exception of the minimum and maximum levels – 13.9 per cent in 1966 and 21.3 per cent in 1983 – depreciation accounted, on average, for about 17 per cent to 18 per cent of net enterprise income.

13 Until 1975, the savings rate also depended on the skill structure of workers. Workers were classified into skill groups, of which the first, that of 'non-skilled workers', was used as a numeraire, by which each other category was reduced to 'non-skilled worker' equivalents, according to determined coefficients. Aggregating across skills gave the 'standardized worker' of an enterprise in 'non-skilled worker' equivalents. The Croatian Social Compact set the maximum level of personal income per standardized worker which

an enterprise could pay, given the enterprise's income per standardized worker; if an enterprise's net income exceeded this level, the difference was divided in determined proportions between personal income and accumulation; thus an enterprise's income performance in relation to other enterprises of the republic sets limits on the extent to which its personal income distribution policy can depart from the republican average, whereas the minimum savings requirement is treated as a residual. The Serbian and Montenegrin agreements, by contrast, set the minimum savings level required of an enterprise, given its income per standardized worker, relative to the average income per standardized worker for the republic (see Dubey (ed.) 1975, pp. 351–3). In 1975 the system was somewhat modified; the basic amount of personal incomes payments is no longer linked to workers' skill structure, but to the personal income fund in the previous period corrected for the rise in the enterprise's net income (see Mramor 1984).

14 The level of depreciation above the legal minimum was exceptionally high in 1975 (over 20 per cent of total accumulation), for the legal rates in that year were low; thereafter they were substantially increased, leading to a drop in this component from 1976 onwards.

15 Productive enterprises' share in gross domestic savings rose from 48.6 per cent in 1961–5 to 51.2 per cent in 1966–70, to 53.6 per cent in 1971–5, and to 54.1 per cent in 1976–80; the share decreased only during the 1980s – to 46 per cent by 1986. In the three five-year periods following the 1966 reform, productive enterprises' share in social sector savings increased from 69.7 per cent to 79.3 per cent and 79.4 per cent respectively (see Narodna Banka Jugoslavije, *Bilten Narodne Banke Jugoslavije*).

16 To give a few examples: the fall in all four savings ratios in the late 1960s can be attributed to the priority given to personal consumption during that period; the policies of the early 1980s (personal income controls, higher depreciation rates) have, in fact, increased enterprise savings ratios; and in 1988, the notable fall in enterprise savings/GMP rate was the direct consequence of a substantial increase in taxes (the share of taxes in enterprise GMP increased by 8 per cent with respect to 1987).

17 These problems are discussed in detail in Lydall (1989), pp. 127–8; Bajt (1988a); Mates (1987); see more in the appendix to chapter 3.

18 These are the latest figures available in one of the last NBY Bulletins published in 1989; since then, due to financial difficulties, the Bulletin has ceased publication and the relevant table has not even been compiled by the NBY for internal use.

19 Indeed, as indicated earlier, 30 per cent to 60 per cent of resources allocated to the business fund and depreciation, which are the principal components of enterprise gross savings, are used for repayment of investment credits.

20 These figures exclude investment for collective consumption purposes, and hence do not raise the problem emphasized by Tyson (1977a) that workers who might be reluctant to save to finance a risky business investment, might

be eager to save to finance the construction of an apartment complex for their own use.

21 Although these figures are therefore lower than the ratios presented earlier, if in Prašnikar's table credits from domestic suppliers are considered as sources provided by other enterprises belonging to the productive sector of the economy, and therefore as a form of internal financing (as opposed to financing through bank credit), Prašnikar's self-financing ratio approaches the self-financing ratio of over 40 per cent recorded at the sectoral level in the late 1970s.

22 This part of self-financed investment need not represent actual *net* investment, because depreciation may not correspond to actual replacement of productive capacity, but this component of enterprise self-financed investment exceeding depreciation is in line with what Stephen considers 'net investment'.

23 According to the definition provided by the Savezni zavod za statistiku (SZS), maintenance refers to the replacement of capital, whereas enlargement includes enlargement, reconstruction, and modernization (such as changes in the composition, technology, and techniques of production), rearrangement of equipment and purchase of new fixed assets within existing working units.

24 A similar conclusion can be drawn from Schrenk *et al.* (1979, p. 153). Depreciation of productive sectors was 49.6 billion dinars in 1966–70, as compared with net investment in both fixed assets and inventories, of 115.3 billion dinars. In 1971–5, depreciation amounted to 156.7 billion dinars, as compared with net investment in fixed assets and inventories of 334.9 billion dinars. The shares of net investment in total gross investment were 69.9 per cent and 68.1 per cent respectively in the two five-year periods following the 1965 reform; the self-financing ratios for these sub-periods (as provided by Schrenk *et al.*) were 66.8 per cent and 63.8 per cent respectively, and net investment financed by enterprise sources was 46.7 per cent in 1966–70 and 43.4 per cent in 1971–5.

25 British firms, for example, tend to rely heavily on retained earnings for financing investment (often approaching 100 per cent), whereas Italian firms had a self-financing ratio of only 19 per cent in 1975 (see OECD 1987b, p. 41).

6 The determinants of investment in Yugoslavia

1 Banks are in principle free to determine the level of interest rates, but lower limits are agreed upon in interbank self-management agreements, while the upper ceiling is set by the Federal Assembly.

2 In the case of households, this is usually the interest rate on time deposits, and in the case of enterprises, the interest rate on short-term credit.

3 Interest rates on savings deposits have been deflated by the cost of living index, while on bank loans by the industrial producers' prices index; a different deflator has for the moment been used only in order to show the

effective losses and gains of the two sectors. In the econometric tests which follow, a single price deflator will be used.

4 Pre-tax profit rate = [(Gross revenue − material costs − net personal incomes − depreciation)/historical value of capital] × 100, referred to in table 6A.1 of the appendix to chapter 6 as Profit rate I.

5 The post-tax profit rate = [(depreciation + allocation to funds)/historical value of capital] × 100, referred to in table 6A.1 as Profit rate II.

6 The fluctuation of workers is an official indicator made available by the SZS, and is calculated as: FW=WL/(WT+WN), where WL is the number of workers leaving during the month, WT is the total number of workers at the beginning of the month, and WN is the number of newly admitted workers during the month.

7 The inadequacy of interest rate policies has been criticized by many Yugoslav economists; see, for example, Ekonomski Institut Pravne Fakultete (1985), or Bajt (1986b) and (1988a).

8 This reverse margin, however, is not a subsidy from households; it is a transfer from banks to the enterprises which own them, i.e. a purely internal transfer within the consolidated banks/enterprises sector.

9 Implicit bank subsidies to enterprises were calculated by deducting total bank losses (the sum of operating deficits, write-off of loans, net deferred foreign exchange losses and the NBY exchange rate loss) from normal bank surpluses.

10 This is in fact predicted by the literature on the labour-managed firm: when no capital rental is paid for the use of capital, the LMF will show a bias in favour of capital-intensive projects. Nevertheless, the lack of capital rental on original capital should not affect the choice of new investment projects.

11 In Serbia the level was set at a maximum of 15 per cent of the worker's monthly personal income in 1990.

12 Nevertheless, in later articles Tyson's views approach our own (see Tyson 1983; Balassa and Tyson 1985).

13 See the 1983 amendments to the Law on the Rehabilitation and Liquidation of Organizations of Associated Labour of July 1980.

14 See the Financial Operations Law adopted in 1989, in *Financial Reform in Yugoslavia* (1989).

15 According to the law, bankruptcy procedures will be initiated if a legal entity has been illiquid uninterruptedly for sixty days, or for sixty days, with interruptions, over a period of seventy-five days; these periods had previously been longer.

16 In the 1979–83 period, 30–7 per cent and 43–52 per cent of total claims against purchases for goods and services were letters of credit and promissory notes respectively; see Knight (1984), p. 36.

17 Thus since 1980, the rise in the ratio of GMP to domestic credit has been largely matched by a fall in the ratio of GMP to the volume of inter-enterprise credit, and thus the overall volume of finance per unit of GMP has not been as effectively restricted (OECD 1987a, pp. 56–7).

18 Tyson (1977b) provides similar data on interfirm credits, but in reference to earlier periods.

19 Of the 125 investment projects, three were still not completed at the time the study was finished, and hence they were excluded from the findings.

20 The sample is quite representative, since it includes all projects undertaken through the Associated Belgrade Bank, which represented 23 per cent to 25 per cent of all investment projects undertaken in 1982–4 throughout Yugoslavia.

21 See the methodologies of the Association of Yugoslav Banks (Udruženje banaka Jugoslavije 1981), of the Associated Belgrade Bank (Lajšić 1984), of the Republican Institute for Social Planning of Serbia (Republički zavod za društveno planiranje 1984), and of the Association of Belgrade Banks (Udruženje bankarskih organizacija Beograd 1985).

22 The compact was concluded between representatives of the federal and of the republican executive councils; see 'Društveni dovogor o davanju mišljenja o društvenoj i ekonomskoj opravdanosti nameravanih investicija', *Službeni List SFRJ*, 20 December 1985.

7 Econometric tests of Yugoslav investment behaviour

1 The problem of how to quantify Furubotn and Pejovich's theory in the most appropriate way has raised many questions, and has suggested a number of alternative approaches to the one that has finally been chosen. One way of proceeding could have been to start with a standard investment model for market economies and adjust it to Furubotn and Pejovich's assumptions; but this procedure would have been biased by our own subjective evaluation of which variables to include. The other way was to construct a simpler model, which nevertheless fully reflects the point of view of the authors. We have opted for the second method.

2 In the regressions which follow, the variable H should be interpreted as the time horizon; in order to avoid confusion in expected signs (since the time horizon is inversely related to labour turnover), it is assumed that $H = 1 -$ labour turnover (see the appendix to chapter 7). Labour turnover is, of course, not the ideal approximation of the time horizon, as employment variability may be related to investment variability because of the influence of investment on both job creation and aggregate demand; nevertheless, in the absence of a better proxy, it is plausible to assume that the time horizon will be longer the lower is labour turnover.

3 Using the formula

$$t = \frac{r}{(1-r^2)/df}$$

where r is the correlation coefficient and df is the degree of freedom, the t test is applied to correlation coefficients (see Mayes and Mayes 1976, pp. 84–6). All reported coefficients proved significant at the 5 per cent level, since the t values obtained were higher than the critical t value (for eighteen observations, two explanatory variables and hence sixteen degrees of freedom, $t>2.120$).

4 In the case of savings, however, the sign of the coefficient is contrary to what is postulated by the theory.

5 The *IR* is expected to influence *SD* positively, whereas the remaining three variables influence savings indirectly, through the investment decision: thus the lower the *LR*, the shorter the *H*, and the lower the *PF*, the less likely is *SFI* and the more likely are *SD*.

6 The lower the *IR* on *SD*, the less likely are *SD* and the more likely is *INV*. The higher the *H* and *PF*, the higher is *SFI* likely to be, and hence also *INV*. As to *LR*, although according to Furubotn and Pejovich's statement the sign ought to be positive ($b_2>0$), its influence on *INV* is indeterminate as it will depend on the extent to which *INV* is financed internally or externally.

7 The lower is the *IR* on *SD*, the less likely are *SD* and hence the more likely is *SFI*. The higher is the *LR*, *H* and *PF*, the more likely is *SFI*.

8 The null hypothesis (H0) of no autocorrelation is rejected, since the probability that it is correct is 0.03 per cent, 0.06 per cent and 0.01 per cent in the three equations respectively, i.e. below 5 per cent.

9 For details concerning each of these tests, see the appendix to chapter 7.

10 Except in one case, where it was at the margin, autocorrelation was confirmed by the DWE, which gave the following probability values: for equation 1.1, 0.15 per cent and 4.25 per cent; for equation 1.2, 0.25 per cent and 0.97 per cent; and for equation 1.3, 0.78 per cent and 5.02 per cent respectively, when including and excluding the first observation.

11 The availability of credit is expected to decrease *SFI*, and hence increase *SD*. As to the effect on *INV*, as in the case of equation 1.2, the effect remains indeterminate as it depends on the extent to which investment is financed internally or externally.

12 Probabilities of 0 per cent, 0.38 per cent, and 0.27 per cent in 1.4, 1.5 and 1.6 respectively.

13 This procedure was also applied to an alternative set of equations in which *LR* was replaced by *DIR*; doing so yielded similar results.

14 All three dependent variables are likely to increase with time.

15 Restrictive policies introduced in the 1980s are expected to influence negatively both *SD* (because of limits on personal incomes), and *INV* and *SFI* (because of various measures aimed at cutting investment demand).

16 For example, in the first group of regressions (1.7, 1.8, 1.9), the variable *H* seemed to be one of the least significant, whereas in the second group (1.10, 1.11, 1.12) it seemed highly significant (although this is approximative because of the presence of autocorrelation).

17 The value of the ARSIM test statistics (1.056) in 1.13a is at the margin for acceptance of autocorrelation (the lower bound DW statistics for eighteen observations and two explanatory variables at the 5 per cent level of significance is 1.05); whereas the value (1.053) in 1.13b lies in the inconclusive region (for eighteen observations and four explanatory variables, at

the 5 per cent level of significance, the lower bound DW is 0.82 and the upper bound 1.87).

18 The value of the ARSIM test statistic of 1.082 lies in the inconclusive region (for eighteen observations and two explanatory variables at the 5 per cent level of significance, the lower and upper bounds of DW statistics are 1.05 and 1.53 respectively).

19 The value of the ARSIM test statistic of 2.333 is higher than 2.06, the upper bound DW statistics for eighteen observations and five explanatory variables, at 5 per cent level of significance.

20 Of course, there is the possibility that, in prosperous times, both may increase.

21 This, however, conforms with Yugoslav practice, since banks are generally willing to lend to enterprises only if they provide a certain proportion of funds themselves.

22 We could have proceeded by including, instead of CR, the alternative variables used before (T, DA), but it is unlikely that the signs of the coefficients would have changed.

23 The ED variable may seem tautological, since it could be interpreted as representing an alternative measure of investment. However, expansion drive does not directly measure investment growth, but reflects the influence of all components of GMP. Alternative specifications could have included lagged ED, or the calculation of ED as the difference between the consumption growth index and the GMP growth index, but this would have taken us away from the original concept of expansion drive in Kornai's theory.

24 It could be argued that this is equally true for any economy, as capital replacement in capitalist economies follows this rule; thus lagged capital stock is consistent with the 'flexible accelerator' theory of investment. Nevertheless, because of the greater emphasis in socialist economies on growth in general, the hypothesis could be considered as applying more to socialist than to capitalist economies.

25 For the correlation between ED and PGMP, $t = 0.16$, i.e. it is lower than 2.12, for sixteen degrees of freedom at the 5 per cent level.

26 SD is expected to increase with increases of disposable income and the rise in GMP, whereas the change in policies is expected to have a negative impact.

27 Expansion drive, increase of fixed assets, stock of unfinished projects, planned investment and GMP growth, are all expected to have a positive influence on INV. The introduction of restrictive policies is expected to negatively influence INV.

28 It may seem simplistic to assume that INV and SFI are roughly proportional, but the portion of fixed assets financed by enterprises' resources in Yugoslavia has not changed much over time (see chapter 5). Under such an assumption, it might have been sufficient to specify only one regression (whether for INV or SFI), but both were needed for our later analysis.

29 For sixteen degrees of freedom (nineteen observations and three explanatory variables excluding the constant), at the 1 per cent level of significance
$t>2.291$.

30 Since one of the regressors is a lagged variable, the DWH test was used for
testing autocorrelation, which gave the probability of 25.19 per cent, thus
confirming autocorrelation.

31 For twelve degrees of freedom (eighteen observations and six variables), at
the 1 per cent level of significance $t>3.055$, at the 5 per cent level $t>2.179$.
Hence, ED, FXA<1>, WIP and PGMP are significant at the 1 per cent level,
and DA at the 5 per cent level of significance.

32 Again, the DWH test was applied for testing autocorrelation, which gave
the probability of 7.09 per cent, thus rejecting it.

33 For eighteen observations and six explanatory variables, and hence twelve
degrees of freedom, at the 1 per cent level of significance $t>3.055$, and at the
10 per cent level $t>1.782$.

34 Again tested through the DWH test, which gave the probability of 26.02 per
cent, thus rejecting autocorrelation.

35 Taking into account only the t statistics in equation 2.3 would have led us to
include ED and WIP, rather than ED and PINV or PGMP. Precisely because
ED and WIP are highly correlated, this procedure, in fact, failed to give
satisfactory results.

36 The DWH confirmed no autocorrelation of residuals (probability of
34.89 per cent).

37 This was to be expected, since the correlation coefficient between these two
variables was 0.968 (see table 7.3.).

38 Again, this was already suggested by the high correlation coefficients
between these variables in table 7.3.

39 The F-statistics give the probability that the H0(1)/H0(2) is correct; if this
probability is higher than 5 per cent, H0 will be accepted as being correct,
implying that the joint effect of this group of variables has no influence on
the dependent variable.

40 DW standard statistics are not directly applicable to regressions without an
intercept. Therefore the DWE was applied; the test gave a probability of
17.91 per cent that H0 on no autocorrelation is correct.

41 The DWH gave a probability of 9.55 per cent, thus rejecting autocorrelation.
However, because of the high value of RHO(1), in order to be sure that there
is no autocorrelation, an additional test (AR) was applied; this test
confirmed that there was no autocorrelation.

8 Early attempts at introducing investment incentives

1 Although the term 'past labour' is effectively a synonym for that part of
capital stock contributed by workers through past investment.

2 For a detailed survey of the discussions on past labour in the late 1960s, see
Burić (1983), pp. 80–108.

3 Among the proposals advanced in the late 1960s for introducing shares in

Yugoslavia, was a proposal by S. Kavčić (who believed that shares would be an adequate way for mobilizing citizens' savings), and a proposal by a Working Group of the Federal Assembly (see Korać 1986, pp. 186–7).

4 For example: 'We have transferred social capital to basic organizations of associated labour (BOALs)' (1978, p. 67); or 'Self-managed associated labour today disposes of the entire social capital, but this social capital is distributed, i.e. decentralized to BOALs' (1978, p. 57).

5 For example: 'Past labour in the wider sense represents that part of value that workers have produced with their current labour, which the society in various ways allocates for accumulation' (1978, p. 52); 'Pooling of income is not investment in another organization, but investment in common social labour' (1978, pp. 39–44); 'From the results of total social labour a worker ought to have a material benefit on the basis of his own past labour' (1978, p. 49).

6 See also the 1971 constitutional amendments and the 1974 Constitution of Yugoslavia.

7 See the 1974 Constitution, Article 20, and ALA, Articles 126 and 129.

8 The only restriction was that these acts could not run counter to social compacts concluded by the enterprise (Article 128, ALA).

9 A worker employed for ten years, for example, would receive an additional 4.5 per cent of his personal income on account of past labour.

10 It does not usually represent more than a worker's monthly, or bi-monthly personal income.

11 On the different versions of and discussions about the new law on past labour, see Burić (1983), pp. 121–5.

12 Of the three criteria that are used to determine a worker's contribution, two are based on his contribution *together* with other workers.

13 Thus short-term instruments (e.g. promissory notes used in direct interenterprise credits), treasury bills of the National Bank of Yugoslavia, or certificates of deposit (issued by banks upon request), all introduced by the 1971 Law on Securities, are not explicitly considered.

14 Our observations have been inspired and are in part based on an excellent discussion of these issues by Babić (1983).

15 'Shares in joint income on account of past labour shall be realized from the part of such income left *after* the allocation of resources for personal incomes . . . ' (ALA 1976, Article 82; see also Article 84).

16 'The right to a share in joint income shall expire upon refund of the value of pooled resources and payment of compensation, or upon expiry of the time limit determined by the self-managed agreement, irrespective of the extent to which the value of pooled resources has been refunded . . . ' (ALA 1976, Article 85; see also Article 83).

17 ALA, Articles 82 and 85.

18 Prior to the 1977 banking law, the number of votes of each founder was linked in theory to the amount of capital contributed; in practice, however, each founder usually had only one vote (see Mramor 1984).

19 1971 Law on Securities, Articles 16–23, 46, 52–5.

20 The first enterprise to issue bonds in Yugoslavia was Crvena Zastava, in 1969.
21 Comparing the value of all securities issued by productive OALs with the value of promissory notes reveals that promissory notes accounted for 60 per cent to 90 per cent of all securities issued by enterprises (see table 6A.4, appendix to chapter 6).
22 I am grateful to Mitja Gašpari for this clarification.
23 Commentators have observed that this is in effect a private enterprise acting under certain legal restraints. Workers sign a contract with the owner, who in turn agrees to conform to self-management rules (Singleton and Carter 1982, pp. 199, 203).
24 'If the value of the resources which the manager has pooled . . . has been paid out . . . the manager's right to a share in income on account of his ownership right shall be terminated' (ALA 1976, Article 315).
25 *Zakon o pribavljanju sredstava od gradjana za proširivanje materijalne osnove organizacija udruženog rada, Službeni list SFRJ* no. 24 1986; see Labus (1987), pp. 139–40.
26 The debates that took place on this issue are reported in detail in Milenkovich (1971), and Stojanović (1964).
27 Professor M. Ćirović is considered one of the major Yugoslav experts on monetary issues, and his views on inflation have had a significant influence on government policies in recent years.

9 Current property reforms

1 On early discussions, see Horvat (1970), pp. 49–52.
2 As a theoretical framework, Milovanović uses the Austrian theory of capital (in a simple Fisher-Hayek form) under conditions of certainty; and under conditions of uncertainty, Hirshleifer's theory of probabilistic decision-making.
3 Milovanović's proposal bears some resemblance to 'entrepreneurial socialism', a proposal made by the Hungarian economist T. Liska in the mid-sixties (see Barsony 1982).
4 This is doubtful, since several economies with share capital, such as Brazil and Mexico, have not avoided the problem of high external debt.
5 Discussions were organized by the Central Committee of the League of Communists of Macedonia (Skoplje, 1985) and Serbia (Belgrade, 1986), by the Presidency of the League of Communists of Yugoslavia (Kumrovec, 1986), and by the Chamber of Commerce (Belgrade, 1986) (see Korać 1986, p. 187).
6 As reported by M. Crnobrnja, then head of the Serbian Commission, in *Ekonomska Politika* no. 1885, 16 May 1988.
7 See the Yugoslav Official Gazette (*Službeni List SFRJ*) no. 77 of 31 December 1988, and amendments to the law in Yugoslav Official Gazette no. 40 of 7 July 1989.
8 See the Law on Banking adopted in February and amended in July 1989.

9 See the Law on the Rehabilitation, Bankruptcy and Liquidation of Banks and other Financial Organizations, Yugoslav Official Gazette no. 84, adopted in 1989.

10 See Yugoslav Official Gazette no. 64 of 20 October 1989.

11 See Yugoslav Official Gazette no. 64, 1989.

12 See Yugoslav Official Gazette no. 84 of 22 December 1989.

13 In Croatia the Law on the Republican Development Fund was adopted (Croatian Official Gazette no. 18, 30 April 1990); and in Slovenia, the Law on the Restructuring Agency (Slovenian Official Gazette no. 14, 1990).

14 See Yugoslav Official Gazette no. 46, August 1990.

15 See Yugoslav Official Gazette no. 37 of 30 June 1990.

16 This limit therefore indirectly links the permissible amount of internal share issues to an enterprise's capital-labour ratio.

17 However, since the dispersion of incomes is not as large as that of capital per man, throughout the whole economy the individual limit will tend to equalize access to ownership by workers operating in sectors and enterprises characterized by widely diverging capital-labour ratios.

18 The intention of this provision is to compensate workers for the reduced self-management rights which will result from privatization.

19 These organizations have the status of a legal entity and perform transactions on behalf of the associated enterprises (see Law on Enterprises, Part Va, Articles 145a–h).

20 Even if workers, citizens and pension funds subscribe to the maximum permissible quantity of internal shares, a substantial part of capital may still remain social property (according to some calculations, around 30–50 per cent of total capital – see Lukić 1990), unless it is sold to external shareholders at auction. However, such sales are likely to be limited to the most profitable firms.

21 The resources of socio-political communities are excluded from social capital that can be sold, but the law gives no clues as to the basis on which the state's share is to be determined.

22 See Slovenian Official Gazette no. 37 of 11 October 1990, and Croatian Official Gazette no. 43 of 24 October 1990.

23 These laws include a law on privatization, a law on the privatization agency, a law on the development fund, and a law on denationalization.

24 For example, on the consultative functions of the Agency, proceeds from sales going primarily to the Republican Fund, the use of the Republican Fund's resources, exclusion from sale of resources contributed by the state, etc.

25 These conditions had to do with the maximum discount, minimum length of employment, part to be paid immediately in cash, and limits on individuals' subscriptions.

26 Kalodjera's model has been elaborated and developed further by a number of economists; see in particular Baletić (1990) and Dubravčić (1990).

27 See Ekonomska Politika no. 2009, 1 October 1990 and Vjesnik, 20 October 1990.

28 The strong role of the state is also suggested by other provisions of the law.

Thus the law allows management rights to be handed over to a minority shareholder; it also lays down that a manager/director can be appointed or dismissed by a decision of the Croatian government (Article 33).

29 The term has been retained in the new Serbian Constitution adopted at the end of September 1990.

30 The Democratic Party has taken inspiration from discussions on privatization in Czechoslovakia, proposing the distribution to all citizens of vouchers which would be exchangeable for shares (see *Demokratija*, 27 September 1990, p. 13).

31 See Yugoslav Official Gazette no. 74 of 23 November 1990.

32 These enterprises include Agrokomerc, IMR, Ekonomska Politika, Jugohemija (Serbia); Fabrika kugličnih ležajeva, Termovent (Voivodina); Rudnik, Istra-Jadran, Croatia Osiguranje (Croatia); Uniskomerc, Šipadkomerc, Energoinvest (Bosnia and Herzegovina); Tito, Priboj (Macedonia); Šport oprema, Kompas Internationala (Slovenia); for other examples, see *Poslovni Svijet* of 21 March, 1991. No official register of these firms exists.

33 See Centre for International Cooperation (1990) p. 12, and *Investing in Yugoslavia* (1989), pp. 18–19.

34 Sekretarijat za informacije Saveznog izvršnog veća (1990) and *Ekonomska Politika* no. 2021, 24 December 1990, p. 20.

10 Specific features of the Yugoslav transition

1 Past economic reforms in Yugoslavia are described in greater detail in chapter 1.

2 SZS, *SGJ 1990*, table 121–11.

3 The federal government has appealed to the Constitutional Court, which is to determine the legitimacy of such republican laws.

4 Similar problems of regional devolution are also present in other transitional economies, particularly the Soviet Union (see *European Economy* no. 45, December 1990).

5 The functions concern convertibility, monetary policy, foreign exchange reserves, ensuring regular payments and the normal functioning of a single market, restrictions on personal and public consumption, further property restructuring, international obligations, national defence and the financing of the Yugoslav Army, rehabilitation of banks, and social security programmes.

6 Some examples include petrol stations of the major Croatian petrochemical company INA, estimated to be worth $150 million; fifty-one textile stores of the Croatian producer Vartex; seventeen offices of Rade Končar, worth $3.5 million; Vesna, Bagat, and others (see *Ekonomska Politika* no. 2034, 1 April 1991).

7 For example, in November 1990 the average wage ranged from 6,702 Dinars in Slovenia, to 3,883 Dinars in Macedonia (*Ekonomska Politika* no. 2027, 4 February 1991, p. 36).

11 An overview of conclusions

1 In addition to active government policies to either institutionalize or encourage forms of economic and industrial democracy in a number of single West European countries, the Commission of the European Communities has for a number of years been promoting workers' participation in decision-making, and has recently also decided to support workers' participation in enterprise results, as stressed in its November 1989 *Action Programme for the Implementation of Social Rights of Workers* and its September 1991 proposal of a recommendation to the Council on the promotion of employee participation in profits and enterprise results (see more in Uvalić 1991a).

References

Aoki, M. 1984, *The Co-operative Game Theory of the Firm*, Clarendon Press, Oxford

Babić, S. 1982, 'On the problem of choice of economic efficiency indicators in the Yugoslav economic system 1976–1980', *Economic Analysis and Workers' Management*, 16 (4)

— 1983, 'Zakon o udruženom radu – Podsticaj ili barijera udruživanju rada u samoupravnoj robnoj privredi?', *Treći Program*, spring

Bajt, A. 1968, 'Property in capital and in the means of production in socialist economies', *Journal of Law and Economics*, 11, pp. 1–4

— 1985, 'Dugovanja i potraživanja u inflatornoj privredi i njihov obračun', *Privredna Kretanja Jugoslavije*, no. 155, October, Ljubljana, pp. 22–49

— 1986a, 'Preduzetništvo u samoupravnoj socijalističkoj privredi', *Privredna Kretanja Jugoslavije*, no. 159, February, Ljubljana, pp. 32–45

— 1986b, *Alternativna ekonomska politika*, Globus, Zagreb

— 1988a, *Samoupravni oblik društvene svojine*, Globus, Zagreb

— 1988b, 'Akcionarske iluzije', *Ekonomska Politika*, no. 1891, June 27

Balassa, B. and Tyson, L. 1985, 'Policy responses to external shocks in Hungary and Yugoslavia: 1974–76 and 1979–81', *Joint Economic Committee Congress of the United States Selected Papers*, October 28

Baletić, Z. 1990, 'Dekolektivizacija društvenog vlasništva', in *Poslednji dani društvenog vlasništva*, Zagreb, Zagrebačka Poslovna Škola, pp. 31–42

Barsony, J. 1982, 'Tibor Liska's concept of socialist entrepreneurship', *Acta Oeconomica*, 28, pp. 422–65

Bartlett, W. 1984a, 'Vanek's theorem on internal and external sources of finance for a labour-managed firm – a critique', mimeo, European University Institute, Florence

— 1984b, 'Enterprise investment and public consumption in a self-managed economy', mimeo, European University Institute, Florence

— 1986, 'Capital accumulation and employment in a self-financed worker cooperative', mimeo, European University Institute, Florence, July

— 1990, 'Economic change in Yugoslavia: from crisis to reform', *Stockholm Institute of Soviet and East European Economics Working Paper*, no. 9

Bartlett, W. and Uvalić, M. 1986, 'Labour-managed firms, employee participation and profit sharing: theoretical perspectives and European experience',

European University Institute Working Paper, 86/236, pp. 1–62, and *Management Bibliographies and Reviews*, 12 (4) MCB University Press, pp. 1–66

Bauer, T. 1978, 'Investment cycles in planned economies', *Acta Oeconomica*, 21 (3), pp. 243–60

1985, 'The new Hungarian forms of enterprise management and their economic environment', Working Paper for the 1985 Radein Research Seminar, presented at the European University Institute, 5 June 1986

Bendeković, J. 1977, 'Ocjena investicionih projekata', *Poduzeće-Banka*, 6, pp. 13–20

Bendeković, J. and Teodorović, I. 1977, 'Osvrt na dosadašnju praksu planiranja investicionih projekata u Jugoslaviji', *Poduzeće-Banka*, 7, pp. 28–32

Bendeković, D., Bendeković, J., Brozović, T., Jančin, T., Nušinović, M., and Teodorović, I. 1987, *Priručnik za planiranje investicionih projekata*, Ekonomski Institut, Zagreb

Bergson, A. 1967, 'Market socialism revisited', *Journal of Political Economy*, 75 (5), pp. 655–73

Bogetić, G. 1987, 'Kako menjati dogovor o dohotku', *Ekonomska Politika*, no. 1823, 9 March

Bonin, J. P. 1985, 'Labor management and capital maintenance: investment decision in the socialist labor-managed firm', in D. Jones and J. Svejnar (eds.), *Advances in the Economic Analysis of Participatory and Labor-Managed Firms*, vol. 1, JAI Press, Greenwich, CT, pp. 55–69

Bonin, J. P. and Putterman, L. 1987, *Economics of Cooperation and the Labor-Managed Economy*, Harwood Academic Publishers, London

Brus, W. and Laski, K. 1989, *From Marx to the Market – Socialism in Search of an Economic System*, Clarendon Press, Oxford

Burić, I. 1983, *Udruženi rad i minuli rad*, Informator, Zagreb

Burkitt, J. P. 1983, *The Effects of Economic Reform in Yugoslavia – Investment and Trade Policy, 1959–1976*, Research Series no. 55, Institute of International Studies, University of California, Berkeley

Čelenković, T., Djilas, M., Tošić, A., and Nešković, V. 1984, *Efikasnost procesa investiranja – Empirijsko istraživanje*, Udružena beogradska banka, Centar za ekonomska istraživanja, Belgrade

Center for International Cooperation and Development 1990, *Investing in Yugoslavia*, Ljubljana

Chilemi, O. 1981, 'Sul regime del capitale nell'impresa autogestita', *Rivista Internazionale di Scienze Economiche e Commerciali*, 28, pp. 151–69

Ćirović, M. 1976, *Monetarno-kreditni sistem*, 2nd edn, Savremena Administracija, Belgrade

Clayre, A. 1980, *The Political Economy of Co-operation and Participation*, Oxford University Press, Oxford

Comisso, E. T. 1979, *Workers Control under Plan and Market*, Yale University Press, New Haven, CT

Commission of the European Communities 1984, *Prospects for Workers' Cooperatives in Europe*, vols. 1, 2 and 3, Office for Official Publications, Luxembourg

1990, 'Stabilization, liberalization and devolution – Assessment of the economic situation and reform process in the Soviet Union', *European Economy*, no. 45, Brussels, December

Connock, M. 1982, 'Capital maintenance and investment in Yugoslavia: two observations', *Economic Analysis and Workers' Management*, 16 (3), pp. 287–98

Constitution of the Socialist Federal Republic of Yugoslavia – 1974, Jugoslovenski Pregled, Belgrade

Conte, M. 1980, 'A theory of investment for a labor-managed firm', mimeo, University of New Hampshire

Crnobrnja, M. 1988, 'Kako oživeti proizvodnju', *Ekonomska Politika*, no. 1885, 16 May

Defourny, J. 1983, 'L'autofinancement des coopératives de travailleurs et la théorie économique', *Annals of Public and Co-operative Economy*, 54, pp. 201–24

Dimitrijević, D. and Macesich, G. 1983, *Money and Finance in Yugoslavia – A Comparative Analysis*, Praeger, New York

Domar, E. 1966, 'The Soviet collective farm as a producer cooperative', *American Economic Review*, 56, pp. 734–57

Drakul, L. (ed.) 1984, 'Economic development 1971–1982', *Yugoslav Economic Survey*, 25 (2), May, Belgrade

Drèze, J. H. 1976, 'Some theory of labour management and participation', *Econometrica*, 44 (6), pp. 1125–38

Dubey, V. (ed.) 1975, *Yugoslavia – Development with Decentralization*, A World Bank Country Economic Report, Johns Hopkins University Press, Baltimore and London

Dubravčić, D. 1990, 'The role of the state in the processes of transformation of social ownership', mimeo, Zagreb, October

Dumas, A. (ed.) 1981, *L'autogestion, un système économique?* Dunod, Paris

Dumas, A. and Serra, D. 1972, 'Modèle d'autofinancement dans l'entreprise autogérée d'un système socialiste', *Revue d'économie politique*, 6, pp. 1022–41

Dumezić, T. 1986, 'Raspodela – Razrada neusaglašenog koncepta', *Ekonomska Politika*, no. 1808/1809, 24 November

Ekonomska Politika, Belgrade weekly, various issues

Ekonomski Institut Pravne Fakultete 1985, 'Negativne kamata ruše osnove društveno-ekonomskog sistema', *Privredna Kretanja Jugoslavije*, no. 157, December, Ljubljana, pp. 24–45

Ekonomski Institut Zagreb 1981, 'Statističko-dokumentacione osnove za sistem proširene reprodukcije 1961–1980', Zagreb

1986, 'Statističko-dokumentacione osnove za sistem proširene reprodukcije 1981–1986', Zagreb

Ellerman, D. P. 1986, 'Horizon problems and property rights in labor-managed firms', *Journal of Comparative Economics*, 10, pp. 62–78

Estrin, S. 1983, *Self-Management – Economic Theory and Yugoslav Practice*, Cambridge University Press, Cambridge

1985, 'The role of producer cooperatives in employment creation', *Economic Analysis and Workers' Management*, 19 (4), pp. 345–94

1991, 'Reform in Yugoslavia: the retreat from self-management', *London School of Economics Working Paper*, no. 79, January

Estrin, S. and Bartlett, W. 1982, 'The effects of enterprise self-management in Yugoslavia: an empirical survey', in D. Jones and J. Svejnar (eds.), *Participatory and Self-Managed Firms*, Lexington Books, Lexington

Estrin, S. and Jones, D. C. 1987, 'The determinants of investment in labor managed firms: evidence from France', mimeo, London School of Economics, January

Estrin, S., Jones, D. C. and Svejnar, J. 1984, 'The varying nature, importance and productivity effects of worker participation: evidence for contemporary producer cooperatives in industrialised Western economies', *CIRIEC Working Paper*, no. 84/4, University of Liège

European Communities 1986, *The Cooperative, Mutual and Non-Profit Sector and its Organizations in the European Community*, Luxembourg, European Communities, Economic and Social Committee

Financial Reform in Yugoslavia 1989, Jugoslovenski Pregled, Belgrade

Furubotn, E. G. 1971, 'Toward a dynamic model of the Yugoslav firm', *Canadian Journal of Economics*, 4 (2), pp. 182–97

1974, 'Bank credit and the labor-managed firm: the Yugoslav case', *American Slavic Studies*, 8 (1), pp. 89–106

1976, 'The long-run analysis of the labor-managed firm: an alternative interpretation', *American Economic Review*, 66 (1), pp. 104–23

1978, 'The long-run analysis of the labor-managed firm: reply', *American Economic Review*, 68 (4), pp. 706–9

1979, 'Decision making under labor-management: the commitment mechanism reconsidered', *Zeitschrift für die gesamte Staatswissenschaft*, 135 (2), pp. 216–27

1980a, 'The socialist labor-managed firm and bank-financed investment: some theoretical issues', *Journal of Comparative Economics*, 4 (2), pp. 184–91

1980b, 'Bank credit and the labor-managed firm: reply', *American Economic Review*, 70 (4), pp. 800–4

1980c, 'Tradeable claims and self-financed investment in the capitalist labor-managed firm', *Zeitschrift für die gesamte Staatswissenschaft*, 136 (4), pp. 630–41

Furubotn, E. G. and Pejovich, S. 1970a, 'Property rights and the behavior of the Yugoslav firm in a socialist state: the example of Yugoslavia', *Zeitschrift für Nationalökonomie*, 30 (3–4), pp. 431–54

1970b, 'Tax policy and investment decisions of the Yugoslav firm', *National Tax Journal*, 23, pp. 335–48

1972, 'Property rights and economic theory: a survey of recent literature', *The Journal of Economic Literature*, 10 (4), pp. 1137–62

1973, 'Property rights, economic decentralization and the evolution of the Yugoslav firm, 1965–72', *Journal of Law and Economics*, 16, pp. 275–302

1974, *The Economics of Property Rights*, Ballinger Publishing Company, Cambridge

Grličkov, V. 1987a, 'Bankarski sistem: propisana samostalnost', *Ekonomska Politika*, no. 1843, 27 July

1987b, 'Bankarstvo – kako do realnog bilansa?', *Ekonomska Politika*, no. 1858, 9 November

Grosfeld, I. 1990, 'Prospects for privatization in Poland', *European Economy*, no. 43, Brussels, March, pp. 139–50

Gui, B. 1981, 'Investment decisions in a worker-managed firm', *Economic Analysis and Workers' Management*, 15 (1), pp. 45–65

1984, 'Basque versus Illyrian labor-managed firms: the problem of property rights', *Journal of Comparative Economics*, 8, pp. 168–81

1985, 'Limits to external financing. A model and an application to labor-managed firms', in D. Jones and J. Svejnar (eds.), *Advances in the Economic Analysis of Participatory and Labor-Managed Firms*, vol. 1, JAI Press, Greenwich, CT

Gujarati, D. 1978, *Basic Econometrics*, McGraw-Hill, New York

Hare, P. G. 1990, 'Reform of enterprise regulation in Hungary – from "tutelage" to market', *European Economy*, no. 43, Brussels, March, pp. 35–54

Hirshleifer, J. 1970, *Investment, Interest and Capital*, Prentice-Hall, Englewood Cliffs, NJ

Hodder, J. E. 1986, 'Evaluation of manufacturing investments: A comparison of US and Japanese practices', *Financial Management*, spring, pp. 17–24

Horvat, B. 1958,. 'The optimum rate of investment', *Economic Journal*, December, pp. 747–67

1967, 'Prilog zasnivanju teorije jugoslovenskog preduzeća', *Ekonomska Analiza*, 1, pp. 7–28

1970, *Privredni sistem i ekonomska politika Jugoslavije*, Institut Ekonomskih Nauka, Belgrade

1972, 'Critical notes on the theory of the LMF and some macroeconomic implications', *Economic Analysis and Workers' Management*, 6, pp. 3–4

1976, *The Yugoslav Economic System*, International Arts and Sciences Press, White Plains, NY

1982, *The Political Economy of Socialism*, Martin Robertson, Oxford

1984, *Jugoslovenska privreda 1965–1983*, vols. 1 and 2, Cankarjeva Založba, Ljubljana and Zagreb

Horvat, B., Vacić, A., Županov, J., et al. 1980, *Il sistema jugoslavo. Dall'impresa alla societa' autogestita – esperienza e progetto*, De Donato Editore, Bari

Investing in Yugoslavia 1989, Jugoslovenski Pregled, Belgrade

Ireland, N. J. 1984, 'Codetermination, wage bargaining and the horizon problem', *Zeitschrift für nationalökonomie*, 44 (1), pp. 1–10

Ireland, N. J. and Law, P. J. 1982, *The Economics of Labour-Managed Enterprises*, St Martin's Press, New York

Jensen, M. C. and Meckling, W. H. 1979, 'Rights and production functions: an application to labour-managed firms and codetermination', *Journal of Business*, 52, pp. 469–506

Jones, D. C. and Backus, D. K. 1977, 'British producer cooperatives in the footwear industry: an empirical evaluation of the theory of financing', *Economic Journal*, 87, pp. 488–510

Kalodjera, D. 1990, 'Otvoreni problemi preobrazde vlasništva', in *Poslednji dani društvenog vlasništva*, Zagrebačka Poslovna Škola, Zagreb, pp. 7–22

Kardelj, E. 1971a, 'O problemima socijalnih razlika i o minulom radu', in *E. Kardelj: Samoupravljanje*, vol. 5 (1979), Svijetlost, Sarajevo, pp. 127–48

1971b, 'Ekonomski i politički odnosi u samoupravnom socijalističkom društvu', Speech on the Second Congress of Self-managers of Yugoslavia, in *Samoupravljanje u Jugoslaviji 1950–1980, Dokumenti razvoja* (1980), Privredni pregled, Belgrade, pp. 237–48

1972, 'Protivrečnosti društvene svojine u savremenoj socijalističkoj praksi', in *E. Kardelj: Samoupravljanje*, vol. 1 (1979), Svijetlost, Sarajevo, pp. 287–405

1978, *Slobodni udruženi rad - Brionske diskusije*, 2nd edn, Radnička štampa, Belgrade

Keren, M. 1975, 'The asymmetry of property rights and the long-run behavior of the labor-managed firm', mimeo

Kessides, C., King, T., Nuti, M., and Sokil, C. (eds.), *Financial Reform in Socialist Economies*, The World Bank, Washington and European University Institute, Florence

King, A. E. 1979, 'Property rights and investment in human capital by the labour-managed firm: a note on Vanek's conjecture', *Rivista Internazionale di Scienze Economiche e Commerciali*, 26 (9), pp. 858–64

Knight, P. T. 1984, 'Financial discipline and structural adjustment in Yugoslavia', *World Bank Staff Working Papers*, no. 705, The World Bank, Washington, DC

Komisija saveznih društvenih saveta za probleme ekonomske stabilizacije 1982, *Dokumenti Komisije*, Centar za radničko samoupravljanje, Belgrade

Korać, M. 1986, *Problemi sticanja i raspodele dohotka u SFRJ. Analiza stanja (1977–1985) i moguća rešenja*, Globus, Zagreb

Kornai, J. 1980, *Economics of Shortage*, North-Holland, Amsterdam

1984, 'The softness of the budget constraint – An analysis relying on data of firms', *Acta Oeconomica*, 32, pp. 223–49

1986a, 'The soft-budget constraint', *Kyklos*, 39 (1), pp. 3–30

1986b, 'The Hungarian reform process: Visions, hopes, and reality', *Journal of Economic Literature*, 24, December, pp. 1687–737

Korže, U. and Simoneti, M. 1990, 'Privatization in Yugoslavia', Paper presented at the Conference on Privatization in Eastern Europe, November 7–8, Ljubljana

Labus, M. 1985, 'The Furubotn–Pejovich effect: some Yugoslav evidence', Paper presented at the Fourth International Conference on the Economics of Self-Management, Liège, July

1987, *Društvena ili grupna svojina*, Naučna knjiga, Belgrade

Lacko, M. 1980, 'Cumulating and easing of tensions (A simple model of the cyclical development of investments in Hungary)', *Acta Oeconomica*, 24 (3–4), pp. 357–77

Lajšić, Dj. 1984, *Metodologija ocene investicionih projekata u sistemu Udružene beogradske banke*, Udružena beogradska banka, Centar za ekonomska istraživanja, Belgrade

Lakićević, M. 1987a, 'Društvena svojina – Vreme za promene', *Ekonomska Politika*, no. 1827, 6 April

1987b, 'Praksa ispred ideologije', *Ekonomska Politika*, no. 1843, 27 July

Lavigne, M. 1962, *Le capital dans l'économie soviétique*, SEDES, Paris

1968, 'Coefficient de capital et politique de l'investissement dans l'industrie soviétique', in *Annuaire de l'URSS 1967*, CNRS, Paris

1978, 'Productivité du capital et efficacité des investissements en URSS', in *Le capital dans la fonction de production*, CNRS, Paris

Lukić, B. 1990, 'Komentar zakona o društvenom kapitalu sa ugradjenim izmenama', *Službeni List SFRJ*, Belgrade

Lydall, H. 1984, *Yugoslav Socialism – Theory and Practice*, Clarendon Press, Oxford

1989, *Yugoslavia in Crisis*, Clarendon Press, Oxford

Madžar, Lj. 1985, 'Revalorizacija zaliha, fiktivna akumulacija i iluzija rasta', *Ekonomist*, 38 (3–4), pp. 327–49

1986, 'Iluzija rasta i iluzionizam njenih analitičara', *Ekonomist*, 39 (3), pp. 237–51

Marglin, S. A. 1963, 'The social rate of discount and the optimal rate of investment', *Quarterly Journal of Economics*, 77, pp. 95–111

Mates, N. 1987, 'Uz nove mjere ekonomske politike', *Naše teme*, 31 (1–2), pp. 3–16

Mayes, A. and Mayes, D. 1976, *Introductory Economic Statistics*, John Wiley and Sons, New York

McCain, R. A. 1977, 'On the optimum financial environment for worker cooperatives', *Zeitschrift für Nationalökonomie*, 37, pp. 355–84

Meade, J. E. 1972, 'The theory of labour-managed firms and of profit-sharing', *Economic Journal*, 82, pp. 402–28

1982, *Stagflation – volume 1: Wage-fixing*, Allen & Unwin, London

1986, *Alternative Systems of Business Organisation and of Workers' Remuneration*, Allen & Unwin, London

1989, *Agathotopia: the Economics of Partnership*, Aberdeen University Press, Aberdeen

Mencinger, J. 1990, 'Dileme privatizacije društvene imovine u Sloveniji', in *Poslednji dani društvenog vlasništva*, Zagrebačka Poslovna Škola, Zagreb, pp. 23–30

Milanović, B. 1983, 'The investment behaviour of the labour-managed firm: a property rights approach', *Economic Analysis and Workers' Management*, 17 (4), pp. 327–40

1990, 'Privatization in post-communist societies', mimeo, The World Bank, October

Milenkovich, D. 1971, *Plan and Market in Yugoslav Economic Thought*, Yale University Press, New Haven, CT

Milošević, D. and Živković, Z. 1984, *Promet, korišćenje, amortizacija i revalorizacija društvenih sredstava*, Stručna knjiga, Belgrade

Milovanović, M. 1986, *Kapital i minuli rad*, Savremena administracija, Belgrade

Miović, P. 1975, 'Determinants of income differentials in Yugoslav self-managed enterprises', PhD thesis, University of Pennsylvania

Morley-Fletcher, E. (ed.) 1986, *Cooperare e competere*, Feltrinelli, Milan

Mramor, D. 1984, 'Analiza banaka kao posrednika kod prenosa novčane akumulacije u Jugoslaviji u razdoblju 1945–1982 godine', M.A. thesis, Faculty of Economics, University of Belgrade

Narodna Banka Jugoslavije, *Bilten Narodne Banke Jugoslavije*, Belgrade, various issues

Nikolić, T. 1986, 'Zablude o svojini', *Ekonomska Politika*, no. 1784, 9 June

Nuti, D. M. 1984, 'Economic and financial evaluation of investment projects: general principles and EC procedures', *European University Institute Working Paper*, no. 84/119, Florence

1985, 'Systemic aspects of employment and investment in Soviet-type economies', in D. Lane (ed.), *Labour and Employment in the USSR*, The Harvester Press, London

1987a, 'Pay-off and recoupment periods as investment criteria', in J. Eatwell, M. Milgate, and P. Newman (eds.), *The New Palgrave: A Dictionary of Economic Theory and Doctrine*, Macmillan, Basingstoke

1987b, 'Financial innovation under market socialism', *European University Institute Working Paper*, no. 87/285, Florence

1988a, 'Progetto per un Fondo Mutualistico per la promozione e lo sviluppo di imprese cooperative', paper presented at the Conference on Cooperatives organized by LNCM, March, Rome

1988b, 'On traditional cooperatives and James Meade's labour-capital discriminating partnership', *European University Institute Working Paper*, no. 88/337, Florence

1988c, 'Remonetisation and capital markets in the reform of centrally planned economies', *European Economic Review*, 33 (2–3), pp. 427–38

1991, 'Sequencing and credibility in economic reforms', in A. Atkinson and R. Brunetta (eds.), *Economics for the New Europe*, Macmillan, London

Nutzinger, H. G. 1975, 'Investment and financing in a labour-managed firm and its social implications', *Economic Analysis and Workers' Management*, 9 (3–4), pp. 181–201

1982, 'The economics of property rights – a new paradigm in social sciences', *Economic Analysis and Workers' Management*, 16 (1), pp. 81–97

Oakeshott, R. 1978, *The Case for Workers' Co-ops*, Routledge & Kegan Paul, London

OECD 1982, *Economic Surveys – Yugoslavia, 1981/1982*, Paris

1983, *Economic Surveys – Yugoslavia, 1982/1983*, Paris

1984, *Economic Surveys – Yugoslavia, 1984/1985*, Paris

1987a, *Economic Surveys – Yugoslavia, 1986/1987*, Paris

1987b, *Economic Surveys – Italy, 1986/1987*, Paris

1988, *Economic Surveys – Yugoslavia, 1987/1988*, Paris

1990, *Economic Surveys – Yugoslavia, 1989/1990*, Paris

Olbina, Ž. 1981, *Investicione odluke u samoupravnoj privredi*, Privredni pregled, Belgrade

Ostojić, S. 1984, *Samoupravne korporacije – Struktura i funkcionisanje SOUR-a*, Marksistički Centar Organizacije SK u Beogradu, Belgrade

Ostojić, S., Vasiljević, V., Djilas, M., Vidić, Z., and Čuturilo, M. 1985. *Investiciona aktivnost privrede UBB u periodu 1981–85*, Udružena beogradska banka, Centar za ekonomska istraživanja, Belgrade

Pančić, V. 1985, *Revalorizacija i amortizacija društvenih sredstava*, 5th edn, Informator, Zagreb

Pejovich, S. 1969, 'The firm, monetary policy and property rights in a planned economy', *Western Economic Journal*, 7 (3), pp. 193–200

  1976, 'The labor-managed firm and bank credit', in J. Thornton (ed). (1976), *The Economic Analysis of the Soviet-type System*, Cambridge University Press, Cambridge

  1986, 'The case of self-management in Yugoslavia', in S. Pejovich (ed.), *Socialism: Institutional, Philosophical and Economic Issues*, Kluwer Academic Publishers, Dordrecht

Petrović, P. and Simoneti, M. (eds.) 1990, *Deoničarski kapital u Jugoslaviji*, Ekonomski Institut, Belgrade

Pindyck, R. S. and Rubinfeld, D. L. 1981, *Econometric Models and Econometric Forecasts*, 2nd edn, McGraw-Hill, New York

Portes, R. 1990, 'Introduction' to *European Economy*, no. 43, Brussels, March, pp. 9–17

Poslednji dani društvenog vlasništva 1990, Zagrebačka Poslovna Škola, Zagreb

Prašnikar, J. 1980, 'Yugoslav self-managed firm and its behaviour', *Economic Analysis and Workers' Management*, 14 (1)

  1983, *Teorija i praksa organizacije udruženog rada*, Centar za kulturnu djelatnost, Zagreb

Prašnikar, J. and Svejnar, J. 1988, 'Economic behavior of Yugoslav enterprises', in D. Jones and J. Svejnar (eds.), *Advances in the Economic Analysis of Participatory and Labor-Managed Firms*, vol. 3, JAI Press, Greenwich, CT, pp. 237–311

Prout, C. 1985, *Market Socialism in Yugoslavia*, Oxford University Press, Oxford

Rankov, I. 1986, 'Inflacija: Osnovni izvori, I & II', *Komunist*, nos. 1533 and 1534

Ranković, J. 1985, 'Obračunski sistem i inflacija', *Ekonomska Politika*, no. 1748, 30 September

Republički zavod za društveno planiranje SR Srbije 1984, *Kriteriji i merila za ocenjivanje efektivnosti i selekciju investicionih projekata*, Belgrade

Rock, C. and Defourny, J. 1983, 'The financing of self-managed enterprises', mimeo, Cornell University and CIRIEC

Round table discussion (1985), 'Ostvarivanje i zaštita društvene svojine', *Socijalizam*, 28 (4)

Round table discussion (1986), 'Mešovita privreda – Šansa ili pretnja socijalizmu?', *Ekonomska Politika*, no. 1801, 6 October

Sacks, S. R. 1983, *Self-management and Efficiency: Large Corporations in Yugoslavia*, George Allen & Unwin, London

Sapir, A. 1980, 'Economic growth and factor substitution: what happened to the Yugoslav miracle? *Economic Journal*, 90, June, pp. 294–313

Savezni komitet za informacije 1976, *Društveni plan Jugoslavije za period od 1976 do 1980 godine*, Jugoslovenski pregled, Belgrade

1981, *Društveni plan Jugoslavije 1981–1985*, Jugoslovenski pregled, Belgrade

Savezni zavod za društveno planiranje, 'Indikatori razvoja', Appendix to *Annual Economic Resolutions*, Belgrade, various years

Savezni zavod za statistiku 1986, *Jugoslavija – 1945–1985, Statistički prikaz*, Belgrade

Savezni zavod za statistiku, *Statistički godišnjak Jugoslavije*, Belgrade, various years

Savezni zavod za statistiku i Savezni zavod za društveno planiranje 1982, *Razvoj Jugoslavije 1947–1981, Statistički prikaz*, Belgrade

Savezno društveno knjigovodstvo, *Bilten SDK*, Belgrade, various issues

Savezno izvršno veće 1990, *Ekonomska reforma i njeni zakoni*, Sekretarijat za informacije, Belgrade

Schall, L. D., Sundem, G. L. and Geijsbeek, W. R. Jr. 1978, 'Survey and analysis of capital budgeting methods', *Journal of Finance*, March, pp. 281–7

Schlicht, E. and Von Weizsacker, C. C. 1977, 'Risk financing in labour-managed economies: the commitment problem', *Zeitschrift für die Gesamte Staatswissenschaft*, pp. 53–6

Schrenk, M., Ardalan, C., and El Tatawy, A. N. 1979, *Yugoslavia – Self-Management Socialism. Challenges of Development, A World Bank Country Economic Report*, The Johns Hopkins University Press, Baltimore and London

Sekretarijat za informacije Saveznog izvršnog veća, *Lična karta reforme*, Belgrade, various issues

Sekretarijat za informacije Skupštine SFRJ 1976, *Zakon o udruženom radu*, Prosveta, Belgrade, 1976; English translation (1977), *Associated Labour Act*, Prosveta, Novi Sad

Sekretarijat za informativnu službu Savezne skupštine 1966, *Društveni plan razvoja Jugoslavije od 1966 do 1970 godine*, Belgrade

1971, *Društveni plan Jugoslavije za period od 1971 do 1975 godine*, Belgrade

Seligman, J. 1986, 'The one share, one vote controversy', The Investor Responsibility Research Center, Washingdon, DC

Sen, A. K. 1967, 'Isolation assurance and the social rate of discount', *Quarterly Journal of Economics*, 80, pp. 112–24

Sertel, M. R. 1982, *Workers and Incentives*, North-Holland, Amsterdam

1987, 'Workers' enterprises are not perverse', *European Economic Review*, 31, pp. 1619–25

Simoneti, M. 1991, 'Privatization in the reforming socialist countries', paper presented at IMD's Conference on Eastern Europe, Lausanne, 6–8 March

Singleton, F. and Carter, B. 1982, *The Economy of Yugoslavia*, Croom Helm, St Martin's Press

Sirc, L. 1979, *The Yugoslav Economy under Self-Management*, Macmillan, London

Službeni List SFRJ, Belgrade, various issues

Sonnberger, H., Kraemer, W., Schraick, W., *et al.* 1986, *IAS System: User Reference Manual*, Institute for Advanced Studies, Vienna, Institutsarbeit no. 234

Štambuk, V. 1988, 'Ustavne promene i akcionarstvo – Treba li zabludom na zabludu?', *Nin*, 27 March

Steinherr, A. and Thisse, J. F. 1979, 'Is there a negatively-sloped supply curve in the labor-managed firm?', *Economic Analysis and Workers' Management*, 13, pp. 23–34

Stephen, F. H. 1978, 'Bank credit and investment by the Yugoslav firm', *Economic Analysis and Workers' Management*, 12, pp. 221–39

— 1979, 'Property rights and the labour-managed firm in the long run', *Economic Analysis and Workers' Management*, 13 (1–2), pp. 149–66

— 1980, 'Bank credit and the labor-managed firm: comment', *American Economic Review*, 4, pp. 796–99

— 1982, 'The economic theory of the labour-managed firm', in F. H. Stephen (ed.), *The Economic Performance of Labour-Managed Firms*, Macmillan, London

— 1984, *The Economic Analysis of Producers' Cooperatives*, Macmillan, London

Stephen, F. H. and Smith B. 1975, 'Capital investment in the Yugoslav firm', *Canadian Journal of Economics*, 8, pp. 609–17

Stojanović, R. (ed.) 1964, *Yugoslav Economists on Problems of a Socialist Economy*, International Arts and Sciences Press, New York

Šuvaković, Dj. 1977, *Samoupravno i kapitalističko preduzeće*, Savremena administracija, Belgrade

Teodorović, J. 1977, 'Ocjena investicionih projekata', *Poduzeće-banka*, 5, pp. 12–26

Thomas, H. and Logan, C. 1982, *Mondragon: An Economic Analysis*, George Allen & Unwin, London

Thornley, J. 1981, *Worker Cooperatives*, Heinemann, London

Tyson, L. D'A. 1977a, 'A permanent income hypothesis for the Yugoslav firm', *Economica*, 44, pp. 393–408

— 1977b, 'Liquidity crises in the Yugoslav economy: an alternative to bankruptcy', *Soviet Studies*, 29 (2), pp. 284–95

— 1980, *The Yugoslav Economic System and its Performance in the 1970s*, Regents of the University of California, Berkeley

— 1983, 'Investment allocation: a comparison of the reform experiences of Hungary and Yugoslavia', *Journal of Comparative Economics*, 7 (3), pp. 288–303

Udruženje banaka Jugoslavije i Ekonomski institut, Zagreb, 1981, *Priručnik za planiranje investicionih projekata*, Privredna štampa, Belgrade

Udruženje bankarskih organizacija Beograd 1985, *Priručnik za primenu jedinstvene metodologije, kriterijuma i merila za analizu, vrednovanje, selekciju, izbor i ocenu prihvatljivosti investicionih projekata*, Belgrade

Uvalić, M. 1986, 'The investment behaviour of a labour-managed firm', *Annals of Public and Cooperative Economy*, 57 (1), pp. 11–33

1988, 'The investment behaviour of the labour-managed firm: an econometric analysis', *European University Institute Working Paper*, no. 88/354, Florence

1989, 'Shareholding schemes in the Yugoslav economy', in C. Kessides, T. King, M. Nuti and C. Sokil (eds.), *Financial Reform in Socialist Economies*, The World Bank, Washington and European University Institute, Florence, pp. 106–25

1991a, *The PEPPER Report: Promotion of Employee Participation in Profits and Enterprise Results, Social Europe*, Supplement no. 3, Office for Official Publications of the European Communities, Luxembourg

1991b, 'How different is Yugoslavia?' *European Economy*, special edition no. 2, Brussels, pp. 199–213

Uvalić, R. 1954, 'The management of undertakings by the workers in Yugoslavia', *International Labour Review*, pp. 235–54

1964, 'Functions of the market and plan in the socialist economy', in R. Stojanovic (ed.), 1964, *Yugoslav Economists on Problems of a Socialist Economy*, International Arts and Sciences Press, New York

Vacić, A. 1989, *Jugoslavija i Evropa*, Ekonomika, Belgrade

Vahčić, A. and Petrin, T. 1989, 'Financial system for restructuring the Yugoslav economy', in C. Kessides, T. King, D. M. Nuti, and C. Sokil (eds.), *Financial Reform in Socialist Economies*, The World Bank, Washington, and European University Institute, Florence, pp. 154–61

Vanek, Jan. 1972, *The Economics of Workers' Management – A Yugoslav Case Study*, George Allen & Unwin, London

Vanek, J. 1970, *The General Theory of Labour-Managed Market Economies*, Cornell University Press, Ithaca

1971, 'The basic theory of financing of participatory firms', *Cornell University Working Paper*, no. 27, Ithaca, reprinted in J. Vanek (ed.) 1975, *Self-Management: Economic Liberation of Man*, Penguin, Harmondsworth

1973, 'The investment decision under labor-management and its social efficiency implications', *Cornell University Working Paper*, no. 55, Ithaca

1977, *The Labor-Managed Economy: Essays*, Cornell University Press, Ithaca

Vanek, J. and Jovičić, M. 1975, 'The capital market and income distribution in Yugoslavia: a theoretical and empirical analysis', *Quarterly Journal of Economics*, 39 (3), pp. 432–43

Vodopivec, M. 1988, 'Productivity effects of income redistribution: an application to Yugoslav firms', Paper presented at the Fourth Annual SSRC Summer Workshop on Soviet and East European Economics, University of California, Berkeley

Vojnić, D. 1986, *Ekonomska stabilizacija i ekonomska kriza*, Globus, Zagreb

Vujović, D. 1978, 'Mesto društvene ocene projekata u sistemu samoupravnog planiranja i upravljanje privrednim razvojem', *Gledišta*, 7 (8), pp. 25–36

Ward, B. 1958, 'The firm in Illyria – market syndicalism', *American Economic Review*, 48, pp. 566–89

World Bank 1983, *Yugoslav Adjustment Policies and Development Perspectives*, A World Bank Country Study, Washington

World Bank 1990, *World Development Report 1990*, Oxford University Press, Oxford

Zafiris, N. 1982, 'Appropriability rules, capital maintenance and the efficiency of cooperative investment', *Journal of Comparative Economics*, 6, pp. 55–74

Žarković, D. and Vujičić, D. 1987, *Amortizacija i revalorizacija društvenih sredstava*, Ekonomika, Belgrade

Zelić, N. 1975, 'Investicioni kriterij u samoupravnoj privredi', *Gledišta*, no. 2

1976, 'Yugoslav firm and theory of behavior of self-management economy', *Economic Analysis and Workers' Management*, 10 (1–2), pp. 61–77

1982, *Efikasnost jugoslovenskog privrednog sistema*, Kultura, Belgrade

Zevi, A. 1984, 'Diritti patrimoniali dei soci e comportamento dell'impresa cooperativa di produzione e lavoro nella disciplina vigente e nelle proposte di riforma', *Rivista della Cooperazione*, 21, Special issue, October–December, pp. 284–308

Županov, J. 1977, 'Mišljenja privrednika o minulom radu', in J. Županov (ed.), *Sociologija i samoupravljanje*, Školska knjiga, Zagreb

Index

accumulation
  and past labour rewards, 163
  of Yugoslav enterprises, 75–80, 81, 91
age structure of workforce in LMFs, 33,
  34–5, 40
aggregate level, Yugoslav savings and
  investment at, 69–73, 88
agriculture, 9
  limits on individual holdings, 182
  selective credits for, 103
ALA (Associated Labour Act, 1976), 161,
  162, 163, 166, 168, 175, 183
Aoki, M., 37
assets
  depreciation of, 32, 42–5
  durability of, 30–1
  investment in fixed assets, 69, 70, 71,
    84–6, 87, 94, 95, 96; see also FXA;
    INV
  liquid, 25, 174, 184
  and LMFs, 20–1, 25, 30–1
  owned and non-owned, 20–1, 102, 103,
    104, 116
  revaluation of, 32, 44–45
  value of, and internal shares, 183–4
  in Yugoslav LMFs, 40, 42–5
Associated Belgrade Bank, 110, 112, 114
Associated Labour Act (1976); see ALA
autonomous provinces in Yugoslavia, 7

Babić, M., 189
Babić, S., 162, 176–7
Backus, D. K., 53
Bajt, A., 45, 60, 63, 72, 179–80
balance of payments in Yugoslavia, 10–11,
  12
bank credit/loans, 25
  financing project overruns, 113
  and interest rates, 98, 99–100, 102, 103,
    116
  and LMF, 24, 36–7, 45

bankruptcies, 106–8, 111, 193, 202, 211,
  212
  and the financing of LMFs, 36
banks, 9, 62, 63, 98, 157, 165, 167, 173–4,
  175
  and investment project selection, 112
  and LMFs, 36–7
  pooling of resources in, 165
  and privatization, 189, 195–6
  securities bought by, 167, 193, 195
  and economic reforms, 6, 7, 8–9, 157,
    183–4, 200, 206–7
  losses, 109–10, 205
  securities, 122–3
Bartlett, W., 41
Belgium, co-operatives in, 47, 48
Belgrade stock exchange, 196, 197
Bendeković, J., 114
black market, 15
BOALs (basic organizations of associated
  labour), 8, 120, 183
Bogetić, G., 163
bonds, 8, 122, 165–6, 180–1, 184, 192, 193,
  194, 195
Bonin, J. P., 29, 30, 31, 36, 37, 176
Bosnia
  bankruptcies, 109
  free distribution of securities in, 192
Britain
  CPF co-operatives, 46, 52
  footwear co-operatives, 53
  ICOM (Industrial Common Ownership
    Movement), 46, 47, 51
budgets; see soft budget constraints
Bulgaria, 198
Burkitt, J. P., 65

capital, 32, 41–5, 60, 61, 63, 212
  allocation and mobility between firms,
    164
  in COALs, 166, 168

22 JAMES RIORDAN
Sport in Soviet society
Development of sport and physical education in Russia and the USSR

The following series titles are now out of print:

1 ANDREA BOLTHO
Foreign trade criteria in socialist economies

2 SHEILA FITZPATRICK
The commissariat of enlightenment
Soviet organization of education and the arts under Lunacharsky, October 1917–1921

3 DONALD J. MALE
Russian peasant organisation before collectivisation
A study of commune and gathering 1925–1930

4 P. WILES (ed.)
The prediction of communist economic performance

5 VLADIMIR V. KUSIN
The intellectual origins of the Prague Spring
The development of reformist ideas in Czechoslovakia 1956–1967

6 GALIA GOLAN
The Czechoslovak reform movement

7 NAUN JASNY
Soviet economists of the twenties
Names to be remembered

8 ASHA L. DATAR
India's economic relations with the USSR and Eastern Europe 1953–1969

9 T. M. PODOLSKI
Socialist banking and monetary control
The experience of Poland

10 SHMUEL GALAI
The liberation movement in Russia 1900–1905

11 GALIA GOLAN
Reform rule in Czechoslovakia
The Dubček era 1968–1969

12 GEOFFREY A. HOSKING
The Russian constitutional experiment
Government and Duma 1907–1914

13 RICHARD B. DAY
Leon Trotsky and the politics of economic isolation

14 RUDOLF BIĆANIĆ
Economic policy in socialist Yugoslavia

15 JAN M. CIECHANOWSKI
The Warsaw rising of 1944